MODERN CATHOLIC
THINKERS
II

hARPER ✦ TORChBOOKS

*A reference-list of Harper Torchbooks, classified
by subjects, is printed at the end of this volume.*

MODERN CATHOLIC THINKERS
II

THE CHURCH
&
THE POLITICAL ORDER

EDITED BY

A. ROBERT CAPONIGRI

HARPER TORCHBOOKS ❦ The Cathedral Library
Harper & Row, Publishers
New York, Evanston, and London

To

THEODORE M. HESBURGH
Priest of the Congregation of Holy Cross
President, University of Notre Dame

*Whose passion for excellence
transforms all it touches*

Table of Contents

EDITOR'S NOTE

This volume contains the two sections of my collection *Modern Catholic Thinkers* that deal with *The Church and the Political Order*. A new preface has been added to this edition. Other sections of *Modern Catholic Thinkers* are available as companion Harper Torchbooks.

Sources and Acknowledgements

"The Church": *Catholicism*, Henri de Lubac, S.J., London: Burns and Oates; New York: Sheed and Ward (second impression 1958), pp. 17–34. Translated by Lancelot C. Sheppard. By courtesy of Burns and Oates and Sheed and Ward.

"The Constitution of the Church": *Under God and The Law*, Mgr Philip Hughes, ed. Richard O'Sullivan, Oxford, Blackwell, 1949, pp. 59–88. By courtesy of Blackwell and the author.

"In the World and Not of the World": *Lay People in the Church*, Yves M. J. Congar, O.P., Westminster, Maryland, Newman Press, 1957, pp. 390–420. Translated by Donald Attwater. Reprinted by courtesy of the Newman Press and the Bloomsbury Pub. Co., London.

"Meaning of the Mass: The Mass and the Church": *The Mass of the Roman Rite: Its Origins and Development*, Joseph A. Jungmann, S.J., New York, Benziger Bros., 1951. Translated by Rev. Francis A. Brunner, C.SS.R. Vol. I, pp. 175–95. Reprinted by courtesy of Benziger Bros., New York.

"The Foundation": *The Church Incarnate: The Sacred Function of Christian Architecture*, Rudolf Schwarz, Chicago, The Henry Regnery Company. Translated by Cynthia Harris, 1958, pp. 3–34. By courtesy of The Henry Regnery Company.

"Politics and Moral Theology": *Les Guerres Modernes et la Pensée Catholique*, Don Luigi Sturzo, Montreal, Éditions de l'Arbre, 1942, pp. 131–71. Translated by A. Robert Caponigri. Reprinted by courtesy of the Istituto Luigi Sturzo, Rome.

"The Democratic Charter": *Man and the State*, Jacques Maritain, Chicago, University of Chicago Press, 1951, pp. 108–46. By courtesy of the University of Chicago Press, Hollis and Carter, London, and the author.

"The Essential Functions of Authority": *The Philosophy of Democratic Government*, Yves Simon, Chicago, The University of Chicago Press, 1952, pp. 19–57; compressed and rearranged by the author. By courtesy of the University of Chicago Press and the author.

"The Freedom of Man in the Freedom of the Church": J. Courtney Murray, S.J., from *The Modern Age*, Chicago, Foundation for Foreign Affairs, Vol. 1, no. 2, 1957, pp. 134–45. By courtesy of the editors of *The Modern Age* and the author.

"The Church and Human Rights": Heinrich Rommen; *The Catholic Church in World Affairs*, Editors Waldemar Gurian and M. A. Fitzsimons, Notre Dame, The University of Notre Dame Press, 1954,

PERSONAL ACKNOWLEDGEMENT

THE expression of gratitude is an ethical duty; it is also the source of the most sincere joy we can experience. Especially is this true in the case of a work like the present, which, of its nature, could only come to be through the selfless cooperation of more persons than it is possible to name here. To all who have extended me this cooperation, friends and colleagues and co-workers, I joyfully offer my most sincere thanks. There are some among them, however, whose contribution to this work has been so great that they must be cited by name no matter what the limits that economy of space imposes. Chief among these is the Very Rev. Martin C. D'Arcy of the Society of Jesus, in whose company the work was planned and who so graciously has contributed an introduction to it. Second only to him, I gladly name Mr. Henry Regnery of the firm of Henry Regnery and Company, Publishers; his interest and encouragement was the main sustaining force which saw the work to its completion. The Grace Foundation of New York generously provided the funds for the research involved and for the preparation of the manuscript; I acknowledge this generosity with the greatest pleasure, with a special acknowledgement of the understanding and interest of Mr. J. B. Murray of New York and Mr. Walter B. Cummings Jr. of Chicago. This work is in its intention a work of Catholic witness. It bears witness not alone to the intellectual efforts of those who are represented in it by their writings, but to the sustaining faith of all these friends as well. Finally, I cannot permit to pass unnoted the silent but ever-present understanding of my wife, Winifred.

A. ROBERT CAPONIGRI

Notre Dame, Indiana
April 20, 1959

Preface to the Torchbook edition

The Church and the Political Order
in
Contemporary Catholic Thought

A FUNDAMENTAL aspect of Catholic thought is its conception of the social order. Although it centers its vision on the individual human person, and places upon him an absolute value as the direct object of God's love and Christ's redeeming passion, it yet sees the fulfillment of the person in the social bonds which link him to his fellows and to God. Catholicism is a religion neither of the individual in isolation nor of the abstract and hypostatized collectivity. It is a religion of the concrete corporate community of men, individuals linked by indissoluble bonds, sharing a common good, aspiring to a common destiny, trusting in a common redeemer.

The concrete corporate community of men has a complex structure. It is wholly immanent in individual human persons: the person sustains all of the relations through which the community, in all of its aspects and forms, may be articulated. Don Luigi Sturzo spoke of society in this sense as the projection of the person onto the plane of collectivity.

The concrete corporate community realizes itself in a twofold social order, because community has a twofold principle in the human person. There is, first, the "temporal" dimension of the community. Its principle is "human nature" not in an abstract and metaphysical, but in a concrete and existential sense. This dimension of community takes form in the historical groupings in which men become associated in response to natural needs and by natural forces alone. These groupings, in order of increasing complexity range from the level of the family to that of the political order. The concrete human community rests also however, on another principle, the principle of grace and therefore is articulated also in another set of relations. In this form it arises in response, not to the simple demands of "nature", but to the potentialities revealed and infused in nature by the redeeming and mediatory actions of Christ; it is effected not by the simple agencies of human nature, but by grace, the continuing presence and power of Christ in history. On this second level, human community finds its realization in a society—the Church; and the Church, appearing in time, space, and history, as do natural societies, has further an inner constitutive dimension that transcends time, space, and history.

Catholic thought does not see these orders of association in isolation from each other either in their principles or in their forms. Avoiding any confusion between them, it sees them on the contrary in the most intimate relation: grace as informing and transforming nature, charity as tempering and elevating justice. Church and natural forms—family, association, state —meet and interact in history through the concrete mediation of the person.

Reflection on the problem may be said to have begun with the saying ascribed to Christ himself: "give to Caesar the things that are Caesar's and to God the things that are God's". Catholic thought has ever since sought to mediate, restate and realize anew the social bonds and forms; a deeper insight into their specific character and mutual relations has been its aim in every age, together with the desire to render Christian social insights as effective as possible under the constantly changing conditions of historical societies and cultures.

The present age is no exception. On the contrary, it might be said that the problem of the social order exercises a particular fascination upon Catholic thought today, perhaps because the Catholic mind senses that the modern world has the power to put Christian insights to the severest test they have yet faced in history.

The writings gathered in this volume seek to document and illustrate current Catholic concern with our theme. They speak for themselves, and are intended to do so.

The constant probing of the Church for her own essence under the changing conditions of history is no accident; it belongs to the basic rhythm of her life. She is not just the repository of the truth and mystery of the Christian faith: she is herself a part of that truth and mystery, the vehicle and embodiment of a divine message and power which have entered into history. The Church belongs both to eternity and to history. She must be mindful of the eternal, so that it may be truly manifested in history; and she must be mindful of history, so that under its constantly changing conditions the divine message and power may reach mankind unaltered and effective.

Our age questions not so much the claims of one Church against those of another, as the very idea of a "church" as a valid and necessary form of human society. Another difficulty has been raised in our time by those who claim to discover in divers forms of "totalitarian" social organization a recrudescence of the notion of "church," thus obliquely investing that notion with the objectionable characteristics of the totalitarian state. These currents have had a marked effect on contemporary Catholic thought. All former reflections and apologetics intended to vindicate the claims of the Church against other churches have become in some degree obsolete. They can have value only when the notion of a church as a valid form of human society is generally accepted; once this general agreement disappears, the notion loses both context and reference. Catholic reflection on the Church has thus been forced to seek a broader context. In addition to a theological ecclesiology, it has had to essay a philosophical and sociological ecclesiology; that is, it has had to create more general theories on the nature and validity of the idea of "church" as a form of human society. There is no doubt that this necessity has brought forth some of the most arresting and persuasive speculations in contemporary thought, such as Don Luigi Sturzo's work *La Vera Vita,* and Henri de Lubac's *Catholicism* from which the chapter entitled "The Church" is reprinted below. We can here mention only the main lines of the argument. The first is the effort to show the church on philosophical and sociological grounds as one of the basic forms of human sociality. The other is the tendency to see in the Church the introduction into historical society of a form unprecedented in history, and incapable of realization through a merely natural social process. These lines of thought produce in turn lines of argument that must deeply affect the notion which the Church holds of herself and of the conditions under which her presence in the world may be authentic and effective.

A second problem that has preoccupied Catholic thought is that of the "constitution" of the Church. By "constitution" we mean the set of structural, dynamic, etc. conditions under which the Church achieves actual existence in all of the dimensions that are implicit in her nature within the context of history. Her constitution in this sense is the means whereby she becomes tangibly present and effective in history. Political constitutions have but one dimension; they are organizations of human presence alone in terms of historical effectiveness. The Church, by contrast, represents the time-historical structure of the transcendent; within the framework of history, that structure is the presence of the transcendent and divine principle which she deploys and renders active and effective. The manner in which her constitution enters into relations with other forms of sociality, altering or qualifying them and in turn being affected by them, ceaselessly presents itself under an almost infinite variety of aspects. Msgr. Philip Hughes, in his essay reprinted below, treats this problem in its most inclusive form.

One of the strongest currents in contemporary Catholic thought concerns the role of the layman. It is now recognized that the distinction within the constitution of the Church between hierarchy and layman, while historically comprehensible and solidly based in doctrine and tradition, does not reveal fully the intention of the faith regarding the Church as a society. The role of the layman, both constitutionally within the Church and in terms of personal vocation, needs to be re-thought with the utmost care; he must be given a far greater effectiveness in the Church. This problem has been the especial concern of some of the most serious minds in the Church. Yves Congar, O.P., has earned the right to speak for them. In his essay here included he attacks the problem at one of its most delicate articulations: the duality of the layman's role. He makes the point that the vocation of the layman is above all to be "in the world and not of it". Under this aspect, the layman directly reflects the constitution of the Church—even more directly, perhaps, than does the hierarchy. For like the Church his role is to make the ideals of Christianity and the power of grace effective under the conditions, not merely of historical, but of day-to-day action. His not-being-of-the-world is not an *absence* from the world; it is a *presence* in the world according to a higher principle which he is called upon to make effective in the world. His being-in-the-world is not a fallen state, such as Plato imagined of man's intellect, but is essential to his nature and his vocation; he is present there not as an alien principle, but as one with a special task under a special seal. One may expect that current reflection within the Church upon the layman's work and vocation will in time have a major effect on the Church's constitution.

The tremendous revival of interest in the liturgy is one of the most significant aspects of Catholic life today. The renewal of the liturgical year, the attempt to bring all of the faithful into the very act of worship has reached down into the life of the humblest communicant. Less clearly understood, however, are the doctrinal and theoretical bases upon which the liturgical life rests. These are closely related to the problem of the constitution of the Church, which involves her presence in history, and her agency in history to do the work of grace. The liturgy brings to the fore in a special manner the form of her presence in its innermost essence. That form of presence is presence as power, but a power of a very special order, the order of sacrificial prayer. It is by her prayerful presence that the Church renders the transcendent present and effective in history. Prayerful presence is indeed deployed through all the phases of the divine liturgy; but it is concentrated at one point: the Sacrifice of the Mass. Here the absolute prayer, Christ's sacrificial self-offering on the cross, is perpetuated and renewed; here, therefore, the constitution of the Church is absolute, for here the absolute form of her constitutional presence is realized. This point is treated with the utmost sensitivity by Joseph Jungmann, S.J., in an essay reprinted from his massive work, *The Mass of the Roman Rite.*

The Catholic Church in its physical character, the actual Church building, from the stately basilicas to the humblest parish structures, is above all one thing: the place where the Sacrifice of the Mass is offered. By this token, it becomes absolutely central to the whole constitution of the Church, as the point in space where the interpenetration of the transcendent and the immanent takes place. The physical form of the Church cannot fail, therefore, to be of the utmost concern to the Church. Contemporary thought on this theme is not widespread; but it is intense and profound, and it may well in time find its concrete expression in a new order of architecture in which the liturgical constitution of the Church is not merely reflected but embodied. The name of Rudolf Schwarz inevitably comes to mind in this context. He combines in himself the roles both of the reflective thinker and of the active builder. From his book, *The Church Incarnate: The Sacred Function of Christian Architecture,* we have selected here a chapter that seems to be its very heart. It takes up the themes we noted: how the whole presence of the Church and her constitution are summed up in the mass, and how they radiate from this center out to the world and up to the divinity. Schwarz's argument is simple: the physical edifice in which this tremendous drama is transacted must itself bond all material elements—space, stone, color—to mirror this tremendous fact. His essay can be read and studied with profit not only for the particular indications it contains, but also for the matchless spirit and vision that illumine it.

The Church as a principle of social life does not stand apart from that "temporal" order which, we noted, comes into being in response to the natural needs of man. It is not a city of the saved, but a saving city; it enters into all the social formations of man's historical life with but one purpose: to make effective in them the power of grace of which the Church is the vehicle. As those social forms are many and diverse, in keeping with the many and diverse needs of men, so too are the ways in which the Christian presence is realized in them. In his essay here included, the noted theologian J. Courtney Murray, S.J., has placed his finger on the basic value for which the Christian presence in the work of the Church has stood and stands. Against the absolute misprision of Dostoevski's "Grand Inquisitor", he sets the sober record of history and theory: the basic value introduced into history by the presence of the Church is freedom. The Church has introduced that freedom first, by being free herself, and next by vindicating her freedom at every point. But this has not been a mere self-vindication—it has been part of her mission. She could render others free only by being free herself. But the full force of her freedom was to be felt not in herself alone, but also in man, the individual, by the way in which she establishes his existence and identity directly on the creative and saving act of God. The Christian concept of man becomes the paradigm of freedom in human association, and has in every crisis represented a force for freedom. The historical presence of the Church has constituted a tremendous lever by which the weight of a thousand serfdoms has been lifted from man's shoulders: not the least of them . . . political bondage. This is the sum of Murray's essay.

The same point is taken up and refined in the essay of Heinrich Rommen. Rommen focuses upon the central point in which the Church's work of freedom has been concentrated: human rights. The foundation is her vision of man as the child of God, whose being flows from none save God and therefore is ultimately subject to none save Him. But on this foundation, as Rommen strives to show, she has, over the centuries, through thought and through action, carefully built an edifice of rights, defined and effectively vindicated, which constitutes the mansion of free man and which has affected the fabric of every free society in the world today. This work of freedom through the identification, definition and vindication of the rights of the person has been slow and laborious, but this is no cause for amazement. What is amazing is the undeviating concentration which the Church, amid countless distractions and temptations, has brought to bear on this point.

The liberating force of the Christian presence in history has been directed principally to the human person, and through him to the transformations of the structure of right and obligation which forms the sinews of all social forms. But the full force of this liberating energy and presence has actually been applied to the central principle of social form itself: the principle of authority. As the essay of Yves Simon indicates, the work of the Church has been fulfilled most completely in the liberation of authority—not, it is to be noted, liberation *from* authority, but liberation within authority. This was achieved by lighting within the consciousness of authority itself the fire of Christian conscience; authority was brought within the presence of God and there compelled to give an account of itself. Inevitably the account differs from what authority may feel compelled to give in the mere presence of man. The presence of God introduced into authority the notion of service and function. Authority, Simon argues, fulfills itself in its functions; these functions are dictated to it, not by its own interest, but by the interest it serves, which is the common good. The common good, in turn, finds realization in the good of the individual. Upon this insight Catholic thought has insisted, opposing, on the one hand, all forms of anarchism, which would dissolve authority, and on the other, all forms of authoritarianism, in which authority becomes self-servant rather than the servant of the common good.

Don Luigi Sturzo has earned the right to speak on the whole range of this issue. Under the heading "Politics and Moral Theology", he treats,

not a narrow casuistic, but the dialectic of principles. He returns to the
starting point of all Catholic thought on these matters, Christ's own
words "give to Caesar the things that are Caesar's, and to God the things
that are God's". One can render to God what is God's only when it is
Caesar himself who is rendered to him. The task of grace is to transform
from within the whole power structure of human society; not, however
by the negation of power, not by its alienation, but by its inward transformation. But this transformation is not sudden and apocalyptic. It
is the work of the Christian conscience working through history, under the
conditions which history, the history of power, dictates: *ipsis rebus dic-
tantibus*. Therefore, the basic dialectic comes into view: the laborious
penetration, case by case, of the human agent in all its transactions with
the principles of right and charity which the Christian presence represents. The process may seem tedious when viewed from without; but it
is as basic and vital as the equally tedious movement of the lifeblood of
man on its appointed way through heart and artery and brain; it is the
very beat of life itself. Sturzo represents the Catholic mind committed
with the full cargo of its message to the labor of the political life, securing
justice, tempering justice with charity, ordering power to right, in the
ceaseless daily struggle of parliament and executive office. His is not a
chamber theology nor a school-book politics. He distills a great deal of the
wisdom gained in a life of study and action, the full force of which was
felt only when, after World War II, and in the twilight of his own life,
in a spent Europe, the creation of his mind and spirit, Christian Democracy, offered the only road to peace and political order.

In the essay "The Democratic Charter", Jacques Maritain makes a
powerful attempt to bring together all of the strands, ideal and historical,
which relate the Church and the political order to each other, and to
chart a path along which the interaction between them might move in the
future. His notion of the "Democratic Charter" is difficult and complex.
The main drift of his thought, however, is compelling. Democracy in the
modern world bears a fundamental, but by no means simple, relationship
to the presence of Christianity in the world and in history; not merely
Christianity in the abstract, as a set of attitudes, but Christianity in the
concrete, in the Church. His development of the theme of sacred and
secular orders involves the transposition of values from one order to the
other. At first glance this might seem contrary to the notion of Catholicism
and its conception of the Church and her work in the world; but when
examined more closely it does not prove to be so. What Maritain en-
visions is precisely what Church and Catholicism have envisioned; namely,
that the values which its presence in the world has initiated and insured
should become so acclimated as to become themselves secular, that is, of
this world. In this sense the democratic charter, as Maritain analyzes it,
represents a true realization and fulfillment of the work in the world that
the Church is present to perform.

The impression which these essays create, when read together and in the
context of each other, is that of a rich, dense, and vital, even electric body
of thought of high seriousness and a vibrant timeliness. It exhibits human
concern, a readiness—even eagerness—to participate in a wider forum of
discussion. It is genuinely speculative, free of apologetic overtones, evoca-

tive of many cognate lines of speculation. It testifies to the fact that the Church of the ages is still the Church of our age, with a rich and urgent message, and a paramount work to contribute. It testifies also to the fact that the most vibrant dimension of the Church and of Catholic life today, as always in the past, is the intellectual life.

A. ROBERT CAPONIGRI

University of Notre Dame

III

The Church

The Church*

Henri de Lubac, S.J.

WE are now in a better position to understand what the Church is. For all dogmas are bound up together. The Church which is "Jesus Christ spread abroad and communicated"[1] completes—so far as it can be completed here below—the work of spiritual reunion which was made necessary by sin; that work that was begun at the Incarnation and was carried on up to Calvary. In one sense the Church is herself this reunion, for that is what is meant by the name of Catholic by which we find her called from the second century onwards, and which in Latin as well as in Greek was for long bestowed upon her as a proper noun. καθολικός, in classical Greek, was long used by philosophers to indicate a universal proposition. Now a universal is a singular and is not to be confused with an aggregate. The Church is not Catholic because she is spread abroad over the whole of the earth and can reckon on a large number of members. She was already Catholic on the morning of Pentecost, when all her members could be combined in a small room, as she was when the Arian waves seemed on the point of swamping her; she would still be Catholic if tomorrow apostasy on a vast scale deprived her of almost all the faithful. For fundamentally Catholicity has nothing to do with geography or statistics. If it is true that it should be displayed over all the earth and be manifest to all, yet its nature is not material but spiritual. Like sanctity, Catholicity is primarily an intrinsic feature of the Church.

The Church in each individual calls on the whole man, embracing him as he is in his whole nature. "People think that you can play on a man as you play on an organ. An organ he is in truth, but a strange and fitful one. He who can play on an ordinary organ will produce no chords from this one."[2] But the Church can play on the organ because, like Christ, she "knows what is in man", because there is an intimate relationship between the dogma to which she adheres in all its mystery and human nature, infinitely mysterious in its turn. Now by the very fact that she goes to the very foundation of man the Church attains to all men and can "play her chords" upon them. Because she is eager to draw them all together she is fitted to do so.

Catholicity was understood in this sense by the great apologists of the first centuries, even though afterwards when the treatise on the marks of the Church came to be written too much importance was attached to geographical considerations. St Ambrose contemplating the Church saw her embracing both earth and sky with Christ set above for sun. He sees her including the whole *orbis terrarum* because he is aware that all, whatever their origin, race or condition, are called on to become one in

* From *Catholicism*; see p. x above.
[1] Bossuet, "Allocution aux nouvelles catholiques" (*Oeuvres oratoires*, Lebarq, t.o., p. 508).
                                    [2] Pascal, Br. 3.

Christ, and that thenceforward the Church is fundamentally that unity. From another point of view the same may be said of Origen, Tertullian and St Augustine. In such expressions as *per orbem terrae ecclesiae latitudo diffusa*[3] Origen states what is a requirement arising from his idea of the Church rather than actual statement of fact. Tertullian, mistaken in this like so many others, celebrated the actual extensive universality of the Church in phrases that were far too oratorical; but over and beyond this he describes that universality "in depth" which he explained by showing its relation with the human soul, everywhere the same and everywhere "naturally Christian".[4] In the same way there is not a little of the same illusion in St Augustine's *Chorus Christi jam totus mundus est*.[5] And yet, though it is not so accurate an estimate of the reality, it was a sound view of the nature of the Church that made the holy doctor add *Chorus Christi ab oriente ad occidentem consonat*. Whatever the number of members—that *Catholicae multitudo* so dear to St Augustine—and however great or small the part of the earth on which she was to be found, the Church still sings the canticle that is never old, the canticle of universal charity: *Pax vinculum sanctae societatis, compago spiritualis, aedificium de lapidibus vivis*. Without restriction of space she extends from "sea to sea", spreading out her song *per universum orbem terrarum*. It is not, then, the small extent of their territory that is the burden of St Augustine's censure of the Donatists but their claim to self-sufficiency, to restrict the Church to their own bounds, *quasi perditis caeteris gentibus*,[6] and of solving all difficulties *inter Afros*.[7] It is their sectarian spirit and parochialism: *et nescio quia ponit in Africa fines caritatis*.[8] On the other hand, what he loves and admires in the *Catholica*, the *Unica Catholica*, is not just here mere universality, open to all men and excluding none—*ad ultimas gentes crescendo porrigitur*—but the bond of peace, that cohesion that is created wherever her sway extends.[9] In the fullest meaning of the word she brings beings into existence and gathers them together into one Whole. Humanity is one, organically one by its divine structure; it is the Church's mission to reveal to men that pristine unity that they have lost, to restore and complete it.[10]

The Church is a mother, but quite unlike other mothers she draws to

[3] *In Genesim*, hom. 2, n. 5 (Baehrens, p. 35).

[4] *Adv. Judaeos*, c. 7, and *De Testimonio*, c. 6 (Reiff., p. 142).

[5] In Ps. 149, n. 7 (P.L. xxxvii, 1953).

[6] See *Sermon.* 128, n. 1 and 10 (P.L. xxxviii, 768) and *Sermon.* 12 *Denis*, c. 3 (P.L. xlvi, 853) for the argument against the Donatists who found in the Canticle of Canticles a prophecy of an African Church. In order to square their assertions with the many texts of scripture quoted against them the Donatists claimed that the Church had already penetrated everywhere, but that thenceforward it was confined to Africa—an idea analogous to that of certain apologists who speak of a transient or precarious Catholicism. Augustine, *De agone christiano*, n. 31 (P.L. xl, 307); *Contra epist. Parmeniani*, lib. 2, n. 38 (P.L. xliii, 79); *Contra litteras Petiliani*, lib. 2, c. 39, n. 94 (P.L. xliii, 294).

[7] *Collatio cum Donatistis*, 3a dies, c. 3 (P.L. xliii, 624).

[8] *In I Joan.*, tract. 10 (P.L. xxxv, 2060).

[9] *Epist.* 140, n. 43 (P.L. xxxiii, 556).

[10] It seems a little inaccurate, therefore, to assert, as a recent author has done, that the "development of the idea of a qualitative Catholicism" in opposition to the idea of a "spatial numerical Catholicism" has found favour in recent years on account of a certain neglect of the patristic sources of doctrine (G. Thils, *Les Notes de l'Église dans l'apologétique catholique depuis la Réforme*, p. 252).

her those who are to be her children and keeps them united together in her womb. Her sons, says St Maximus, come to her from all sides:

> Men, women, children, profoundly divided in nationality, race, language, walk of life, work, knowledge, rank or means . . . all these she recreates in the Spirit. On all in the same measure she imprints a divine character. All receive of her a single nature which cannot be divided and by reason of which their many and deep differences can no longer be held in account. By it all are brought up and united in a truly Catholic manner. For (in the Church) no one is in the slightest degree separated from the community, all are fused together, so to speak, one in another, by the mere and undivided strength of faith. . . . Christ is also all in all, for he encloses all in himself by his sole power, infinite and all-wise in its goodness, like the centre to which all lines converge, so that all the creatures of the one God should not be strangers or enemies to each other without common grounds whereon to show their friendship and the peace between them.[11]

That was the mystic reality, with its visible result of fraternal charity, a radiant novelty in the midst of a world grown old in its divisions, that aroused the enthusiastic admiration of such as St John Chrysostom or St Augustine. Chrysostom exclaims in his commentary on St John, when he reaches those words "to gather together those who are high and these who are far off": "What does that mean? It means that of one and all Christ makes a single body. Thus he who lives in Rome may look on the Indians as his own members. Is there any union that may be likened to this? Christ is the head of all."[12] And St Augustine, again extolling the Church in his well-known hymn in the *De moribus ecclesiae*: "You unite together the inhabitants of the cities, the different peoples, nay the whole human race, by belief in our common origin, so that men are not satisfied in being joined together, but become in some sort brothers."[13]

*   *   *

Through a symbolism the origins of which seem to go back to the first Christian generations, this Catholicism found expression in the miracle of Pentecost. For in very early times the scene that occurred then must have been compared with the account in Genesis of the scattering of the peoples and also with that in Exodus of the giving of the Law on Sinai. The tongues of fire proclaim the gift of tongues that are to come; we have here indeed a parable in action which signifies and ordains the world-wide preaching to the gentiles. For these gifts were in fact scattered on the Apostles[14] simply that they might carry out a mission of unity: the Holy Spirit, manifested through them, is about to re-establish mutual comprehension among men, since each individual will understand in his own language the one truth which is to reunite him to his fellows:

"Let us go down," said the Holy Spirit to the other persons of the Blessed Trinity, "and there confound their tongue, that they may not

---

[11] *Mystagogia*, c. 1 (P.G. xci, 665–8), slightly abridged translation.
[12] *Hom.* 65, n. 1 (P.G. lix, 361–2).
[13] *Lib.* 1, c. 30, n. 63 (P.L. xxxii, 1336).
[14] In Acts 2. 3 "the choice of the term διαμεριζόμεναὶ cannot be without significance. It is the word which, in the Song of Moses, is used for scattering of the nations, Deut. 32. 8" (Cerfaux).

understand one another's speech . . . and therefore the name thereof
was called Babel, because there the language of the whole earth was
confounded" (Gen. xi, 7, 9). And behold, once again at Pentecost the
Holy Spirit comes down from heaven. He does not merely come down,
he falls down, *cecidit*. He rushes down like a thunderbolt; he restores
these "parted tongues" (*dispertitae linguae*) to the Church that they
may be the fire of a single furnace.[15]

There are twelve Apostles in the same way that there are twelve tribes
of Israel, and the number twelve signifies the universality of the world,
for the twelve are to go everywhere, teaching all nations and bringing
them back to unity. Each of them speaks all languages; one man, alone,
speaks all languages because the Church is one, and she must one day
praise God in all the tongues of the earth. "And even now all these
tongues belong to each one of us, since we are all members of that one
body that speaks in them."[16] So the miracle of Pentecost heralded, in
symbolic abridgement, the fulfilment of the promise made of old to
Abraham, and the infant Church herself, on the day of her birth, proffered
a living likeness of her nature and her end.

For just as after the flood the wicked pride of men built a high
tower against the Lord, and the human race then deserved to be divided
by means of a diversity of languages so that each people speaking its
own tongue was no longer understood of the others; so the humble
piety of the faithful has made these diverse tongues combine in the
unity of the Church, so that what discord had broken up charity should
reunite, and the scattered members of humanity, as members of one
only body, should be bound up together in Christ, the only head, and
forged together in the fire of love to make the unity of this holy body.[17]

This unity is so close that the Church is constantly personified. She is
the betrothed, the bride that Christ has chosen, for the love of whom he
gave himself up, whom he had made clean by baptism.[18] She is the
"chosen people", the "son of God", etc.[19] She appears to Hermas in the
guise of an aged woman "created before all things".[20] And here we are
not dealing with mere metaphor. The emphasis that is laid in this way
on the universal destiny of the community is a genuine legacy from the
Old Testament, a doctrinal legacy and not merely a literary one. It is
said in St Matthew that the Kingdom "shall be given to a people bringing forth the fruits thereof", not ἔθνεσι " to the Gentiles", but ἔθνει "to
a new people" of God.[21] St Paul especially, unrivalled opponent as he
was of Judaism, pours Christian teaching, so to speak, into the moulds
that this very Judaism had providentially made for it. The novelty of
Christianity consists in its being a transfiguration rather than a fresh
creation. To St Paul the Church is the People of the New Covenant.
Israel according to the Spirit takes the place of Israel according to the

---

[15] Paul Claudel, *Introduction au livre de Ruth*, p. 93.
[16] Augustine, *Sermons* 266-9 (P.L. xxxviii, 1225-37).
[17] Pseudo-Fulgentius, s. 51 (P.L. lxv, 918).
[18] Eph. 5. 25-32.
[19] Irenaeus, *Adv. Haereses*, 4, 33, 14 (P.G. vii, 1082).
[20] Vision 2, c. 4, n.1 (Lelong, p. 23).
[21] Matt. 21. 43. And compare also Deut. 7. 6; 14. 2; and 1 Pet. 2. 9.

flesh: but it is not a collection of many individuals, it is still a nation albeit recruited now from the ends of the earth; "the tribe of Christians", says Eusebius, for instance, "the race of those who honour God".[22] The Old Covenant is entirely oriented towards the preparation of the New—and it is in this that it achieves again its full meaning at the very moment when, as such, it ceases to be. The promise was made to Abraham and his seed. The biblical text, remarks the Apostle in a piece of subtle exegesis, does not speak of seed in the plural, as if there were several heirs of Abraham; it is put in the singular. This one seed in Christ.[23] Where Christ is, and there alone, can be found the true Israel, and it is only through incorporation in Christ that participation in the blessings of Abraham may be obtained. "The real spiritual people of Israel is to be found in us":[24] that will be the Christians' calm assertion. "We are the true people of the Circumcision, the chosen people, the nation of kings and priests." Gentile converts can say quite naturally, speaking of those we still call nowadays the patriarchs and the princes of Jewish history, "our fathers, our forebears".[25] In the prayer of the liturgy we still beseech the Lord that the peoples of the world may become the children of Abraham and may be led *in Israeliticam dignitatem*.[26]

Thus, just as the Jews put all their trust for so long not in an individual reward beyond the grave but in their common destiny as a race and in the glory of their earthly Jerusalem, so for the Christian all his hopes must be bent on the coming of the Kingdom and the glory of the one Jerusalem; and as Jahwe bestowed adoption on no individual as such, but only in so far as he bestowed universal adoption on the people of the Jews, so the Christian obtains adoption only in proportion as he is a member of that social structure brought to life by the Spirit of Christ.[27]

Seen like this, Jewish nationalism, which taken by itself would stand for so narrow and incomplete a doctrine, finds its full meaning in an anticipatory symbolism. It was not merely of service, as is generally admitted, for the upholding of the chosen people, a necessary condition for the maintenance of their religion. The national character of the kingdom of God, in apparent contradiction with its world-wide character, was an antidote to all attempts at interpretation in an individualist sense. Made spiritual and world-wide, as the prophets had indeed foretold,[28] Judaism passed on to Christianity its concept of salvation as essentially social. If, having regard to the greater number of the faithful, the Church derives more particularly from the Gentiles—*Ecclesia ex gentibus* —the idea of the Church, none the less, comes from the Jews.

*　　　*　　　*

No doubt if they had taken greater care many historians of primitive Christianity would not have connected its universalism with that of contemporary pagan mystery cults. For this one word "universalism" denotes two realities which, in spite of certain common attributes that

---

[22] *Historia Eccles.*, passim.　　　[23] Gal. 3. 16; Gen. 15. 18.
[24] Justin, *Dialogue with Trypho*, c. 11, n. 5 (Archambault, p. 54).
[25] So Eusebius, *Praep. evang.*, lib. 1, c. 5 (P.G. xxi, 44–8).
[26] Cf. Collect on Holy Saturday (after fourth prophecy).
[27] Rom. 9. 5; Gal. 3. 25, 29; Eph. 2. 12.
[28] See particularly Isa. 19. 23–5, and Jer. 23. 38–42.

there is no question of denying, profoundly differ: on the one hand it denotes a vague cosmopolitanism, on the other hand Catholicism. From the very beginning the Church by her visible, intimate structure, as by the very concept which she had of herself, was apart, right outside the limits of Hellenistic religion. Combining at the same time a certain looseness of organization with the maximum of centralization, she appears to the observer as a type of society like no other.

For the redeeming Act and the foundation of this religious society have an extremely close connection. These two works of Christ are in truth but one. All that we have said so far applies equally to the visible Church and to the invisible body of Christ, and any attempt at separation will in this case run counter to the facts of history. No more to St Paul than to the other witnesses to the early faith is the Church a sort of "aeon", a transcendent hypostasis which really existed before the work of Christ in the world. But neither is she a mere federation of local assemblies. Still less is she the simple gathering together of those who as individuals have accepted the Gospel and henceforward have shared their religious life, whether in accordance with a plan of their own or as the occasion demanded, or even by following the instructions of the Master. Neither is she an external organism brought into being or adopted after the event by the community of believers. It is impossible to maintain either of these two extreme theses, as it is impossible to keep them entirely separate. Yet that is the vain endeavour of most Protestant theology.[29] Paradoxically enough, on the other hand, it is precisely Protestant studies, completing and sometimes correcting Catholic work in the field of history or philology, that strengthen the traditional view on this important point. It emerges particularly that the primitive idea of the Church is in direct continuity with the Hebrew concept of "Qahal", a word translated in the Septuagint by ἐκκλησία "Qahal" does not mean a restricted group or a purely empirical gathering, but the whole people of God, a concrete reality which, however small it may seem outwardly, is yet always far greater than it appears.

The Greek word accepted from the Septuagint was suitable, too. because it emphasized another essential aspect of the Church. The man who hears the "glad tidings" and gives himself to Christ answers a call. Now by reason of the connection between the words (it does not appear in English) "to be called" is to be called to belong to the Church. The Ἐκκλησία that neither Paul nor any other of the first disciples ever imagined as an entirely invisible reality, but which they always understood as a mystery surpassing its outward manifestations, this ἐκκλησία is in logical sequence to the κλητοί she convenes them and gathers them

[29] As, for example, Theodore of Beza, *Traité de l'autorité du Magistrat en la punition des hérétiques*: The Church "is our Christian republic, and consists of several companies of citizens assembled together. The Church is the reunion of Christian cities." "The Church", said Edmond Scherer, "is an abstraction by which the churches are considered as one whole." *Esquisse d'une théorie de l'Église chrétienne*, p. 4. Still more recently Emil Brunner, after saying "The Church is not only the totality of individuals who have been separately selected in the world and designated as heirs presumptive of the heavenly kingdom", and again "The Church is the mother of all believers, she exists before every believer", adds a little further on: "The community must of necessity create an organism for itself, an 'exterior' organ by which it manifests its life", *Le Rénouveau de l'Église* (1935), pp. 12, 14, 23.

together for the Kingdom.[30] She is a *convocatio* before a *congregatio*. Isidore of Seville, for example, faithfully interpreted primitive Christian thought when he risked the following definition, so often to be quoted in the course of the following centuries: *Ecclesia vocatur proprie, propter quod omnes ad se vocet, et in unum congreget.*[31]

She summons all men so that as their mother she may bring them forth to divine life and eternal light. Now this part of a mother is indeed allotted to the visible Church. This "Jerusalem from on high, our mother", who makes of us free men, is not envisaged by Paul as being merely in some far off heavenly future; he sees it rather on the earth, in every city that has received the Gospel, already beginning its work of liberation; she it is who speaks by the mouth of the Apostles and of the heads of churches. And when the Christians of Lyons write concerning their brethren who at first gave way but had afterwards offered themselves for martyrdom, they say: "It was a great joy for our virgin mother when she received back alive those whom she had cast out from her womb as dead."[32] Irenaeus too speaks of the living faith on which the Church alone feeds her children.[33] And Origen tells his hearers, "May you, as a new Isaac, be the joy of your mother the Church. But I fear she must yet give birth in pain and sorrow."[34] When Cyprian lays down the principle that will be echoed throughout the Christian centuries, "He cannot have God for Father who has not the Church for Mother";[35] when Basil upbraids Julian the Apostate, "You have turned against God and you have insulted the Church, the mother, the nurse of all";[36] when Augustine, Optatus, Fulgentius and Caesarius extol the *Catholica mater*,[37] their filial fondness and their unswerving fidelity go out to that society whose witnesses they are in the face of paganism, whose defenders they are against schism.

It was the unanimous language of tradition which came spontaneously to Paul Claudel when he wrote in praise of his refound faith, "Blessed be that mother at whose feet I have learnt all". A Protestant, Karl Barth, more than anyone else on his guard against the attraction of Catholicism, recognized this in his own fashion when he wrote, "If we seek to solve the question of the unity of the Church by appealing to an invisible church, we speculate as Platonists instead of listening to Christ."[38]

*   *   *

Of course—and this remark has often been made before—just as Christianity is not the Church, so the Church, in so far as it is visible, is not

---

[30] L. Cerfaux, *op. cit.*, pp. 188–91. "These three terms, convocation, Church, Kingdom, are mutually dependent, and one defines the other; each of the three is necessary to the whole conception, and taken together they evoke one of the predominating trends of primitive Christian thought. . . ." See also *Théologie de l'Église suivant saint Paul*, pp. 143 and 149–50. (But we have been unable to utilize this important work.) Cf. 1 Thess. 2. 12.

[31] *De ecclesiasticis officiis*, lib. 1, c. 1 (P.L. lxxxiii, 739–40).

[32] In Eusebius, *H.E.*, lib. 5, c. 1, n. 45 (Grapin, vol. 1, p. 35).

[33] *Adv. Haereses*, 3, praef., and 3, 24, 1 (P.G. vii, 843 and 966).

[34] *In Gen.*, hom. 10, n. 1 (Baehrens, p. 93).

[35] *De catholicae Ecclesiae unitate*, c. 6.

[36] *Epist.* 41, n. 1 (P.G. xxxii, 345).

[37] Optatus, *De schismate donatistarum*, lib. 1, c. 11 and lib. 7, c. 5.

[38] *L'Église et les églises*, trans. Moobs, *Œcumenica*, t. 3, p. 141.

the Kingdom, nor yet the Mystical Body, though the holiness of this Body shines through its visible manifestation. Do not the two terms "visible" and "mystical" bring out this distinction? Yet confusion may creep in here from the fact that in theological literature the same word "Church" is used with varying meanings.[39] For was not Christianity itself in its double aspect and double power—spiritual and temporal—for long just called "the Church"? Another source of confusion is that the Mystical Body is sometimes considered as it appears in its transitory, imperfect state and sometimes in its complete, spiritual, definitive state. So it happens that conclusions are drawn which seem at first sight contradictory. For a distinction must be made not indeed between two realities with no intrinsic connection between them, but as it were between a series of parallel conclusions none of which exactly corresponds to its opposite number. Firstly, for example, the Church is, in an objective sense, *congregatio generis humani*, the assembly which results from the reuniting of all peoples: *Ecclesia ex circumcisione, ecclesia ex gentibus*; yet in the second place it is she on the contrary who summons them, and she it is *ex qua credunt homines*. She is baptized and also she baptizes. The one metaphor of the Bride conjures up two contrary visions, both founded on scripture and both frequently portrayed: the wretched being on whom the Word took pity and whom he came to save from prostitution at his Incarnation;[40] on the other hand, the new Jerusalem, the bride of the Lamb "coming out of heaven from God";[41] the daughter of strangers or the daughter of the king. On the one hand we have the assembly of sinners, a mixed herd, wheat gathered with the straw, a field with tares growing in it: *Corpus Christi mixtum*, the ark which shelters clean and unclean animals; on the other we have an unspotted virgin, mother of saints, born on Calvary from the pierced side of Jesus, or else the very Assembly she has made holy: *Ecclesia in sanctis, virgo mater*. In the first case a group with fixed laws and well-defined frontiers; a peculiar "sect", if we may be allowed the expression, in the midst of other sects, a proper subject for sociological investigation. In the other we perceive a vast spiritual organization, unseen even by those who are its members, which is known only to God. From yet another point of view, she is either an historical institution or else she is the very city of God. In the first case, as a society founded by Christ for the salvation of men, she labours to bring them to it; she is then a means, and we can say with Pius XI: "Men were not made for the Church, but the Church was made for men: *propter nos homines et propter nostram salutem*."[42] A necessary means, a divine means, but provisional as means always are. Whereas in the second case, since the Bride is henceforward but one with the Bridegroom, she is that mysterious structure which will become fully a reality only at the end of time: no longer is she a means to unite humanity in God, but she is herself the end, that is to say, that union in its consummation.

---

[39] It will be noticed that St Augustine, for example, makes a clear distinction between the Church, which is the Body of Christ and the City of God, and the visible Church as she is contained with certain limits of space and time. In Ps. 90, *Sermo* 2, n. 1 (P.L. xxxvii, 1159).

[40] Ambrose, *In Lucam*, lib. 1, n. 17 (P.L. xv, 1540).

[41] Apoc. 21. 9; cf. 3. 12; Gal. 4. 26.

[42] Allocution to the Lenten preachers of Rome, 28 Feb. 1927.

Christus propter ecclesiam venit. Thus Clement of Alexandria writes: "In the same way that the will of God is an act and it is called the world, so his intention is the salvation of men, and it is called the Church."[43] That too is the idea expressed by the second vision of the Shepherd in which Hermas unites, that he may apply them to the Church, what the book of Proverbs sings about Christ, together with what Judaism taught about Israel itself or the Law. He beholds an aged woman whom at first he does not identify.

" Who is this aged woman, think you, from whom you received the little book?"

"The Sibyl," I replied.

"You are wrong," said the Shepherd, "for it is not she."

"Who is it then?"

"The Church."

"Why is she aged?" I then asked.

"Because," he answered, "she was created first, before all else; that is why she is aged. It was for her that the world was made."[44]

So we must be careful not to confuse these aspects, which are so very different despite their correlation. The danger of such confusion is by no means an imaginary one, and its consequences may be serious, as the history of Donatism or Jansenism demonstrates. But provided the requisite distinctions are made, and not forgotten when they are needed, it is no less important to construct a synthesis. The Church on earth is not merely the vestibule of the Church in heaven. She is not unlike the Tabernacle of the desert compared with Solomon's Temple, for she stands to our heavenly home in a relation of mystical analogy in which we should perceive the reflection of a profound indentity. It is indeed the same city which is built on earth and yet has its foundations in heaven; and St Augustine, who has taught us most of the foregoing distinctions, could exclaim with justice: "the Church of today is the kingdom of Christ and the kingdom of heaven". The Church, without being exactly coextensive with the Mystical Body, is not adequately distinct from it. For this reason it is natural that between her and it—as within the Mystical Body itself—between the head and the members—there should arise a kind of exchange of idioms: *Corpus Christi quod est ecclesia.* "I am Jesus whom thou persecutest." "He who beholds the Church," says Gregory of Nyssa, "really beholds Christ." And just as the term "supernatural" is applied equally to the means that shape man on his course towards his end and to that end itself, so the Church is properly called Catholic, and it is right to see in it in truth the Body of Christ, both in its actual and visible reality and in its invisible and final achievement. For between the means and the end there is not merely an extrinsic relationship. *Gratia inchoatio gloriae.* Since we are dealing with two states of the same body, we might use a closer comparison; we might say that just as our poor fleshly body is the same one that, in a spiritual state, will have its lot in glory—*corpus humilitatis nostrae configuratum corpori claritatis Christi*—so the Church which lives and painfully progresses in our poor world is the very same that will see God face to face.

---

[43] *Paedagog,* lib. 1, c. 6.
[44] *Vision* 2, c. 4, n. 1.

In the likeness of Christ who is her founder and her head, she is at the same time both the way and the goal; at the same time visible and invisible; in time and in eternity she is at once the bride and the widow, the sinner and the saint.

In the interests of refuting such chaotic concepts as those which see a divine Church only in a "Church of the saints", an entirely invisible society which is nothing but a pure abstraction, we must not fall into the contrary error. The Church "in so far as visible" is also an abstraction, and our faith should never make separate what God from the beginning has joined together: *sacramentum magnum in Christo et in ecclesia.* Nor do we claim to prove this union by an explanation of it for the mystery of the Church is deeper still, if that were possible than the mystery of Christ, just as that mystery was more difficult to believe than the mystery of God, a scandal not only to the Jews and Gentiles, but also for too many Christians. *Avocamentum mentis, non firmamentum.* For no one can believe in the Church, except in the Holy Spirit. That, at any rate, is not "to deify her visibility" as we are sometimes reproached with doing. We do not confuse the "institution of the Papacy and the kingdom of God". We do not "attribute to the Church what belongs to God alone". We do not adore her. We do not believe in the Church in the same sense in which we believe in God, for the Church herself believes in God, and she is the "Church of God". All the more then do we reject Monophysitism in ecclesiology just as we do in Christology, but none the less strongly do we believe that dissociation of the divine and the human is in either case fatal. If necessary, the experience of Protestantism should serve us as sufficient warning. Having stripped it of all its mystical attributes, it acknowledged in the visible Church a mere secular institution; as a matter of course it abandoned it to the patronage of the state and sought a refuge for the spiritual life in an invisible Church, its concept of which had evaporated into an abstract ideal.

But the Church, the only real Church, the Church which is the Body of Christ, is not merely that strongly hierarchical and disciplined society whose divine origin has to be maintained, whose organization has to be upheld against all denial and revolt. That is an incomplete notion and but a partial cure for the separatist, individualist tendency of the notion to which it is opposed; a partial cure because it works only from without by way of authority, instead of effective union. If Christ is the sacrament of God, the Church is for us the sacrament of Christ; she represents him, in the full and ancient meaning of the term, she really makes him present. She not only carries on his work, but she is his very continuation, in a sense far more real than that in which it can be said that any human institution is its founder's continuation. The highly developed exterior organization that wins our admiration is but an expression, in accordance with the needs of this present life, of the interior unity of a living entity, so that the Catholic is not only subject to a power but is a member of a body as well, and his legal dependence on this power is to the end that he may have part in the life of that body. His submission, in consequence, is not an abdication, his orthodoxy is not mere conformity, but fidelity. It is his duty not merely to obey her orders or show deference to her counsels, but to share in a life, to enjoy a spiritual union. *Turpis est omnis pars universo suo non congruens.*

*   *   *

This makes it possible to understand why schism has always inspired the true believer with horror, and why from earliest times it has been anathematized as vigorously as heresy. For destruction of unity is a corruption of truth, and the poison of dissension is as baneful as that of false doctrine. Nor is it only a pastor, the responsible head of a church, like Cyprian of Carthage, who thinks in these terms. Clement of Alexandria is not a whit less vehement against those who, faithless to the unity of the Church, attack, so to say, the very unity of God. We may recall Origen's emphatic commendation of that *consonantiae disciplina* without which no offering can be acceptable to the Lord—without which, indeed, a proper idea of God is wanting. For they who do not give him glory do not know him, and this glory can be given to him only in the Church— *Ipsi gloria in ecclesia!* And did not the Lord appear to Moses in a burning bush to teach us that as a general rule he does not reveal himself elsewhere save in the Church, that is to say, in the midst of that Assembly where burns the fire of the Holy Spirit?

It follows that the schismatic or the provoker of dissension outrages what is dearest to Christ, for he commits a crime against that "spiritual body" for which Christ sacrificed his carnal body. It is a violation of that vital charity which is the guardian of unity. Conversely he who does not keep charity cannot speak in the name of unity. Woe to the *perditor caritatis!* For if the charity that depreciates unity is never authentic, there is only a seeming unity where charity does not reign—*Caritas unitas est ecclesiae. Sive caritatem, sive unitatem nomines, idem est, quia unitas est caritas, et caritas unitas.*[45] Injury done to the one or to the other— and one is never injured without injury to the other as well—is to rend the Church, the seamless robe that Christ willed to put on that he might dwell among us. It is a rending so far as it is in man's power, of the very body of Christ—*Corpus Christi ecclesia est, quae vinculo stringitur caritatis.* It is an onslaught on the very society of the human race. In truth it is self-destruction, in that the schismatic cuts himself off from the tree of life: "If a member is separated from the Whole he ceases to live."

On the contrary, in the man in whom the grace of Christ triumphs over sin it will be seen that the most spiritual inwardness is coincident with the fullness of the Catholic spirit, a spirit, that is to say, of the broadest universality coupled with the strictest unity. No one has a better title to the fine name of "churchman" than this truly spiritual man, and no one is more removed than he from whatever smacks of sectarianism. For the fact that he "has received the Spirit of God and that the Spirit of God dwells in him" may be recognized precisely in this: "the love of peace and unity, the love of the Church scattered far and wide over the face of the earth". This love makes him clear-sighted, for gradually he regains the eyes which man possessed in his state of innocence wherewith in the mirror of his soul he could contemplate the

[45] Hugh of St Victor, *De Sacramentis*, lib. 2, p. 13, c. 11 (P.L. clxxvi, 5440).

glory of the Lord. Once more he becomes aware of the truth of his being, and the divine Image that has been restored in him disperses the illusions created by sin. For him, then, begins once more the restoration of that pristine harmony of human nature, together with those new splendours which are the work of sacrifice and charity. It is a foreshowing, dim but certain, of a new paradise. In the midst of a world impervious to the light and generally hostile, he has already recovered his lost unity—*per communionem quidem gratiae incipit reparari communio naturae.*[46] He knows that in Christ the faithful are truly present to each other, and that for those who live by his love the good of each is the good of all: "If you love unity, whatever in it is another's is at the same time yours."[47]

A medieval author, taking his cue from Claudianus Mamertus, expressed this view of the faith very well when he wrote as follows is a Christian addressing his brother in Christ:

> When you are at prayer you are in my presence, and I am in yours. Do not be surprised because I say *presence*; for if you love me, and it is because I am the image of God that you love me, I am as much in your presence as you are in your own. All that you are substantially, that am I. Indeed, every rational being is the image of God. So he who seeks in himself the image of God seeks there his neighbour as well as himself; and he who finds it in himself in seeking it there, knows it as it is in every man.... If then you see yourself, you see me, for I am not different from you; and if you love the image of God, you love me as the image of God; and I, in my turn, loving God, love you. So seeking the same thing, tending towards the same thing, we are ever in one another's presence, in God, in whom we love each other.[48]

What that monk wrote to another monk, every Christian should be able to say to his fellow Christian. He should try to make it understood by all men.

[46] Baldwin of Canterbury, *Tractatus de vita coenobitica* (P.L. cciv, 562).
[47] Augustine, *In Joan*, tr. 32, n. 8 (P.L. xxxv, 1646).
[48] *Meditationes piissimae de cognitione humanae conditionis*, c. 15, n. 14 (P.L. clxxiv, 496).

The Constitution of the Church*

Mgr Philip Hughes

I AM invited to speak about "The Constitution of the Church" to an audience of men of the law; and the first expectation, I presume, which the title of the address must raise is that I shall be occupied with a description of the various institutions and laws through which the 400,000,000 members of the Church are governed. For, roughly, that is what we mean when we speak of constitutions—the totality of a state's public institutions, and the laws which establish these and maintain them in being; and behind these, that which is their inspiration and their life, namely, certain principles of politics, of ethics, certain ideas about right and wrong, about rights and wrongs, about the nature of authority and of freedom—a social philosophy indeed.

And, in truth, some such description must form a part of my paper; however summary and insufficient, it is a necessary part of it.

But—and it is here that my difficulties begin—I must so describe these institutions and laws that they are seen in relation to that from which they take their rise; and that from which they take their rise is not a political philosophy, nor indeed a philosophy at all—but a religious belief. The "Constitution" of the Church founded by Christ Our Lord, cannot be rightly described, nor understood, without reference to that great mystery of the unity of the Church—the fact that the Church continues, after nineteen hundred years, to be one thing; the marvel of this visible, external oneness; and the cause of the eternal unity that brings this about: the mystery of what it is that *constitutes* the Church. And, as we continually find to be the case, whenever we begin to uncover the appearances of our religion, the consideration of any one mystery speedily leads to the discovery that it is so interwoven with other mysteries that, if considered by itself, it cannot be understood at all. You are, I am afraid, in for quite an amount of theology—and, I make my excuses, I am far indeed from being a theologian.

We must then—in this preliminary unfolding of the subject—look at the Constitution in a very different way from that which usually occupies the Constitutional Historian, or Constitutional Lawyer. We shall need to take the word as meaning that which *constitutes* or makes up the Church, antecedently to any laws or external activity; asking ourselves what the Church itself is, according to an analysis that is structural; and here we come to such dichotomies as the hierarchy and its subjects, the *ecclesia docens* and the *ecclesia discens*, the clergy and the laity. You see how rapidly the complications of the subject multiply! There is the arrayed authority, and the arrayed theology; the public aspect of religion and the private aspect; and, at the heart of it, that for the sake of which, after the glory of God, it all exists, the rights and the needs of the indi-

* From *Under God and the Law*; see p. x above.

vidual soul for its own individual and wholly personal interior life with God. Somehow I ought, in this paper, to show how all these are parts of a single whole: the Church is a unity deriving from the single purpose of the divine Wisdom which created it, and which indeed became incarnate for no other reason; for the Church, as a fact of history, is nothing else than the continuation through space and time of the Incarnation.

I propose to attempt this task by saying something (I) of what is actually meant by the unity of the Church—analysing, according to good authority and not proposing any discoveries of my own, all that is contained in this notion; by relating (II) this mystery, which is the foundation and root of the Constitution in a "legal" sense, to that which is its principal support and strength and cause—namely the sacrament of the Holy Eucharist—and thereby to what is the beginning of all our life with God, namely the sacrificial Passion of Our Lord. Then (III) I will describe the "legal" Constitution of the Church—in its essentials (which are of divine creation) and in those accidental features which are modified to suit the special needs of different ages. And finally—but with reference to this last section—I will try to say something about the inter-relation of the elements revealed in the structural analysis, and of the latest, contemporary development of the Constitution.

I

First of all, may I say that the considerations now put before you are not a mere theological décor—an appropriate and seemly setting for the tableau of a great ecclesiastical organization. On the contrary, here is the *ratio* of the whole thing. For, wrapped up in the mystery of the unity of the Church—an essential component of that mystery—is the revealed truth about God's plan for the unity of government in the Church; about the sovereignty, divinely created, in that government, and the divinely decided place in that government where the sovereignty has its being; and there is wrapped up in it the fact that Catholics accept the unity of government based on this sovereignty as part of the faith divinely revealed—that is to say, they accept, as a truth of faith, that God meant the whole Church of Christ on earth to be ruled by the papacy.

If we look at the faithful as a body, we find there three things. First of all, there is a unity in the theological virtues and in the sacraments: for each of them believes the one thing, hopes the one thing and loves the one thing, namely, God who is Trinity and Unity; and they all have the same sacraments—and if the faithful had not any other unity than this, the Church would not, properly speaking, be thereby *one thing*: all that this would amount to would be that the faithful would be alike, in these various respects. We are not then surprised to find, secondly, that there is between them a unity in accepting a single head—not only a single head in heaven, Christ Our Lord, but a single head on earth, a Vicar of Christ. From this, second, unity there comes to each of the faithful a relation of subordination to the one head—there are lawful commands, there is dutiful obedience. For each of the faithful is moved by the Holy Spirit not only to believe the one thing, to hope the one thing and so forth, but also to be obedient to one and the same head, the Vicar of Christ. But even this, if this were all, would not mean that the Church *is* one, but only that it was ruled by one: the faithful would, if this were all, be no more than so many kingdoms, as it were, ruled by the one king. And so it is that our examination discovers, thirdly, that there is also a unity in the collectivity of all the faithful—a unity, that is to say, from which there comes to each of the faithful a relation to every other one of the faithful; it is a relation whereby each realizes that he is a part of a people that is one people. And, thereby, there results for each a dependency upon, or from, the whole; and also there comes a rule in all that they do or endure. For the faithful are moved by the Holy Spirit to the various acts of their religious life—believing, hoping, loving, sanctifying, obeying, *commanding*,[1] or illuminating through a conveyance of revealed doctrine—in such a way that it is as active parts of a single whole that they do these acts: the Holy Spirit not merely moving the faithful to do these acts, but to do them in this way. For the Holy Spirit has willed that the Catholic Church—that is to say, the Church as a whole —shall be one thing and not several things. And thus it is that he moves each of its members to act in this precise way that—whether their activity be interior or external—they act as parts of a whole, and for the sake of the whole, and according to the whole: they believe, they hope, they administer the sacraments, they receive them, they teach, they learn and the rest—according to the faith and tradition of the whole.

And so it comes about that between churches which seem to be altogether cut off from one another, as for instance the churches of Spain and the churches of Scotland, there is not only an agreement in belief, in hope and in charity, in the use of the same sacraments and in their obedience to the one head, but there is also a clinging of every part of the one to every part of the other, in a congregation that is numerically one, which congregation has for its first and principal ruler the Holy Spirit.

Now—of all those things that make for the good of one's neighbour, this unity of the Church of Christ is the greatest; for what it effects is the good—the spiritual good—of the whole world. It is the very being—this unity, that is to say—it is the very being of the Church considered as a thing which is a single whole.

Nor is this all. But, first, in passing, and as throwing more light on the nature of what we are analysing, it may be pointed out that here lies the reason why schism is held as a sin against charity, rather than a sin against faith. For that unity from which the schismatic separates himself is a unity that is the work of charity. What is it makes a schismatic? Simply this, that a man who believes in the Church, one of the faithful, refuses to act as part of the whole; he refuses, that is to say, at a given moment, for one reason or another, to regard himself as a part of the one only Church; whatever the diversity of opinions, or of preferences, it is just in so far as, or inasmuch as, a man wills to sanctify others or to be sanctified himself, to teach or to be taught, to provide for others or be himself provided for, not as a part of the Catholic Church but as

[1] Italics mine.

something distinct and separate: it is just in so far as this is his mind that, from being a Catholic, he becomes and is a schismatic.[2]

II

And here we make a transition to our next consideration about this mysterious unity of the Church. We have seen it as a unity bound up with identity of faith and worship, with obedient acceptance of one ruling authority, and with the acceptance of the role, under that authority, of a part within the whole; our next stage is the relation of that unity to charity.

Very simply indeed can the principle be stated—there can never be unity where there is no charity. This unity in the Church whereby the Church is one thing is a spiritual unity; and such spiritual unity is the fruit of charity—the virtue that is first infused into the soul by the reception of the sacrament called Baptism. It is through the charity of the faithful—that is, through their love of God, above all things, for his own sake and their love of their neighbour as themselves for God's sake—that the Holy Ghost brings it about that each of the faithful is willing to be, and to live, as a part of that single Catholic collectivity of which the Holy Ghost himself is the life, and thereby to make up the Catholic Church.

And here, in order to bring out more explicitly what otherwise may have sounded but a truism—whereas it is, of course, a major and most vital truth, practical no less than speculative—something needs to be said of another truth about the Church of Christ, namely, that the Church is a thing constituted by the faith of Christ and the sacraments of the faith. This will lead us to a consideration of the place of the Holy Eucharist, not of course in the general system of the Church, which is not our subject, but rather of its place in the production and preservation of unity regarded as the fruit of charity.

The Church—it is St Thomas who says it, with the simple sureness of genius—is "the faith of Christ and the sacraments of the faith".[3] This is what the Church is—and what else does the Church do, except teach the faith and administer the sacraments? In this phrase, indeed, there is resumed all that the Church is, and all that for the sake of which it was called into being. And it is as doing this, that another great summary description of the Church was long ago coined, namely, that the Church is the continuation through space and through time of the Incarnate

---

[2] This analysis of the truth "the Church is one", is a résumé of the classic commentator of St Thomas Aquinas, Thomas de Vio, Cardinal Cajetan (1469–1534), commenting the *Summa Theologica*, part II-II, q. 39, a. i, the 2nd objection: Leonine Edition of St Thomas, vol. VIII, p. 307 (Rome, 1895).

[3] *Summa Theologica*, part III, q. 64, a. 2, a reply to the 3rd objection. St Thomas has been showing how it is that only God can institute sacraments. The objection is then suggested that since the Apostles were given God's place on earth (vicem Dei gesserunt in terris) they could institute new sacraments. The answer to this, based on the principle that what was given over to the care of the Apostles was a Church fully constituted, is worth transcribing in full: "Ad tertium dicendum, quod Apostoli et eorum successores sunt vicarii Dei, quantum ad regimen Ecclesiae constitutae per fidem et fidei sacramenta. Unde, sicut non licet eis constituere aliam Ecclesiam, ita non licet eis tradere aliam fidem, neque instituere alia sacramenta; sed per sacramenta quae de latere Christi pendentis in cruce fluxerunt, dicitur esse fabricata Ecclesia Christi."

Life of God the Son. And if we turn from these sublimities to what, at first sight, seems but a poor relation indeed, to the Canon Law, we find that, excluding the procedural law, nearly two-thirds of the whole code are taken up with laws to promote this divine work, to protect it, and to ensure, if not its *esse*, certainly its *bene esse*.[4]

It is by our receiving the sacraments—I quote St Thomas once again—that there is linked up with ourselves the power of the Passion of Christ:[5] and, in keeping with a traditional way of speech that is much older still, he goes on to say how this was prefigured when, from the side of Our Lord, as he hung on the cross, in the very moment of the consummation of his sacrifice for us, there flowed out water and blood, types in particular of the two chief sacraments, Baptism and the Holy Eucharist.

The faith of Christ; the sacraments of the faith; the Church of Christ: the connection, and the common construction which these three make up, is brilliantly set out by the declaration that to teach another faith, to institute other sacraments, to found another church are but three ways of saying the same thing.[6]

These seven sacraments, in the administration of which the practical side of the Church's office towards man's salvation can thus be resumed, are not of equal importance in that work of salvation, though all seven are equally sacraments; and above all the rest, in infinite distance, there towers the Holy Eucharist. This sacrament is above all the rest, and it must be so, if only for this reason that whereas all the sacraments give grace and, as the phrase goes, "contain" grace—the Holy Eucharist contains not only grace, but the very Author of Grace, really and objectively present in the very sacrament, and not merely in the one who receives the sacrament. So much is general sacramental theology. But with reference to our inquiry about the mysterious unity of Christ's Church, about that unity considered as an interior thing, and a fruit of grace, as the working out in practice of a *fiat* of the Most High, from this point of view the sacrament of the Holy Eucharist has a role that is all its own; for to promote this unity is one of the two main purposes for which, as a sacrament to be received, the Holy Eucharist was instituted.

May I illustrate what I mean by a series of very simple citations from the classic authority here—St Thomas Aquinas? "In this sacrament," he says, "the whole mystery of our salvation is contained"[7]; the whole mystery—namely, our relation to the passion of Our Lord, to the one Church of Our Lord, and to Our Lord as our future eternal bliss; our relation to the promise, to the means, to the fulfilment.

It is to the "Church relation" that we must, tonight, rigidly confine ourselves; and so we learn that "by the sacrament of the Eucharist what is signified is the unity of the Church".[8] Again, "This sacrament has a triple significance (that is, for the past, for the present, for the future).

---

[4] Cf. Yves Congar, O.P., "des études recentes portant sur le contenu du Droit actuel aussi bien que sur l'histoire, ont montré combien foi, discipline et liturgie se compenetrent, et combien de Droit de l'Église est, à titre essentiel, une organisation de son culte sacramental"; *Pour une théologie du laicat in Études*, January 1948, p. 42.

[5] *Ibid., Summa Theologica*, part III, q. 62, a. 5.

[6] Cf. the last note but two.

[7] *Summa Theologica*, part III, q. 83, a. 4. [8] *Ibid.*, q. 65, a. 3.

. . . In respect of the present, it signifies the unity of the Church, to which men are by this sacrament aggregated; for by this sacrament we communicate with one another and are united one to another".[9]

"Iube haec perferri per manus sancti angeli tui in sublime altare tuum", the priest says in the Canon of the Mass, mysterious words; but for St Thomas, so insistent on this aspect of the sacrament, by the word *haec*—these things—it is the Church that is meant, the prayers of priest and people, of that mystical body of Christ for the sake of which the real Christ is now there before the priest upon the altar by virtue of the sacramental words. It is for the mystical body the priest begs that its prayers be carried on high, says the saint, because "it is this which is signified in this sacrament".[10]

The Holy Eucharist is "the sacrament of ecclesiastical unity"[11]—*tout court*; it is "the sacrament of the whole ecclesiastical union".[12]

Again, when St Thomas comes to consider the effects which the sacrament was instituted to produce, the same idea is no less evident to him. "The effect produced by this sacrament is twofold: one effect is something which the sacrament signifies and contains, namely, Christ himself; the other effect is something which the sacrament signifies but does not contain, namely, the mystical body of Christ"[13]—i.e. the Church. "The unity of the mystical body is the fruit of the reception of the real body."[14] With this declaration we approach the very heart of the teaching: "The effect of this sacrament is the unity of the mystical body."[15] And all this is but reasonable, natural, what might be expected, since, in another place, is this key thesis, "The effect of this sacrament is charity, not only charity as a habit, but charity also in act, which activity is by this sacrament aroused."[16]

One last point I must not omit, lest I give a wrong impression about the Holy Eucharist as a principal, divinely wrought means of the unity of the Church through charity—and as illustrating the teaching that the Church is, in fact, nothing more than the faith of Christ and the sacraments of the faith. It is this: The union with Christ Our Lord which this sacrament signifies and actually brings about, is not just *a* union with Christ Our Lord—but, precisely this, a union with Christ Our Lord self-immolated, self-offered for us, as a willing victim, in loving propitiation for our sins. The new strength, the nourishment, all that the Holy Eucharist does as a sacrament for those who receive it and for the Church, it does in the closest possible relation with its other role, namely that it is a sacrifice, that it is also the Mass—it is because it is a union with Christ Our Lord as offered to the Father in the Mass, that our union in Holy Communion is effective. This should never be out of mind. Always, "It is the Mass that matters"—even though we receive Holy Communion apart from Mass and outside Mass; and the Mass "matters", not just because it is thereby that Holy Communion becomes a possibility, but

[9] *Summa Theologica*, part III, q. 73, a. 4.
[10] *Ibid.*, q. 83, a. 4, the reply to the 9th objection.
[11] *Ibid.*, q. 80, a. 5, the reply to the 5th objection.
[12] *Ibid.*, q. 83, a. 4, the reply to the 3rd objection.
[13] *Ibid.*, q. 80, a. 4.
[14] *Ibid.*, q. 82, a. 9, the reply to the 2nd objection.
[15] *Ibid.*, q. 73, a. 3.   [16] *Ibid.*, q. 79, a. 4.

because it is through a union with Christ Our Lord sacrificially offered in the Mass, that the union achieved in Holy Communion is fruitful. The Mass—again this is not a digression—is never a private devotion: that "private" Mass, about which, in the sixteenth century, there was so much hostile comment and controversy, is, in the nature of things, an impossibility. For *Ubi missa, ibi ecclesia*—in this sense, namely, that it is by the Church's authority that every Mass is offered, in the Church's name and for the Church, for the whole Church. And, in a very important sense—and here I rejoin my thesis—there can be no such thing as private devotions in the Catholic Church: whatever our devotions, if they are lawful we do them as Catholics; and whatever we do as Catholics cannot but be done in function of our membership; all is part of the Constitution of the Church, it is the unity in action—for it is precisely by these activities that the living Church is constituted.

III

I come now to speak of the Constitution in the ordinary legal sense which this word has—to say something of those institutions and laws through which lawful authority rules this unity. May I repeat that what has been said so far is no mere décor of seemly theology for the somewhat less inspiring business of describing human beings as they carry out, *in concreto*, the plan that is divine? I am emboldened to take a simile from your own learned profession. The foreigner who wishes to know how England is governed may be taken down to the House of Commons; and, if his guides are intelligent, to the Old Bailey also, and even to those Courts in the Strand where the great fortunes are made of which—when you are promoted—we read in the evening papers. Even so, that is not enough. If he is really to pierce below the surface, and to understand what he has spent the day observing, our foreign friend must ask his guide to take him to the Inns of Court where he will find, not merely lawyers, even distinguished lawyers, but the law itself, enshrined in a living tradition that never dies; where he will find doctrines centuries old, and corporations of which these doctrines are the life, and which in turn ensure the future of the doctrines: you notice I say *doctrines*, for, in one way or another, lawyers *teach* law to one another; and it was one of the greatest of all of your profession who told the world the great secret that it is taught law which is tough law.

This is in part excuse, in part explanation—or my justification—for the long theological excursus: this excursus is really the heart of my paper. *My* tour I have begun in the Temple; and I ask your patience as, in my turn, I prepare to cross over the Strand.

I must begin by saying that the warrant for the external thing which I am about to describe, its basis and the source of its life is, necessarily, an act of the divine will. The basis of that unity among us, so often commented on, is not discipline accepted but truth believed, not acts of the will but acts of the intelligence—for it is the intelligence that is the seat of faith: that unity is not a natural phenomenon but a supernatural effect, and so is inexplicable in terms of the natural. The beginning of it all, historically, is God's creation of the episcopal office: the divine arrangement that the Church should consist of groups of the faithful, each group taught and ruled, in all that belongs to "the faith and to the sacraments of the faith", by one who is commissioned divinely for the work and who receives the sacramental power necessary through a sacramental imposition of hands. These rulers are the bishops; and it is in this idea, that it is the ruler who is the teacher and the teacher who is the ruler, that Harnack has seen the "core" of Catholicism. No bishop is more a bishop or less a bishop than any other bishop, whether he rules over hundreds of thousands from palatial chanceries with a trained secretariat and all the apparatus of a prosperous industrial corporation or whether, like the Chinese bishop revealed to us recently by the Congregation of Propaganda, he sits on his porch in an old cotton suit spinning flax for a living.

All bishops are equal in their episcopal quality and, with a solitary exception, they are equal in their jurisdiction. The exception is, again, a divine creation—sovereignty over all other bishops (and indeed over the whole Church of Christ on earth) is part of the office of the bishop who is successor to that Apostle to whom it was said, "Thou art Peter, and upon this Rock I will build my Church, and to thee I will give the keys of the kingdom of Heaven." This, evidently, is a disciplinary regulation. But it is a disciplinary regulation that has God for its author, and that is known to man through God revealing it and through man's believing God revealing; in other words, it is a truth of faith. And as a truth of faith it is an *internal constituent* of the religion of Christ Our Lord—it is, indeed, that internal constituent which, taken and believed by all who believe God revealing his mind about his Church, serves first of all as the *immanent* spiritual link between them all, and makes of them all that one thing, the single universal Church. The universal jurisdiction of the papacy could not function as it does were it no more than an external link, imposed on the universal Church from without, even though accepted willingly and gladly. And if there were not that internal thing which the universal papal jurisdiction in fact is, then there would not be a *church* of Christ, but merely so many unities of individuals faithful to his words, more or less, each according to his lights. "Alas, Mr Bonvisi," said St Thomas More to his lifelong friend, "whither was I falling, when I made you that answer of the primacy of the Church?[17] I assure you, that opinion alone was enough to make me fall from the rest, for that holdeth up all."

[17] Viz.: that the papal supremacy was a mere human ordinance, "for the more quietness of the ecclesiastical body"; cf. Chambers, *More*, p. 196, referring to Strype, *Eccles. Mem.*, 1822, vol. III, pt. ii, pp. 491–3. Cf., for a modern, classic (and authoritative) statement of the role of this truth of faith in relation to the rest, the encyclical letter *Mit Brennender Sorge* (1937) of Pius XI, published by the Catholic Truth Society as *The Persecution of the Church in Germany*, pp. 18–19. Also a brilliant page of Newman (*Development of Christian Doctrine*, standard edition, pp. 154–5) explaining how "it is impossible, if we may so speak reverently, that an infinite wisdom, which sees the end from the beginning, in decreeing the rise of an universal Empire, should not have decreed the development of a sovereign ruler", p. 155; "A political body cannot exist without government, and the larger is the body the more concentrated must the government be. If the whole of Christendom is to form one Kingdom, one head is *essential*; at least this is the experience of eighteen hundred years. As the Church grew into form, so did the power of the Pope develope [*sic!*]; and wherever the Pope has been renounced, decay and division have been the consequence", p. 154 (italics mine).

All the complex of officers, laws, administration, courts and the rest is but the human development, through nineteen hundred years, of the means by which this divinely created authority—of the bishops and of the pope—takes effective shape.

The papacy has always been there, the Bishop of Rome, that is to say, who, "successor to Blessed Peter in the primacy, has not only a primacy of honour, but the supreme and full jurisdiction over the whole Church, as well in all that belongs to faith and morals as in what belongs to the discipline and ruling of the Church throughout the whole world",[18] and at no time, so history seems to show, has any Catholic who publicly denied the supreme authority claimed by the popes been allowed to "get away with" his denial.

In the course of the nineteen hundred years of its history, this supreme authority has been exercised through a variety of systems. The present form of the administration goes back to the century of the reforming Council of Trent; and the law it administers goes back, substantially, for yet another five hundred years, to the greatest of all papal reformers, St Gregory VII, Hildebrand, the contemporary of our own William the Conqueror.

To Hildebrand, in fact, facing the task of pulling religion out of the slough of "the century of iron", an age when Europe all but succumbed, under a long succession of barbarian assaults, of famines and of plagues, an age when the Church was truly "in the layman's power",[19] it became more and more evident that the reforms needed to be seen, by those upon whom they were imposed, as that restoration of an earlier, better state of things, which they were in fact. He realized that nothing could be more useful than the re-publication, after generations of oblivion, of the Church's own ancient laws, the decrees of popes, the canons of councils, the *dicta* of ancient fathers and saints. Whence, side by side with those external activities that took popes and legates into every country of the north and west, there began a vast activity of scholarly research in libraries everywhere—an enterprise no less important in the sequel than the better known, and vastly more dramatic, scenes where popes and emperors confronted each other in open conflict. It was from this research, begun in the mid-eleventh century, from these labours which came to fruition in the very generation that saw the return to European life of the scientific law of imperial Rome, that the Canon Law, as an ordered system, was born.

As a symbol of that early research I recall to you the familiar name of Lanfranc; and along with the names of Gratian, whose fundamental *Decretum* appeared in the opening years of our King Stephen (1142), and of Gratian's greatest pupil Roland Bandinelli in whom, as Pope Alexander III, this Canon Law first—and in what constructive power!— ascended the throne of St Peter, I recall the name of another Archbishop of Canterbury who was also perhaps Gratian's pupil, and certainly his disciple, the one time chancellor of King Henry II, St Thomas Becket.

[18] The quotation in the Canon Law statement of this truth of faith (Codex of Canon Law, c. 218, I).
[19] Cf. the title of a masterly book on this subject, *L'Église au pouvoir des laïques* (888–1057) by E. Amann and A. Dumas (Paris, 1943).

Upon the papacy as St Gregory VII (1073–85) and his successors re-organized its universal supremacy, cases and questions now poured in by the hundred and the thousand, for judgement and for solution, from every part of the Church. Particularly was the flow of business strong in the reigns of Alexander III (1159–81) and Innocent III (1198–1216), and it was very largely from their decisions, set out in decretal letters to particular bishops,[20] as well as from the canons of the General Councils which these two popes assembled,[21] that the first official code of Canon Law, universally binding, was compiled in 1234, at the command of yet a third great papal canonist, Gregory IX (1227–41), by the genius of the Spanish Dominican St Raymond of Peñafort. Sixty years later Boniface VIII (1294–1303) added a first supplement to this—the *Sext*[22] as it is called—and in the fourteenth century two more were added, the constitutions, *Extra Vagantes*, of Clement V (1305–14) and of John XXII (1316–34).

All this legislation is set out after a pattern that derives from the classic *Personae-Res-Actiones* of Justinian, and which a doggerel verse conveniently summarized for the sudent as *Iudex Iudicium Clerus Connubia Crimen*, i.e. the law was set out in five books that dealt with law, its sources, and the holders of lawful authority; with judicial procedure; with the clergy as individually subject to law; with marriage and all that belongs to marriage; with the punishment of lawlessness.

This law-making, sometimes indeed original, but more often developing existing law, went forward, as is the wont of all law-making, in the company of administrative development. Here, the most striking novelty of all was the emergence as the second power in the Church of what, for centuries now, has been known as the Sacred College of Cardinals—the *corpus* of the seven bishops of the sees closest to Rome, of the priests of certain Roman churches, and of the deacons associated with other churches of the same rank. When, in 1059, one of the reforming popes of the time, the Burgundian Nicholas II (1058–61), solved the major practical anxiety of many centuries by reserving to the cardinals the right to elect the pope, he created out of hand the immense importance of the Sacred College which has endured ever since. From this time onwards, it is, more and more, with the cardinals gathered round him as his permanent council that the pope governs the universal Church: in the hey-day of medieval Catholicism they sit indeed as a body under his presidency, and so form that *consistory* in which all important business is transacted; they also sit, by his commission, to judge special cases; they go forth from Rome as the pope's personal representatives, to act in his name and with his powers in all the ecclesiastical provinces of Christendom; from them the pope chooses those officers who gradually build up the administrative system. We can, in fact, as we look at the *Sancta Romana Ecclesia* in the age of Glanville and Hubert Walter and

---

[20] Maitland (*Canon Law in the Church of England*, pp. 122 and foll.) has drawn attention to the high proportion of judgements in English cases that went to make up the new *corpus*, e.g. 180 of the 470 of Alexander III's decretals that appear in it.

[21] Third Lateran in 1179, Fourth Lateran in 1215.

[22] Very largely made up of the decretals of Innocent IV (1243–54), for Maitland "the greatest lawyer that ever sat upon the chair of St Peter" (*Selected Essays*, p. 228) and of the canons of his General Council (Lyons, II, 1245).

Pateshull and Raleigh and Henry of Bracton, see there also that same fullness of dual development, law expanding logically and producing a system of administration, and administrative needs calling for and producing a further development of law.

By the time of the Reformation the legal system is as full—and as complicated—as any lawyer, any legal archaeologist, could desire. The popes still transact their major business sitting with the cardinals in *consistory*. Their chief permanent officers—cardinals all—are the Chancellor, the Datary, the Penitentiary and—most important of them all, for many reasons besides the most obvious reason—the Camerarius, who is in charge of the finances. There is a co-ordinated system of law courts, and at its summit the so-called *Segnatura*, where the cardinals are judges; and the Consistory itself.

To say that in the 300 years between the publication of Gregory IX's Five Books of Decretals (1234) and the Fifth General Council of the Lateran (1512–17) that all but coincided with Luther's revolt, much of the law had got in the way of justice, and that much of the administration had become a source of evils as mischievous as those it was designed to check, is to say that there had happened what is to be expected everywhere, so long as men remain free to choose wrong rather than right; it is to repeat what, in a general sense, everyone knows already. It is also a matter of general knowledge how the Council of Trent (1545–63) not only re-stated the traditional doctrines lately jettisoned by Lutherans, Calvinists and the rest, but also made a gigantic effort to renew a right spirit within the central administration; and how, in the lengthy debates and conferences of those years, a far-reaching reconstruction of the principal organs of government was foreshadowed.

From all this there emerged, in the generation that followed the Council, a system and principles which, substantially, are those that still function. The great officers are still there, the Chancellor, the Datary, the Penitentiary and the Camerarius. But the Consistory, as the main organ of everyday government, now disappears. In its place is a new invention, the Congregation—a permanent committee of cardinals, with its own permanent officials and with a permanent body of expert advisors attached to it, the *consultores*, who give their advice in written memoranda. It was Sixtus V (1585–90) who, more than any other pope, fixed for centuries the character of the Roman government of the universal Church by instituting no less than fifteen of these congregations.[23] At the same time he fixed the number of cardinals at seventy. The Curia Romana remained pretty much as he left it until, in the early years of this present century, Pius X (1903–14), the greatest constructive reformer in practical matters since Sixtus, remodelled it entirely.[24] Some congregations this pope suppressed entirely; he changed the work of others, created new congregations, and by restoring the tribunal called the Rota to its ancient importance as a court of appeal from all the diocesan courts of Christendom, he inaugurated what must in the end prove to be one of the strongest natural forces that safeguard the practical working out of the doctrine of the Roman primacy.

[23] By the constitution *Immensa*, 23 March 1588.
[24] By the constitution *Sapienti Consilio*, 29 June 1908.

Today there are eleven of these Congregations; in the order in which they were founded they are: (i) the Holy Office (1542) or Inquisition, for the protection of the true doctrine about faith and morals; (ii) of the Council (1564), originally for all questions arising out of the disciplinary decrees of the Council of Trent, and so, nowadays, for the whole general discipline of the Church; (iii) of Rites (1587), among whose major duties is to conduct the legal investigations that precede the canonization of saints; (iv) for the affairs of Religious Orders (1587)[25] whose title explains the field of its work; (v) of Ceremonial (1588); (vi) the Consistorial Congregation (1588), charged with the appointments of bishops and the founding of new sees, everywhere except in missionary countries, and with all questions relating to the way in which sees are governed—the supervision of episcopal government, in fact; (vii) Propaganda (1622), which has entire charge of Catholic life in all missionary countries; (viii) for Extraordinary Ecclesiastical Affairs (1793), a Congregation which is a kind of annexe to the office of the Secretary of State; (ix) for Seminaries and Universities;[26] (x) for all that concerns the discipline of the Sacraments (1908); (xi) for the affairs of the Eastern Church, to which come all questions that concern those Catholics who belong to the sees of non-Latin rite. Three of these congregations—the Holy Office, the Consistorial and the Eastern Church—have the pope himself for their president.

The four great offices of the medieval organization still remain, each still held by a cardinal: the Chancellor, charged with the preparation and dispatch of such documents as papal bulls; the Datary, for the business of all lesser benefices than those granted in consistory: the Camerarius (or Camerlengo) responsible for the administration of the temporal properties of the Papacy, a personage of the first importance during vacancies of the Holy See; and the Penitentiary, whose business is those matters of conscience which cannot properly be dealt with by ordinary public legal procedure. A fifth office has developed since the middle of the sixteenth century which, in publicity at all events, has outstripped all the rest—the Cardinal Secretary of State, who is, in practice, the reigning pope's Prime Minister, and around whom turns the papal diplomatic system.[27]

The vast administrative reforms of Pius X had as their complement—and as a security against future sterility—the greatest re-modelling of the law itself seen for seven hundred years, for this same pope set up a commission to codify the truly labyrinthine Canon Law.[28] Pius X died as the new code was completed; it was his successor who published it on Whitsunday, 27 May 1917, to come into force at the following feast of Pentecost, 19 May 1918. Already the fruits of this great measure are evident,

[25] Founded by Sixtus V as the *Congregation for Bishops and Regulars*, remodelled by Pius X in 1908.
[26] Founded first by Sixtus V, remodelled in 1824 by Leo XII, and again by Benedict XV in 1915.
[27] It is under Gregory XIII (1572–85) that the system of resident nuncios first attains its permanent importance and extension.
[28] Never more baldly described in all its *vitia* than in the preface written by Cardinal Gasparri for the new Code. Much of the law was obsolete, it is there declared, there were practical problems for which no legal solution was possible, and in matters of the highest importance there was no longer any certainty what the law was.

the unmistakable signs not only that the rule of law is everywhere steadily displacing the bad tradition of personal administration, but signs also of a new general awareness that unless law is studied and appreciated— loved even—in its own right and for its own intrinsic value, it can never be so known as to be administered in the only spirit that makes administration fruitful, and that safeguards administrators from the perennial curse of *libido dominandi*.

The universal Church is made up of the hundreds of local churches over which the bishops preside, church of Westminster, church of Paris, church of Milan, church of Cologne, church of New York and the rest. And the authority of the divinely instituted diocesan episcopate is organized in each of these churches in a fairly uniform manner. Here, to complete the account of the Church's constitution in the legal sense of the term, is the pattern, briefly described.

The normal bishop of the Canon Law is a priest five years ordained, at least thirty years of age, and technically qualified by a university training in theology and canon law or by expert knowledge of these sciences[29]; and he is appointed by the pope to whom, on appointment, he links himself not only by a public profession of the Catholic faith but by a personal oath of fidelity. For all the Catholics of the territory committed to him by this papal nomination the bishop is legislator and judge, in all that pertains to the faith and the sacraments of the faith; and he is the administrator of all the temporal properties belonging to the see. All other administrators of the diocesan properties have authority only in so far as he commissions them.

To set out in any detail what this episcopal authority means in practice would, of course, take far more space than is allowed. It may be noted, however, that the bishop must keep to the general law of the Church— he may make special laws for his diocese (and when he does so he is *solus legislator*) but he cannot forbid what the general law positively allows, nor allow what this forbids; and he is not free to rule without the assistance of other personages as determined by the general law of the Church. These are: (1) the canons of the cathedral chapter (or, where there is no chapter, the body of Diocesan Consultors) whose opinion the bishop must ask, if his act is to have legal value, in ten important matters which the Code specifies, and whose consent too is needed before he can act lawfully in another four cases; (2) the officials who, by the general law of the Church, make up the normal diocesan curia, and whose intervention is essential for the legality of many public acts. These officials are: (a) *for the administration*, the Vicar-General, the Chancellor, the Synodal Examiners (4 to 12 in number, as the bishop chooses), the Consultor-Parish Priests (also 4 to 12 in number); (b) *for the bishop's judicial power*, the personnel of the diocesan court, viz. the Officialis, the Synodal Judges (who may be as many as 12), the Promotor Justitiae, the Defensor Vinculi, the Auditor, the Notary (the last four named need not be permanent officers, but may be specially named for each case). The Vicar-General, Officialis, Synodal Judges and Auditor are, of course, as is explicitly enacted, presumed to be skilled canonists. The well-being of the

[29] Code of Canon Law, canon 331, 1.

universal Church presupposes the rule of law, and this presupposes everywhere the presence of trained lawyers.

The foundation of all this elaborate system, it is relevant to recall, is a
divine command and a divine creation, the commission to the Apostles
and the institution of the episcopate and of the Roman primacy. It is
relevant to recall this because, in the course of nineteen hundred years,
the human beings with whom the exercise of authority has lain have
made their mistakes, and have even committed sins, in their very exercise
of this authority; because the scandal caused thereby, and the scandals of
contemporary errors and sins, still echoes and re-echoes in men's minds
everywhere, and, very really if not at all logically, gives immediate right
of hearing to the specious objection that "all this" is very remote from
Galilee and the four gospels. For those who urge that "the Church" is an
obstacle to the life of "Christianity", as to those who urge that "Theology"
is a barrier to "Religion", we might answer that what, in their view,
really needs to be abolished is not either the "Church" or "Theology"
but human nature itself—man, in fact, who cannot think and who needs
organization because it is his nature to be social.

That the history of the rulers and administrators is so often scandalous
in the literal sense of the word,[30] should be no surprise to anyone clear-
minded enough to grasp the implications of the fact that "men not
angels are the ministers of the gospels",[31] and candid enough to consider
the gap between his own beliefs and the actions of his life. The peculiar
danger of the ecclesiastical ruler was long ago vividly labelled by the
genius of St Bernard—*libido dominandi*; and centuries before St. Bernard,
another *doctor ecclesiae*, one indeed divinely inspired, set out the cause
of the difficulty for all time when he wrote that "the letter killeth, it is
the spirit that giveth life".[32] The main difficulty, of course, for the ruler
no less than for the subject, is to live at once according to the letter and
in the fullness of the spirit. The performances of the mere zealous
disciplinarian—and have they abounded!—are not thereby Christian
activities any more than are those of the sergeant-major on the barrack
square. "The benignant idea of a father in God and a shepherd of souls,
with the tenderness and patience which it implies, no doubt existed in
theory. But the prevailing aspect of the Bishop's paternity was its severity,
and in the attitude of the pastor to his flock the spirit of correction was
more prominent than that of compassion ... their pastoral care was dis-
charged, not in evangelical exhortation and pious encouragement, but
in bringing their subjects to book for defaults against the spiritual
code. ..." So a scholar, expert in the matter, has written of the bishops
of England as they were on the eve of the Reformation.[33] They were not
such because they were bishops, nor because they were Catholics: but
because they were men still not entirely brought captive to the charity of
Christ crucified. And nothing is more instructive than to note how the
liberators of mankind from the yoke of pope and bishops had no sooner
accomplished the revolution, than they turned to devise new machinery
for the same purpose, where they, the liberators, should now in their

---

[30] Scandal, i.e. a stumbling block.   [31] Cf. Newman's sermon, so entitled.
[32] 2 Cor. 3. 6.   [33] A. Hamilton Thompson.

turn give *libido dominandi* all its opportunity—this time, of course, on the basis of their own private judgement.

Administration-mindedness (I am speaking to lawyers) is always dangerous to those whose task it is to provide, by means of administration, for the safety of an ideal. The main danger that ever threatens them seems to be the growth of what is in reality a cult of the administrative machinery for its own sake.[34] In the churchman the contest has been frequent, between administration-mindedness and pastoral-mindedness. Where the first is victorious, the "brainy" begin to be trained with a view to produce administration-mindedness, and all the "brainy" tend to become, by training and by employment, administration-minded; and only the less "brainy" are directed to the pastoral cares which are the real business of the priest. In no country more than our own is the witness of history more startling of the ills such a monstrous perversion must bring in its train.[35] And all this is, no doubt, one reason why the administrator par excellence, the diocesan bishop, needs to be and—so it is stated[36]—actually is, in the divine view of things, a man already formed and perfected in charity, the *uomo completo*, the saint. Sanctity possessed—a soul utterly surrendered to grace—is the only adequate protection for human nature against the temptations that beset the ruler of his fellows *in spiritualibus*; as essential to the bishop, if he is to do a bishop's work, as a knowledge of music is essential to whoever will conduct a symphony.

"Nothing is more helpful than to look on things as they really are", a modern pope has reminded us. The Church is both divine and human; and all of us need to consider its constitution in both the senses outlined in this paper, and to bear in mind that these are not two points of view, but the two halves that make up the single truth, if we are to understand the past of Catholicism, or its present action, or if, with intelligent loyalty, we are to play our own part as members of the Church, to live consciously as members of Christ, to live by "the faith of Christ and by the sacraments of the faith".

The Church when presented, or regarded, as a divinely founded institution, operative upon man, external, visible and humanly organized, can so fill the imagination that this view of it may dominate the mind exclusively—half the truth coming, in practice, to obscure the whole—to the great detriment of any wholly fruitful Catholic practice. The Canon Law is a reality, and so too are the officials through whom it is effective. But the Church of Christ is not a society in which there is a governing class—it is the Church alone who is the real ruler; and every member of

[34] "And, we may think, the movement of reform in the thirteenth century had in it a fundamental flaw—a flaw that ran through so much of the official religious achievement of the time, even through the work of Gregory IX, of Innocent IV, of Grosseteste and of Haymo of Faversham: the substitution, that is, of a legal, calculated, logical programme, apparently capable of rapid and complete execution, for the ardour of a call to the ideal, based not upon law but upon love." Knowles, *The Religious Orders in England* (1948), p. 25.

[35] This very day we are admonished of a similar ill that threatens in the world of education, "a system in which third-rate teachers are told what to do by first-rate administrators". (The High Master of the Manchester Grammar School in *The Sunday Times*, 31 Oct. 1948, p. 4.)

[36] Cf. St Thomas Aquinas in the *Summa Theologica*, part II–II, q. 185, a. 1 ad 2 ". . . ad statum episcopalem praeexigitur vitae perfectio. . . ."

the Church is, ultimately, the Church's subject, all being equally dependent on the Church's teaching, on the Church's sacraments, on the Church's discipline; and the very pope as much a *fidelis* as the little child preparing to make his first confession. And as it would argue a superficial understanding of the facts to identify *ecclesia docens* and *ecclesia discens* with governing class and subject class, so too would it be superficial, and very mischievously so, to equate cleric and lay with roles in the Church that are active and passive. The cleric is a cleric by grace and not by nature; he is a cleric for the sake of both cleric and lay—that should be evident; in no sense is his rank his own, is his function himself; he has not a property in either; really a priest, and no less really a teacher, these are realities committed to him as a trust; what makes the cleric a cleric, what gives the priest his power of sacrifice and the bishop his tenure of divine authority, is a reality accidental to the holder of either. And of that something else for the sake of which this hierarchy exists, the cleric stands as much in need, and will to the last moment of his life stand just as much in need, as the layman to whom it is his function to minister.

The cleric exists for the service of the *fidelis*—not of the layman as such: he absolves other clerics as well as laymen; he gives them holy orders, the priesthood to the deacon, the episcopate to the priest; he gives to them their last communion in the Holy Viaticum and he gives them, too, Extreme Unction; he says Mass for them during life and after their death; and to clerics also, no less than to the layman, does the cleric bring that other mystery, the divine word; as a *fidelis* the cleric himself is as fully dependent on clerics "for the faith of Christ and the sacraments of the faith" as is the *fidelis* who is a layman.

Nor would it be a true view that saw in this *receiving* of sacraments—whether by layman or cleric—a mere passivity. For all sacraments are, by their nature, acts of divine worship. To receive a sacrament is to do something for God; it is, necessarily, to make an offering; to go to confession, to make the sacramental act of contrition, is not only to receive an absolution, to say a prayer, to make a resolution to receive the graces appropriate to all this: it is also an act of priesthood, akin to that offering a sacrifice which is the specific act of priesthood. This is not just the picturesque language of a writer whose fervour has momentarily got the better of him. It is the sober, solid fact of the matter; the fact being that that sacramental character impressed on the soul by Baptism, that image of Christ which thenceforward marks the soul for ever and is the Christian's title to grace, is not just any image of Christ but is, specifically, the image of Christ as priest. By receiving the sacrament of Baptism the Christian becomes a real sharer in the priesthood of Christ Our Lord, a part actor in that priesthood which is itself eternal activity, eternally offering; and the character—"an image by which a thing is marked out as designated for a particular purpose"[37]—stamps the Christian as one set apart for all that belongs to worshipping God.[38]

The character conferred by the sacrament of Confirmation is, again, a "participation in the priesthood of Christ, a participation that derives

[37] "Signaculum quoddam quo aliquid insignitur, ut ordinatum in aliquem finem", St Thomas Aquinas, *Summa Theologica*, part III, q. 63, a. 3.
[38] ". . . deputatur quisque fidelis ad recipiendum vel tradendum aliis ea quae pertinent ad cultum Dei; et ad hoc proprie deputatur character sacramentalis"; *ibid.*

from Christ himself"[39]; and the character received in Holy Orders is yet a third participation in it.

It is this doctrine that we shall find the key to all the problems of cleric versus layman, and the rule for the conduct of each *vis-à-vis* the other; we shall also find, in the neglect of the cleric to understand this doctrine, to preach it and to apply it, the solution of many dark mysteries in the past history of the Church.

It only remains, in conclusion, to relate this doctrine to the latest phase of the Church's development of her constitution—to changes proceeding before our very eyes,[40] in which we may discern something of the shape of all the next centuries, a pledge of survival through troubles that at times might seem to presage the end of all, and an augury of yet further triumphs for the cause of Christ Our Lord. This is that movement so widely spoken of and—in this country—so little studied, to which the name Catholic Action has been given.

This twentieth century is now all but half way through its course. We are just seventy years from the election of the great pope, Leo XIII, whose reign future historians will surely set by the side of the reign of the pope who summoned the Council of Trent, and of the reign of Hildebrand himself, as a real turning point of history. Those seventy years have seen great revivals and far-reaching reforms: the return of the theology of St Thomas Aquinas to its rightful place in the *schola*; the deeper understanding of the meaning of that devotion to the Sacred Heart of Christ that characterizes the activity of all the modern popes; the revival of frequent and even daily communion as a practice of ordinary Catholic life; the renewed vigour in Scripture studies; the return to the liturgy, and the re-discovery of the science of plainsong; the new Canon Law; the masterly papal leadership (all too slowly understood by too many) in the application of the gospels to solve the social problem; the truly unprecedented growth of the foreign missions, in China and Africa particularly, the great host of the modern martyrs: it is hard to find a parallel to this in any century since that of St Dominic and St Francis; and never has the Church been more beholden to its chiefs for clear, continuous, practical guidance and encouragement.

With such a revival in full progress—a progress that the two greatest wars of history have not checked—it was but a matter of time until, in its turn, there re-emerged, in a form suitable to the new age, the ancient truth that the layman's share in the priesthood of Christ is meant to bear fruit in an activity that is directly apostolic. By Baptism he shares that priesthood which in Holy Orders is given full (though sacramental) reality: it is but logical that he be called to share the apostolate which

---

[39] *Summa Theologica*, part III, q. 63, a. 3: "Character Christi, cuius sacerdotio configurantur fideles secundum sacramentales characteres, qui nihil aliud sunt quam quaedam participationes sacerdotii Christi, ab ipso Christo derivatae."

[40] Of which, as of all, we may say, *mutatis mutandis*, what Newman says about the Papal Supremacy: "*The Sacramentum Unitatis* was acknowledged on all hands; the mode of fulfilling and the means of securing it would vary with the occasion; and the determination of its essence, its seat and its laws would be a gradual supply for a gradual necessity ... St Peter's prerogative would remain a mere letter, till the complication of ecclesiastical matters became the cause of ascertaining it. ... The *regalia Petri* might sleep ... not as an obsolete, for they had never been carried into effect, but as a mysterious privilege, which was not understood; as an unfulfilled prophecy"; *Development of Christian Doctrine*, pp. 149, 150.

is the function proper to the sacramentally empowered hierarchy. With Pius XI this truth was boldly revived, and in so actual a form as to be something of a shock to those for whom the most blessed thing about religion is that it preserves untroubled the whole universe of their childhood.[41]

The layman *as such* has his *ius* in that particular ecclesiastical activity —the realization of the divine prayer "Thy Kingdom come on Earth"— which is the very *raison d'être* of the Church of Christ; the layman, too, is an ecclesiastical person. And the *radix* of his rights and duties as such, to the exercise of which the popes invite and urge him, is a character given him by sacraments—by the sacraments of Baptism and Confirmation. The sacrament of Confirmation, in particular, is a kind of consecration for this very work. The character received through this sacrament is, above all, a reality that is orientated socially—it is something given for the service of the Church as a whole, and for the good of mankind as a whole. If it be permissible to say of these three, character-conferring sacraments, that each produces a type, then the type produced by Confirmation is the Catholic realizing his Catholicism in Catholic Action. This sacrament institutes a state, and places those who receive it in a new, special situation with regard to the Church and to society in general.

The laymen who thus rise to the fullness of their vocation have a real place in the hierarchy's business of "apostolizing"; they are an organism of the Church, and not a mere organization within it; and they are thus more important to it than when simply organized in unions for the promotion of their own piety; and, within the scope assigned it by the hierarchy, this lay apostolate is autonomous. As in the thirteenth century the popes did a revolutionary thing by calling in an order of priests for the express purpose of sharing duties until then regarded as specifically episcopal, viz. the preaching of doctrine, so now in the twentieth century the popes invite the layman to take his place—his own place, that none but a layman can fill—in the general task of evangelization.

Such is the principle: the "ecclesiastical" quality of the layman's Catholicism is proclaimed as the basis of the new forward movement. And in studying the nature of Catholicism—the Constitution of the Church, whether in the structural sense or the legal sense—this fact, and the truth which is its basis, will need to be more carefully considered than has so far been the wont of students.

There is surely nothing more remarkable in contemporary Catholicism than this development. For few things will the Church ever be more indebted to the popes of our own time. There is no more evident sign that the Holy Spirit is guiding the Church through the popes. How the principle needs to be applied in detail, in what way it is being applied

[41] Cf. the words of the Cardinal Archbishop of Paris (1 Jan. 1931) to his clergy, "You are going to have a ministry that will be, in some sense, a new thing. So far, you have been the undisputed masters, almost, as it were, kings by divine right. . . . Once the laity take their place at the side of the hierarchy to direct the Catholic Action upon the world outside, you will be, thenceforward, constitutional monarchs": quoted in *La Vie intellectuelle*, December 1946, p. 24. There is scarcely one of Pius XI's major encyclical letters that does not preach Catholic Action. See especially the four letters to the Cardinal Archbishops of Breslau, Toledo and Lisbon, and to the bishops of the Argentine, translated in the Catholic Truth Society pamphlet *The Pope and Catholic Action*.

in those countries where the papal direction has been seized upon, studied and put into the beginnings of action, this is not the place to tell. Already, wherever the popes have evoked such a response, a new spirit is evident at work, and especially a new spirit of active general charity that often touches the heroic; and the lines of a new kind of world are faintly discernible. That world is, very evidently, not going to be such a restoration of medieval Christendom as our grandparents began to dream about when, one hundred years ago, Pius IX replaced the regime of vicars-apostolic by a hierarchy of diocesan bishops; it will not be a new age *à la* William Morris. The aim of Catholic Action is not the production of a layman who will be a kind of clergyman: the role destined for the layman of the new age is one that he can only fulfil in the measure that he is wholly a layman. And the world in which he will live is this same secular world which we know—a world of the natural, with its own rights as such, rights given it by its Creator, a world, interesting for its own sake, to be studied for its own sake no less than for its relation to its Creator, and to be used according to its own character; a world that lies (and has always lain) outside the domain of the cleric, whose *regimen* is restricted to "the faith of Christ and the sacraments of the faith". Over these the cleric will continue to reign—by virtue of the special character conferred by the sacrament that sets him apart as a cleric—and he will continue to minister them to the layman, who, thus nourished and fortified, will go forth to his life in that world where, by the nature of things, the cleric as cleric cannot count. The layman will not strive to achieve the impossible task of producing out of that world, a new, clergy-dominated universe, but representing in that world the primacy of the spiritual, and ultimately ensuring it, he will link that world as a means to ends that are supernatural, and will thereby fulfil, as none but the layman can fulfil it in the realm of nature, that reconciliation to which Our Lord's words surely point, "Thy Kingdom come, on Earth as it is in Heaven".

In the World and Not of the World*

Yves M. J. Congar, O.P.

WE can see that the problems of lay sanctification arise with unexampled acuteness today as a consequence of engagement in the work of a world that is thoroughly secular. But the world had not become secular overnight. The more that scholars make known the real twelfth century, the clearer we see that it was marked by a rediscovery of nature and a more positive appreciation of the things of this world. With the thirteenth century this process was strengthened, and our attempt to examine the problem of a properly lay spirituality can invoke the aid of him whom the Church has made her "Common Doctor", St Thomas Aquinas.

His importance in this connection has been shown by Father R. A. Gauthier in his full study of magnanimity.[1] It is from that unexpected—and perhaps rather narrow—angle that the question of the Christian and moral value of earthly work is tackled. The word seems a bit too much in the style of Corneille; conformably with its real meaning, it can be expressed in terms of human hope, spirit of enterprise, man realizing himself through his engagements; one might almost say, in terms of man's demiurgic function but that it is a question of a humanist value for life rather than of external actualization. Pagan magnanimity envisaged man's greatness, a greatness he found in himself through his own efforts; it expressed the ideal of a humanism of man only. Brought up on the Bible, wherein man is good, strong, holy only through God who alone is good, strong and holy, the Fathers transposed this ideal of magnanimity into terms of relationship with God, in what he does for man and in man. While the pagan philosophers were concerned only with man's greatness and a pure humanism of human endeavour, we find in the Fathers and the monastic ideal what may be called a pure "divinism" in which everything is looked at from the angle of an immediate ordering to God, of an *immediate* adherence to him: no attention is paid to any greatness *of man himself*. Father Gauthier takes the ideas about the historical signification of Thomism that have been brought out by Father Mandonnet, Professor Gilson and Father Chenu, and extends them to his own field; he shows how in St Thomas there are affirmed an autonomy and a value of created things *in themselves*, and most particularly of man. The Fathers and the monks had simply laid the foundations of a spirituality of immediate adherence to God, implying renouncement of the world. In medieval Christendom this spirituality was lived as fully as possible, and earthly society itself was conceived in

---

* From *Lay People in the Church*; see p. x above.
[1] *Magnanimité: L'idéal de la grandeur dans la philosophie païenne et dans la théologie chrétienne* (Paris, 1951). There must be no illusion about St Thomas's earthly humanism: not only is he theocentric, he is basically monastic in his concrete ideals, which were embodied in St John the Baptist, St Antony, St Benedict. Cf. I. Eschmann in *Medieval Studies*, vol. vi (1944), p. 106; *Sum. theol.*, II–II, q. clxxxviii, a. 8; *Polit.*, i, I.

function of it; this was expressed "through the absorption of society into the Church and the effacing of secular tasks and aims by supernatural tasks and aims". Father Gauthier goes on:

> St Thomas does not belong to those middle ages; indeed, the proper import of his teaching is to sound their knell and usher in the modern world. Following Aristotle, he restored credit and its own value to nature, in particular to man's nature, and by so doing he in effect laid down the constitutive principle of modern society: the whole historical process of this society is simply a translation of its principle into fact, ever since the end of the thirteenth century secular structures have been receiving their autonomy. The thomist teaching on magnanimity supplied this nascent world with the spirituality that it called for. Of course, as we have already emphasized, St Thomas in nowise disowned the spiritual doctrine of the Fathers. His teaching on the theologic virtues (Christian hope, in this case) not only kept all its religious wealth, but he set it forth with greater clarity and force than did the Fathers themselves. But—and this is his particular work—he adopted a "humanist" spirituality, showing how it could be reconciled with the "divinist" spirituality of the Fathers. Therein lies the whole significance of St Thomas's doctrine of magnanimity. By it he made possible, side by side with the monastic spirituality made for those who have renounced the world, which is characterized by an almost exclusive dominance of the theologic virtues which order us *immediately* to God, he made possible the emergence of a typically lay spirituality: a spirituality characterized by the place given to the virtues which, animated like all Christian virtues by the theologic virtues, seek God, but seek him, not *immediately*, but through something other than him, through man and through the world which are their proper object. Now, on the plane of individual life, the first of these virtues, governing all the others, is magnanimity, just as on the plane of communal life it is social justice.

Like so many other aspects of St Thomas's wisdom, these views were not fully elaborated and applied at once. New things are first lived in individual minds and consciousness before they are expressed in social history. Time had to go by, and several stages be lived through,[2] before a really lay world would emerge, and not without men's violently throwing off monastic and theologic tutelage and experimenting with a pure humanism without God. Here would be the place to go over the stages of this "recovery of the human" which had been swallowed up in the divine and, in this sense, as it were, made alien to it. But it is sufficient to recall the elements of its "prehistory" and the inevitable character of the process.

The first movement of faith is to give all to God. What Pascal lived

---

[2] The writings occasioned by the troubles of Philip the Fair and Lewis of Bavaria with the papacy are generally considered only from the viewpoint of political theory; but fundamentally they involved a vindication of the autonomy of the lay order and a refusal to see it as receiving its validity from the priesthood. As well as the *De potestate regia* of John of Paris, see book iii of Occam's *De potestatae papae*. Here the way St Robert Bellarmine speaks of the laity is again interesting. He was writing only from the point of view of their temporal and political role, but in a measure it was an acceptance of progress made since St Thomas; in a measure only, for Bellarmine was dominated by the mentality of hierocratic Christendom even when his principles were beginning to anticipate Leo XIII's teaching on the autonomy of the temporal in its own order.

through alone during the night of 23 November 1654, the Church has lived collectively and numberless souls have lived at the beginning of their Christian life: "To forget the world, to forget everything, except God. . . ." From a purely eschatological and monastic point of view, the less of the world, the less of the body and earthly activities, the better: primitive monachism was a total withdrawal from the world, and this has always been held in honour in the Church as a vocation and an example. But in the religious life itself there has been a progressive movement away from this absolute attitude towards a certain being in the world. First, agricultural work in common was introduced, then intellectual and cultural activities, then, with the Preaching Friars, scientific work of the reason (this raised protest and opposition). We are seeing experiments with religious life "in the world", truly lay. At the same time there is a rediscovery of the excellence of marriage, and of the excellence of the body, round which a kind of theology and spirituality are being made. Christians, who had said No to so many things, are gradually coming to say Yes to them; a recovery of the human and of nature is at work in history. And so, little by little, the Church enters into the experience of a secular world and of a fully lay condition of the faithful in this secular world. For the purely human humanism of paganism she substituted the pure "divinism" we have referred to; then came the Renaissance and the emergence of a new, godless humanism; and now, recognizing the fact of a secular world and an order of properly human and earthly values, she faces the task of developing a suitable programme for its hallowing, for a God-centred humanism and a "christofinalized" human work on earth which yet remain truly human and of this world.

This task is largely unprecedented, for, in our opinion, there has been a secular world and a fully lay life only since the time that social and political life was laicized, and especially since the inauguration of a mechanized civilization which, born outside the Church, has never been consecrated and regulated by her. One is extremely conscious of this when, mixing with the crowd on a workmen's train or when a factory knocks off or at a football match—still more, no doubt, if one is engaged in business or industrial production—one asks oneself what is the relation of all that with the Church and with her sacral life and priesthood. We know well enough that men are turning away from God and that the contemporary world is a world of unbelief, of rationality turned in on itself, bent on the use of its demiurgic powers and the pursuit of happiness, all without God. But there is more to it than that. There is the fact that, for the first time, the Church is really confronted by a secular world, and by the task of developing a fitting spirituality and means towards the reign of Christ in the lives of those engaged in the work there. It is not difficult to see that new forms of holiness are called for and that, if they are really to touch men where they actually live and move, the clergy have to find not only new pastoral forms but even new forms of priestly life.

*   *   *

There is only one Christian life, which is developed according to the conditions and requirements of particular times and callings. The signs of the quest for new actualizations of holiness that is going on today can be grouped under three main heads.

(1) For a time and as a whole, Christians did not react in face of a laicized daily life. They asked no questions, and in practice accepted a division between their religious life, consisting chiefly of obligatory cultural observances, and their daily earthly life of work, family, recreation. Between the years 1925 and 1935, Catholic Action struck a heavy blow at this calamitous attitude. Catholic Action marked the simultaneous realization of the secular condition of the contemporary world, consciousness that it must be hallowed and that we must sanctify ourselves in it, and the rise of a laity which, with its clergy, was seriously considering the problem of its Christianity. During those ten decisive years, the theme of exhortations, of writings, of retreats and days of recollection was unwearyingly the same: Put Christ back into the whole of life; don't be Christians only on Sundays; the faith is not an overcoat, to be hung up in the cloakroom of office or factory, it is a total quality which must inform the whole personality and its integral life.

Thus was spread the idea that daily life, working, civic, domestic, is simply an aspect and a part of one single Christian life in which the faithful have to sanctify themselves and give glory to God—after all, a rather strange idea to the old monastic world, and still more to the laicized world between a dying sacral Christendom and the first hints of a new Christendom.[3]

This awakening of Christian consciousness was not without its dangers. There was—there always is, of course—profound truth in the things so often heard during those years: "When you are at the factory, it is Christ who is there"; the criticism of a "disembodied Christianity"; the idea of a "continued Incarnation". But there was also—and there is always—a danger, when the secular order and the Christian's full engagement therein were (re)discovered, of reducing Christianity itself to that: a danger of identifying the mystical Body with industrial work "christofinalized" in the soul of the Christian worker; of seeing in holiness an exaltation of man, a service of men, and of this service itself being humanized and laicized, in the bad sense of those words ("I've done with a faith; I'm at the service of a social world"); a danger, finally, of believing that the maximum of Christianity is necessarily found in a maximum of effective engagement in the world's work. These dangers were and are real; many concrete examples of them could be given, and they have been severely denounced.[4] But it must also be stressed that they have been effectively set off in individuals and groupings by a very active life of prayer, frequentation of the sacraments and union with Jesus Christ and his cross. Among the Young Christian Workers in particular, the eucharist, prayer and Calvary in their purest form have never been separated from the truth that they extend to the daily life of work and human relations.

[3] We have pointed out that the patristic era and the Middle Ages did not ignore the sanctification of professional and family life, but even to that they brought the points of view of their monastically-dominated spirituality. The differences between then and now are obvious. Compare how medieval lay groups were drawn to the religious orders, the rise of the third-orders (tertiaries), for instance.

[4] See, e.g., especially A. Z. Serrand in *Vie intellectuelle*, October 1945, pp. 40–61, and L. Bouyer in *Revue des sciences relig.*, 1948, pp. 313–33.

(2) During the war of 1939–45 and the years that followed there was a deepening of the consciousness of the secularity (*profanité*) of the world and of the full "laicity" of the faithful; but there has been added thereto consciousness of the missionary commitment of the Christian and the Church, and, too, a probing of the mystery of the Church and of the fact that the laity as laity are "of the Church". Hence the desire of so many lay people for a spirituality that would enable them to answer their call to holiness in their own way, by being adapted to their lay condition and to their responsibilities as real members of the Church, the people of God and the Body of Christ. They have a new awareness of being called to holiness, to a holiness not less than that of priests and religious, but doubtless a little different. Many people have now got over the idea that evangelical perfection, particularly the spirit of the Beatitudes and what are called the counsels, is not for them. Accordingly, they feel an inadequacy in the classical classifications, the distinction between the evangelical life, identified with monasticism, and the life of Christians in the world, or the distinction—often leading to separation—between action and contemplation. To deserve the name of contemplation, need prayer, the adherence of mind and will to God, grow somewhere between Heaven and earth, feeding solely on speculative considerations? Cannot it be nourished by all the doings of a dedicated life, dedicated to God in himself and in our brethren, God sought "on earth as in Heaven"? There is only one God and there is only one holiness, and it consists in total cleaving to God, who alone is holy, holy by himself and in his existence, simply, in his own "order".

Today search is being made for an understanding and a living of this holiness that properly befit the lay person and lay service in the Church.[5] In the Middle Ages a man who felt the hand of God answered by "leaving the world", he was converted and did penance by renouncing earthly things to the uttermost; and we have seen how Pope St Gregory VII reacted from this in favour of militant and missionary engagement. Today, when the hand of God touches a man, he certainly thinks of the priesthood or the religious life: sometimes right away, like Lacordaire; sometimes after first thinking of remaining a lay man, and then realizing that a total commitment of service and godliness is required of him elsewhere. But many people, often by express choice, remain in the lay state, there to try to live Christ's holiness. They want to serve God and to be wholly his in the state of life wherein his call has come to them. Lay saints, "among working people, scouts, students, fathers and mothers . . . , in every social class, and in the trades and professions which seem never to produce saints . . . , holy men and women who have lived their lives in the ordinary conditions of the world . . .". We think of our Lady St Mary, queen of all saints, who was the first lay person in the Church and who led a perfect life in those ordinary conditions. At the present time, a desire for service and Apostleship is very often added to the seeking of holiness "in the world". In a medieval world imbued with Christianity, the God-touched man devoted himself to God alone. Now, in a world not simply "pagan" and indifferent but godless, it is still like that; but the man also—perhaps especially—wants to be an apostle, to

[5] Cf. *Vie spirituelle*, February 1946, pp. 312 ff.

bear witness, to serve others, to live and bring to them the saving love of Jesus Christ. Canon F. Boulard has rightly written that, "Other ages were inspired by the superhuman virtue of the solitary and the ascetic; ours is won over by all-embracing charity and goodness". As we shall see, service of others as well as being in the highest degree evangelical is a crucial part of lay "spirituality".

(3) Contemporary aspirations would seem to receive divine guidance particularly through the example of the saints who have been given to our age and through the directions of pastoral authority.

It is clear that, looking at holiness in practice, there is something new about it, in the way that new things come about in the Church: that is, they do not abolish the old, they simply develop to meet a new situation those given resources that are beyond the reach of time.[6] It is said that St Aloysius Gonzaga would not look his own mother in the face, that the Curé of Ars would not kiss his; but Piergiorgio Frassati, who is recommended to us as a model today, did not avoid young women and went camping with them. St Katharine of Siena lived like a nun "in the world" and engaged in all sorts of difficult affairs; but when she undertook the spiritual direction of a Florentine lawyer, the first thing she told him to do was to give up his wife and his profession. Such a thing could happen today, but we lay special emphasis on the home and professional duties, on sanctification through the family and one's work. A hundred years ago a religious man, retired from work, would spend his time in devotional observances and in the company of other like-minded persons; today we are urged to be up and doing among men in a world of men, to use our energies to the full in the field of apostolic work.

Would it be wrong or exaggerated to say that fresh values are being recommended to the faithful in view of new calls of grace in these times? We are thinking of the many writings which, without for a moment forgetting the law of the Cross, offer Christians a humanist ideal, a candid engagement in earthly activities and a positive view of their worth.[7] We are thinking of the renewed vision of the world of nature, the keen concern about work and the world of work, the interest taken by the clergy in men's real life. We are thinking of the many pronouncements in which the leaders of God's people, and notably Pope Pius XII, declare the goodness of earthly activities, of the body and of sport, of marriage as being in its own way an occasion and means of perfection.[8] We are thinking of that impressive collection of texts in which the Church's pastoral magisterium encourages the faithful to recognize the value of initiative, of strength, of confidence, of cheerful and energetic collaboration in human work and earthly progress. All this is supported by the actual lived experience, not of lukewarm lay people of "worldly" tendencies, but of those who are very fervent and deeply committed Christians. It is

[6] See the passage in Newman's essay on the mission of St Benedict where he contrasts the characteristics of Benedict, Dominic and Ignatius Loyola.

[7] See, for example, the references given by S. Ligier in *L'adulte des milieux ouvriers* (Paris, 1951), p. 162, n. 2; the work of Fr P. Doncoeur in France, of Fr A. Rademacher in Germany, and others.

[8] Pius XII in *Doc. cath.*, 1945, cc. 513–18; and his address on 3 Mar. 1940, when he spoke of that charity "which affection does not corrupt but enlivens, which the marriage bed does not contaminate but heightens".

plain that all these things mean something and indicate a current that is being providentially guided in the Church of our time.

We have already remarked how canonizations and examples of holiness have a significance equivalent to providential guidance. The Church's life had always included many examples of holy life "in the world", the greater part of them, however, belonging to that *turba magna* spoken of in the Apocalypse and the liturgy of All Saints known in their glory only to God;[9] but during the past few generations it seems that a new series is being opened in the shining roll of holiness. As we have said above, the hagiography that is represented by the Breviary *legendae* presents a type of holiness that is expressed in special ways, those of asceticism and monasticism; and the laity accordingly often get from it an impression of unreality and unapproachability. God now seems to be giving us, beside the saints of the sacral ages, examples from among people whose holiness was achieved through ordinary activities, just the same as those to which we are called, but carried out for the sake of God and his reign, with perfected love and obedience to his holy and hallowing will. Such persons as St Antony Claret, St John Bosco, the boy St Dominic Savio and our contemporaries St Pius X, Bd Contardo Ferrini and St Teresa of Lisieux, she whose way of childhood would appear to be an interpretation of the evangelical ideal given by God to our world and lit up by a wonderful shining holiness. And perhaps among the saints of tomorrow there will be such as Ozanam, García Moreno, General de Sonis, Philibert Vrau, Leo Harmel, Frassati, Elizabeth Leseur, Marius Gonin, Jaegr, Brother Mutien, Antony Martel, Father Maximilian Kolb and some of the stalwarts of Catholic Action (only yesterday, John Colson).

If one examines, from the point of view with which we are concerned, the canonizations carried out by the twentieth-century popes, one will notice, as a Protestant observer has done,[10] a sort of "politics of canonization": it consists in giving contemporary people models of holiness and patrons for the different conditions of their vocation, occupation and duties. These patterns are not so much in line with asceticism and unusual deeds as with St Teresa of Lisieux's childlike spirit, in complete giving of oneself to God's will, the exact doing of the duties of one's state, the following of Jesus in his love and humbleness.

Dostoevsky sometimes had strange ideas but he was often prophetic about the state of the world, and in *The Brothers Karamazov* he sketched the idea of a new Christian vocation. The old monk Zossima, on his death-bed, tells his disciple Alyosha to leave the monastery and return to the world; there, in contact with evil, he will have to fulfil his vocation of raising up a reconciled and brotherly mankind: he will have to serve God in the persons of men. Zossima dies; and Alyosha, after reading the story of the wedding at Cana beside the body, throws himself to the ground and kisses the earth in a passion of love. Dostoevsky did not write the continuation of a story in which life would no doubt reveal more

---

[9] [Perhaps attention may here be drawn to the people of godly life who are publicly venerated because they accepted martyrdom. An outstanding example is St Thomas More.—*Translator's note.*]

[10] H. Hermelink, *Die katholische Kirche unter den Pius-Päpsten des 20 Jahrhunderts* (Zurich, 1949).

about things than do books. But the broad outline of the idea is clear enough to enable us to see the pattern of the whole.

SANCTIFICATION IN THE WORLD

It is easy to define the two sides of our inquiry. We learn from the Bible and from the experience of the Church of the saints and martyrs that the Christian, while living in the world, is not of the world—he is in it as a stranger and sojourner. Recent experience, especially of new demands made on Christians, speaks to us of sanctification through our very employment in the world and involvement in its affairs. The first of these voices has an absolute value, as a permanent imperative; the second is a relatively new imperative, made manifest in an historical situation which Christians had not yet fully experienced; the first is the expression of a universal law, covering all cases, the second is a full valuation of the particular aspect, included in the universal law but hitherto less realized, expressed in God's own word: "I pray not that thou take them out of the world . . ." (John 17. 15); "Increase and multiply, and fill the earth and subdue it . . ." (Gen. 1. 28). How can the truth of these two voices be reconciled, how can both be obeyed at once? How can the lay man fulfil his calling to be fully a citizen of the City that is to come, not in spite of his commitment to the earthly City but actually in it? There are some answers offered to this question that do not entirely satisfy us.

Some are too optimistic; they put forward service of God in and through the world's work in such a way that this work seems to be identified with that of the Redemption and of the Kingdom of God: they would, as it were, see most Christianity there where there is most effective engagement in the business of the world. Convictions of this kind make ready appeals to the ideal of Catholicity and of "continued Incarnation". But this is to forget that the Church is a different thing from the world, and that the world is not holy by itself but has to be hallowed and saved from without, by Jesus Christ. The Son of man, the New Adam, does not come from the earth but from on high; his work is not the world's work, which also is not holy by itself: it has to be hallowed by being put into relation, in a way that remains in a sense external to it, with the unique holiness of God and Jesus Christ. Moreover, many great lay saints, beginning with the Virgin Mary herself, while they were sanctified in the duties of their state, yet did not undertake big things from the point of view of the world's demands.

Other answers seem too negative, or at least too dualistic. First among these is the ascetico-monastic answer. When for instance St Gregory the Great resolves the Christian antinomy (to be in the world—not to love the world—to use it as not using it) by saying that earthly things are there for the Christian to use according to his needs but not for him to desire and cherish, we are in general agreement but not completely satisfied. For we are seeking a spirituality that shall recognize more worth in earthly things than St Gregory accords them: we want the Christian to be able to put his heart into the world's undertakings and achievements but without being enthralled by them as if they were a last end. St

Gregory's solution is wholly monastic; at bottom, it assumes that there is only one order of values, that of supernatural life, faced by which the use of temporal things is no more than an indulgent concession; eventually, it leads to what has been called "political Augustinism", whereby temporal power itself has only the consistence it receives from the supernatural order. But this was given its death-blow by the great thirteenth-century doctors, Albert, Thomas and after them John of Paris and many others. We have learned that though the work of the world is not the last end, neither is it *solely a means*; subordinate to the absolute end, it partakes of the character of means, but also of *intermediate end*, having its *own* value in its order. Accordingly it is appropriate that our commitment to it—in complete subordination to our supreme commitment to the faith—should be real and valid in its order too. We are engaged neither as to sheer means nor as to absolute end, but as to an intermediate end.

The "cosmic incarnation" position does not sufficiently distinguish between Church and world. The monastic solution does not see the whole of the Church's mission to the world: to the world as sinful, to preach repentance to it, yes; but also to the world as cosmos, to achieve its purpose in Christ Jesus. The one explanation has an idea of Catholicity that is too wide; the other has an idea of holiness and of Christ's work that is too narrow, in as much as it makes the monastic ideal that of all Christian life, even lay. Jesus is the saviour *of the world*, his incarnation and his cross are to restore creation in accordance with God's design. This restoration is indeed eschatological; but not in such a way that the work of Christians engaged in the world is unconnected with it: it is particular material of holiness and Christian value to those who are called to it.

So we have to find a way between positions that are too favourable to the world or too negative, which, however, at least remind us that the antinomy of the Christian condition here below is irreducible. St Paul was not just playing at paradox or literary conceits when he wrote of this condition in dialectical terms: having as having not, weeping as weeping not, using the world as not using it, treated as deceivers and yet truthful. It is all quite true, and we can add to St Paul contradictions inherent in the conditions of our life today: finding life hard yet being assured, worried for our children yet full of trust, badly off but finding the wherewithal to give. . . . This is perhaps to go beyond St Paul's strictly personal terms of reference, as it is to extend his thought to speak, with Walter Dirks, of the Christian being lost to the world and at the same time the friend of every created thing.[11] There is no world-loving spirituality for lay people, he writes, for they too have to renounce the world and set it at naught; but, unlike monks, they have to work in it, to use it and to serve God without cutting down their earthly commitments. Once again, to be of it and not of it, to be truly of it and truly not of it. How?

We have to start from the will of God, for it is that that sets the Christian apart from the world to make him a citizen of another City and, at the same time, does not withdraw him from the world but leaves him

[11] "Der Welt verloren und aller Welt freund", in *Geist und Leben*, vol. xxiii (1950), pp. 288–98.

to work therein. To all, God directs a call that raises them above the world; it is this call that properly constitutes the people of God, following that first call by which this people came into existence in the person of our father Abraham, father of believers: "Go forth out of thy country and from thy kindred and out of thy father's house."[12] Nobody who fails to answer the call is fit for the Kingdom of God; but neither is everyone called to work for that kingdom *directly and exclusively*. Those to whom the call comes in this sense must answer to it: no yoke of oxen to be tried, nay, not even a wife to be cherished, may be allowed to come between the Lord and them (Luke 14. 16 ff.; etc.). Others have to work for the Kingdom without leaving family and relatives, business and property— their "nets". John the Baptist sent the tax-gatherers and soldiers back to their occupations, only telling them to be more honest in their dealings (Luke 3. 10–14). Jesus did not call the centurion away from his command or Nicodemus and Joseph of Arimathea from the respectable positions or the ordinary people who listened to him from their hardworking lives; he sent the paralytic back home, the woman taken in adultery and the Samaritaness too. St Paul wrote that it does not matter whether we eat and drink or whether we abstain, he told the faithful to stop where they were; and it is clear the Apostles did not alter the state of life of those whom their preaching numbered among the faithful.

After having set the faithful apart from the world by his call, God puts them back there and assigns to each a task and duty which also is, in its order, a vocation according with the divine will. God leaves the monk in the world, but here the world is only a setting; he leaves, he sends, the apostle—priest or lay person—in the world, but here the world is only an object on which one works in view of something else; he leaves, or rather he puts, a vast number of men and women in the world, assigning to them the task of co-operating in the work of the creation in such a way that it is not alien to their sanctification and salvation, to their co-operation in the Kingdom of God.

The Christian is in the world and does its work in conditions very different from those of the man who knows not the living God. The Christian's engagement therein is real, but it is not to a closed world, regarded solely in itself and as final and definitive, but as being under the will of God, a temporary world, which man can look after lovingly but wherein he is awaiting a call whose delay does not hide its real imminence. "All things are yours", writes St Paul, "and ye are Christ's, and Christ is God's." That does not mean that every earthly joy is to be banished, that everything is to be decked in ashes and to take on the mourning of Good Friday. People are afraid of that, partly through worldly attachment to loveless pleasure, partly through wrong understanding of what for us is "being Christ's", and for Christ is "being God's". We are much too inclined to separate Good Friday from Easter; we do not perceive the deep bond between the redeeming Incarnation and the Creation, that the second requires the first, not that it may be rejected and destroyed but that it may be saved and fulfilled in truth.

---

[12] Gen. 12. 1; cf. Heb. 11. 8–10. This is in line with the well-known texts Luke 14. 26; 9. 62; 18. 29; Mark 10. 29. The association of the word ἐκκλησία itself with the idea of calling together should be noticed.

It therefore seems to us that the paradox of the Christian condition can be resolved by starting from God's will, which gives or restores the world to us as duty and as task. From this first great unbreakable link the main elements of a "spirituality" of Christians "living in the world" follow like a chain thus: the holy and hallowing will of God $\longrightarrow$ vocation $\longrightarrow$ service and its demands $\longrightarrow$ engagement and responsibility: the whole beneath the sign of the Cross.

The Will of God. When we set ourselves to learn how the Bible understands things, in particular such fundamental notions as faith, truth, holiness, the word, strength, we arrive at the following general idea, which in its simplicity lights up many texts[13]; God is the primary and supreme source of all activity, nothing has life and dynamism except through him; he alone is wise, mighty, good and man is wise, mighty, good *only through him.* God alone is holy, and especially is nothing holy except through him, that is, by belonging to and partaking of him. Now, in God, holiness is not an attribute that can be explained by another attribute, indeed, it hardly is an attribute: it is in Pascal's sense of the word, the order proper to God, his order of existence, wherein he is grounded as an inexistence itself, necessarily, by reason of what he is. It is a mystery, his mystery, a mystery being something whose explanation is carried in itself. Surely there are few verses more expressive of biblical spirituality than Psalm 18, verse 10 (Vulgate): "The judgements of the Lord are true, justified in themselves". God's will is holy; not because it is good by reference to a right and good object, but because it is the Lord's will, he who is in himself absolute holiness.

Nothing is holy unless in dependence on and in conformity with God, who alone is holy: and accordingly spiritual men all declare obedience to his holy and hallowing will to be the content and final test of holiness. Is not this what all the prophets preached, beginning with the first, Samuel? "Obedience is better than sacrifice. . . ."[14]

God's will is a will of love. As Father F. Varillon has said, love is not an attribute of God, it is his very name, that is to say, his essence, and the classical attributes (justice, all-powerfulness and the rest) are rather the attributes of love. "God is *agape*", wrote St John, precisely that source of goodness whose loving movement is directed and justified by itself, like water rising from a spring: God's love is not aroused by the existing goodness of what it sees: flowing from the source of all goodness, it makes good that which it freely loves. God loves and sheds goodness everywhere because he is God. There is no need to stop at the philosophical aspect of certain passages of St Thomas which invoke the Dionysian axiom that the good communicates itself[15]; he uses these perfectly valid philosophical notions only in order to elaborate an exposition of the most fundamental data of the Judaeo-Christian revelation. This revelation shows God, perfectly blissful and self-sufficient in the absoluteness of his glory, freely making creatures, and in particular a creature of his own image, in order that he may communicate his goodness to them.

[13] Cf. J. Pedersen, *Israel, its Life and Culture* (2 vols., London, 1940).
[14] 1 Sam. (Kings) 15. 22–3. Cf. Osee 6. 6; Amos 5. 21 ff.; Isa. 1. 10 ff; Mich. 6. 6 ff.; Ps. 49. 9; 1. 18; Matt. 9. 13.
[15] See particularly *Sum. theol.*, III, q. i, a. I, with Cajetan's comments; and C. V. Héris, *Le mystère de Dieu* (Paris, 1946).

In a succession of ever higher and more beautiful degrees, God gives his creatures being: not simply the minimum of being necessary for existence, but with the ability further to perfect their being through their own activity, to accomplish themselves and the world through a demiurgic power that is in them. Yet more, God made man in the divine image, destining him from the first to be raised to sonship, in such a way that he could accomplish himself and the world by his efforts *freely*. For freedom is the mode of action that befits a spiritual being and a person who exists in his own being, with choice and judgement of his own activity. By a further communication of God's goodness, man is called to do his work of accomplishment not simply through the exertion of the demiurgic energies implanted in him and the world, but according to another scale of knowledge and powers, that of the divine intercourse that we call grace: on the basis of a choice, a call, a personal communication through his word, then of the gift of his own Spirit, grace is a new and more intimate communication by God of his goodness.[16] That goodness goes further still, even to a real and substantial communication of himself to mankind through the union of the person of the Word with the son of David, in Mary's womb. Nothing more could be given, for this union is the only communication of his divine being itself that God could make short of pantheism.

These communications are so linked up that the first trends towards the second and finds its meaning there; together they show forth the bounty of God's successive approaches. They make part of a single design, which can be expressed, as by St Thomas, in terms of that which comes from God returning to him, or in terms of temple, as summed up by St Paul, "All things are yours, and ye are Christ's, and Christ is God's": Christ gives back to the Father all over which he has established his reign, that God may finally fulfil the communication of his goodness in blessedness and glory, and that his reign may be ours too.

Such, so far as we can know it, is the general effect of God's holy and hallowing will. It is expressed for each individual in a variety of ways in his daily life, particularly in that which may well be called a vocation. We shall come back to that. But all vocations have their place within the total purpose that embraces the whole destiny of the created universe, so that God's will for each one always involves imperatives having in view the actualizing of his mercy for the whole world and for all men. To each he accords gifts, possibilities, opportunities, which are the setting for the fulfilment of oneself, of one's task and one's happiness,[17] but also of one's part in the accomplishment of God's will for the whole world: the will that all things that breathe shall be filled, that all men shall be saved and come to the knowledge of truth.

Every believer must needs be a servant of this holy, sanctifying will, and find a cheerful strength from the certainty that, whatever form it takes, it is a loving will. We know, and they know, that lay people do not

---

[16] Chrysostom distinguishes God's kingship exerted over his creation according to demiurgy and according to "familiarity": *In i Cor.*, hom. xxxix, n. 6 (P.G., lxi, 341). Cf. the *Journal of Theological Studies*, 1948, p. 59.

[17] Some wise man has said that "The secret of happiness is to love one's duty and to try to find satisfaction therein." In the collect of the 13th Sunday after Pentecost we ask "ut mereamur assequi quod promittis, fac nos amare quod praecipis".

have a special "spirituality". They nourish their spiritual life and seek their sanctification by turning ever more directly towards God's will, lovingly endeavouring here and now to co-operate with it on earth as in Heaven. That is the essential consideration in a "spirituality" of Christians busied in the world: it is hardly its "own" or its "proper" value, for it is not peculiar to that "spirituality", but it may be said to be the most sufficient and the most fitting to it. In the inquiry conducted by *La Vie spirituelle* already referred to (note 5, above), it is noticeable that obedience to God in one's state of life is very often put forward as the proper characteristic of holiness. And it is noticeable, too, that several answers personify this ideal in our Lady St Mary: she "led a normal life in obedience and detachment . . . in the world, amidst the day-to-day comings and goings of an artisan's household"; but above all, perfectly in right relation towards God from her conception, she was at every moment exactly what he wanted her to be. One answer invented a word that is expressive, even if not beyond criticism: it spoke of "the Blessed Virgin's increasing participation in the grace of *immaculization* of the will", meaning thereby growth in perfect conformity to what God wills for us at every moment and in all circumstances of life.

It is also to be remarked that the aspect of God's will has been stressed whenever there has been a call in the Church for service that is militant, and therefore temporal and generally lay. Pope St Gregory VII, for example, wrote that "It is not for a man to decide what path he shall take; he has to accept the decisions of him who directs his steps". Nowadays people like to refer themselves to Christ the King, to the rule of his sacred heart; and French scouts have made their own a prayer of St Ignatius Loyola: "Lord Jesus, teach me to be generous, to give without counting the cost, to serve you as you ought to be served, to fight without caring about wounds, to work without respite, to spend myself without looking for any reward except the knowledge that I am doing your holy will".

Vocation. We might say that everything is vocation, as George Bernanos said that everything is grace. Bernanos was no Father of the Church, but the Fathers and many of the great scholastics would not have disowned him. However, there are narrower and more precise meanings of the words grace and vocation. The term "vocational council" points to the sense of vocation as profession, trade, occupation, "calling" in fact, and that usage is fully justified. But when we speak in French (and English) of "the work of vocations", or say that so-and-so has, or has not, got a vocation, we are thinking solely of the priestly or religious vocation, the "call to higher service". Accordingly there are some who want to reserve the name of vocation to the priestly and religious state of direct service of God and rejection of temporal things, and refuse it to lay life and to marriage. Others, on the contrary, speak of vocation to marriage and to the various states of life characterized as callings, and point out that the very existence of celibacy implies a vocational character in marriage. Surely these are two elements or aspects of a truth to each of which, here as elsewhere, justice must be done, while keeping them together in an integral synthesis.

This is not so difficult if we start with God's will as pursuing the realization of a design which is carried on at two different levels but is none the less one in the end. Every man has a vocation, because there is a will of God in respect of each one, ordered to the carrying out of that design. This will may be manifested in a particular way; but ordinarily it is expressed in the inclinations which an individual gets from his temperament, education and circumstances, in the invitations he receives, expressly or tacitly, from others, and so on. That is St Thomas's idea, and at bottom it is the idea of Catholic tradition. It may be remarked that it is especially preaching religious, spiritual writers and mystics who have held to this idea of a vocation of every man according to his state, and of sanctification in carrying out the duties of that state "in God's name", that is, in loving obedience to his will. We find it, for instance, in Eckhart and Tauler: when a man turns to God, God gives him the world anew as a duty and service. Tauler speaks of this explicitly as a call or vocation from God.

The Bible enables us to distinguish the two different planes on which the single design is worked out. Genesis, the Book of Beginnings, sets forth, in their relation to God and his to them, the origins of two orders of things; it deals with them in successive parts, the first comprising chapters 1–11 of the book, the second being from chapter 12 to its end—or even to the end of the whole Bible, where the "unveiling", the Apocalypse, of the purpose announced at the beginning is completed. The first eleven chapters of Genesis explain—essentially from the point of view of God's free and gracious willing—how there came into being what may be called the creational order, all those things that man experiences about him in the world: an order, moreover, that is disturbed by sin, deprived of its "integrity" and in bondage to "vanity", in the sense of those words given in our third chapter. Genesis explains the cosmos itself, the earth, light and darkness, the firmament, land and water, life vegetable and life animal, and then man, with his spiritual nature, his male and female forms, the mutual attraction of man and woman, marriage, work as creativeness: and then sin, evil, pain and affliction, work as a burden, sexual shame; finally, the seeds of war and death in the world, something of a mechanized civilization, differences of race, the variety of language that makes a barrier between peoples, with whose multiplicity and dispersion the section ends.

But with chapter 12 something absolutely new begins, a new creation, as one may say: "The Lord said to Abram: 'Go forth out of thy country and from thy kindred and out of thy father's house and come into the land which I shall show thee. And I will make of thee a great nation.' ..." It is no longer a matter of the creational order, with its surroundings and laws whose regularity was guaranteed by the Noachic covenant: so far as a collective economy is concerned, the order of free purpose of grace has begun. God no longer acts simply as Cause of all things, but as Lord, as the living God. Freely he chooses and calls, with a word he makes this choice and calling known. It is the beginning of the history of the people whom God summons, whom he calls from the world to his service (*ecclesia*): to correspond with the creational order, it may be called the vocational order, the order of the purpose of grace whose story fills the Bible and which is actual today in the Church.

It would seem that this distinction of two orders can be helpfully applied to the matter of vocation. It shows us vocation in a wide sense, depending on the creational order and God's general providence; and vocation in a strict sense, properly and directly ordered to the realization of the purpose of grace, depending on a special intervention by God. God's call to those whom he has chosen to work for his purpose and reign is clearly presented as vocation in the Scriptures: all the faithful (who as such are called) and the instruments or ministers whom God joins with himself as collaborators.[18] If the word vocation has been more particularly applied to the monk, to the extent of being almost reserved to him, it is not (as K. Holl supposes) through an ignoring of the faithful people and an improper confining to some of what belongs to all: it is principally because the monk's life realizes the Christian vocation integrally and to the letter. God's word to Abraham, quoted above, has been traditionally applied to monks. Holl was making the most of the views of Luther who, as against what he believed to be the traditional meaning, denied that monk or priest has any special Christian vocation different from that of a cobbler or a housewife. But it is the opinion of contemporary exegesis that Luther exaggerated the importance he attached to states of life "in the world" as Christian vocations, these things not being so strongly brought out in the Bible.[19]

Vocations to the direct service of God's purpose of grace have something special about them. They are much more imperious. They are organized socially in and by the Church, which thus again collaborates with God and again carries out visibly what the Holy Spirit does inwardly; they therefore entail entry into an "institution" and there constitute a particular sacred state.[20] Nevertheless, the tasks willed by Providence in the creational order for the fulfilling of the whole divine plan are also the object of true vocations, though in a less strict sense and in a less urgent way. There are as many of them as there are men and women, for God calls each one by his name, but they have a common object and they can be arranged into several large categories.

Their common object is to seek the perfection and harmonization of the creational orders by striving to withdraw them from "vanity" and so far as possible to procure its "integrity" for everything: this can be done only by putting a thing in its right place with regard to other things (peace, unity), especially with regard to that which is above it (order). This, as we have seen, constitutes a preparation of the Kingdom of God in respect of the cosmos. Concretely, it is man's effort to liberate and

---

[18] Use of κλῆσις for the faithful: Rom. 11. 29; 1 Cor. 1. 26; Eph. 1. 18; 4. 1, 4; Phil. 3. 14; 2 Thess. 1. 2; 2 Tim. 1. 9; Heb. 3. 1; 2 Peter 1. 10. Use of κλῆρός Rom. 1. 6, 7; 8. 28; 1 Cor. 1. 2, 24; Jude 1; Apoc. 17. 14; and the numerous use of καλέω For the collaborators, cf. for example Abraham, Gen. 12; Isa. 51. 2; Moses, Exod. 3; Samuel, 1 Kings 3; Isaias, Isa. 6; Jeremy, Jer. 1; the Apostles, Matt. 4. 21; Mark 1. 20; 3. 13; Paul, Rom. 1. 1; 1 Cor. 1. 1; Gal. 1. 15.

[19] K. Holl, "Die Gesch. d. Wortes Beruff", in *Ges. Aufs.*, vol. 3, pp. 193, 196. Cf. Kittel's *Wörterbuch*, vol. iii, p. 493, note.

[20] Writing of the priestly and the religious states, Fr de Montcheuil observes that "One does not enter them simply at will, and one cannot leave them at one's own pleasure".

develop the energies latent in the world (demiurgic power), to free himself from the world, to accomplish creation and accomplish himself by giving, at the call of his Creator, the free response of his co-operation and self-dedication, as leader in a world that he draws after him in the wake of his own destiny. Here we would draw attention to all the texts of the Old and the New Testaments that sound a note of "cosmism": they encourage a very positive idea of the Christian's creational vocations.

These vocations may be distributed accordingly as they belong to the elementary human, the political or the economic organisms. The elementary human organism includes the states of husband and wife, of father, mother and child. All the states we are going to mention here can be called "orders", in the sense explained. But the state of husband and wife, being consecrated by a sacrament of the Church, constitutes an order not only in the world but in the Church; it is traditionally so called in a sense that has an ecclesiological as well as a sociological significance. On the other hand, the governmental and civic states of the political organism have no ecclesiological significance, except possibly that the sacring of sovereigns may institute them in a sacred office and dignity. The economic organism includes the states of employer and employed, or rather, within an enterprise, of an initiator and director and of the co-operators; and this organism also includes the different trades and professions that are integral parts of it (the first division is rather that of its potential parts).

These great categories, and others, were seen of old as so many "orders" or "estates". The word *ordo* had more than one meaning: in a general sense, recognized in the secular as well as the ecclesiastical sphere, it signified a state of life corresponding to a function (*officium*), having defined conditions of life and its own regulations. Accordingly, *ordo* was at one and the same time (e)state (*status*), charge (*officium*), business or profession (*ministerium*), dignity and honour (*dignitas, honor*), and with all that, vocation. *Ordo* was grounded in a certain state or condition which involved a given way of life, emoluments, expenditure and honours, but also duties (to live according to one's condition or state), and it represented a certain degree (*gradus*) in a social hierarchy that was highly organic. Every man had his place and his function: the carpenter, the mason was carpenter or mason of a community that also had its fighting men, its judges, its king, its men of prayer and its priests. Each one represented this or that function or service for the others. This notion of an organism is always cropping up in the mind of the Middle Ages; it is the secret of a society whose fixity rather repels us but whose essential idea was perfectly sound.

The Middle Ages thought of sacred functions and secular functions as completing each other to build up one single society, as the north and south sides make up a church building or the right and left sides a human body. We cannot follow that era in giving the name Christian Commonwealth or even Church, to the whole of which the orders of labourers, soldiers and the rest would be members side by side with the orders of monks or of nuns. But we can do justice to the deep element of truth expressed in this view; after sharply distinguishing the vocations of the creational order from those directly referred to the purpose of grace and the Kingdom of God, we can agree that the first of these orders is not unrelated to the second.

We have only to recall what has been said in Part One, Chapter III. We saw that the Incarnation has a relationship to the Creation, that Christ "brings all things to a head", so that in him Creation is accomplished and finds its full meaning. Thereby the creational order, the order of explanations and techniques, receives a divine *significance*, which belongs to the wisdom of faith and answers to that "supplement of soul" of which Bergson speaks; it was Bergson, too, who did not hesitate to call the universe "a machine for making gods", thus recalling many passages in the Fathers. "Just as God's will is an act and is called the world, so his intention is man's salvation and is called the Church", wrote Clement of Alexandria. It is very remarkable to see how the ancient liturgies, no doubt taking a theme from Jewish prayer, put thoroughgoing Christic praise into a setting of cosmic praise. So far as we know, this point has not been studied; but it is important and deserves careful examination. One can speak of an "Adamic function" of creation and a "Christic function" of redemption, provided that the connection of the first with the second is made clear, and that they are not referred respectively to the laity and the clergy: creational tasks ("Adamic function") are more especially the business of the laity, but their final meaning is in Christ and they do not prevent lay people from having their part in the redemptive function and the duties of the Church, as we hope we have shown. In any case, the creational function or vocation of the laity is itself in one sense a function or vocation of the Church, or at the very least in the Church. Not only does spiritual vocation generally find its place in the natural vocation that arises providentially from our gifts, opportunities, etc., but it is each one's providential "Adamic tasks" that provide the setting of the laity's mission of "being the Church", in the sense of Pope Pius XII's words. Care, then, must be taken in distinguishing the two planes of vocation, lest we put too far from one another what God himself brings together in that unitary design wherein the same creation that was lost is to be saved in Christ.

In this matter of vocation, one of the most necessary of priestly duties is to give the faithful an over-all view of God's design for the world, to help them to find their place in that design and to learn what is the Christian's service and responsibility in the world.

Service and its demands. We are emancipated from the tyranny of the world by the call from on high; but God gives the world back to us as our task, and we accept it as his holy and hallowing will, with the vocation to co-operate with Love's design for his creation. That is the field of the engagement for which we have been set free, in which we exercise that Christian freedom spoken of before with reference to our spiritual kingship.

Christian freedom is not the freedom of a man without responsibility or of a tourist—we are pilgrims, travellers, in the world, but not in that sense. Ours is the position of one who, delivered from bond-service, is given a new task, or simply the same one, as a vocation and labour of love. For the Father does not restore the world to us as selfish, worldly beings but as his children, his family, the body of his only-begotten Son, to us-all-as-a-single-one, to us as living in charity: "ut te tota virtute diligant, et quae tibi placita sunt, tota dilectione perficiant", says the Missal. And what is restored to us is the same world and not the same world: it is the world as realm of the Father. Every part of it belongs to him: we live there very happily, as children with their Father, but in as much as, babes as to malice, we are grown-up in mind (cf. 1 Cor. 14. 20), we indeed also live there as stewards of the things that are not ours but the Father's, intended by him for all his family.

Such is the very profound meaning of the parable of the Unjust Steward. We have seriously to strive for life everlasting by making use of goods that, radically, do not belong to us but to the Father of all. It is service, therefore, *of God* and of our brethren, his children, not solely in themselves but in that part of the common estate which it has fallen to us to take care of; this, of course, without detriment to direct service of God and neighbour, in which the part of the clergy and religious is more especially found. The fact that all this is service of God does not mean that nothing else is added to it, especially at the inspiration of God himself, who is the author of all healthy natural inclinations (interest in things, fellow-feeling, love for the world of men); nor does it mean any lack of enjoyment of the work given us to do. It is right and proper that we should come from prayer or the eucharist with a longing, like Dostoevsky's Alyosha, to kiss the earth: for we have just communed with the source of all fellowship and with the will of him who day by day, together with the day's bread, gives us all things for our task: "Give us this day our daily bread"; "My food is to do the will of him that sent me and to accomplish his work." [21]

The Christian's position as God's faithful servant in the world makes two principal demands, corresponding respectively to an aspect of detachment or transcendence and one of engagement or immanence. In relation to engagement, that is, fidelity of service and its discharge taken in themselves, the great requirement is to have respect for things and to be competent and efficient. To serve God in the care of his household and children certainly means referring and offering the work to God in prayer; but it also means, essentially, to do the work well: one must be prepared to work for it, work hard at it, and so far as possible be well qualified for it. It is the same for any other employment—teaching, research, journalism, commercial or industrial activities. . . . How often do forms for examination of conscience in our prayer-books take notice of this aspect of our duties? Who ever questions and accuses himself on this head? [22] Why is it that so often good intentions are a substitute for a serious effort to be technically efficient, and that the motive of God's service is a cover for mediocrity, uninterestedness and sometimes real

[21] John 4. 34. On the daily bread, see V. Solovyev, *God, Man and the Church* (London, 1938), pp. 45–6; this is a book well worth reading. See, too, M. Glanndour, "Notre messe continue", in *Vie spirituelle*, 1951, pp. 466–71.

[22] [It was not always thus. In the examination of conscience in the first edition (1740), of Bishop Challoner's *Garden of the Soul* there occurs the question: "Have you profess'd any art, or undertaken any business without sufficient skill or knowledge? And what prejudice has your neighbour suffer'd from it?"—*Translator's note.*]

objective dishonesty? Péguy went to the heart of the matter when he wrote:

> If one would raise oneself to the eternal, it is not enough to de-
> preciate the temporal. To raise oneself to grace, it is not enough to
> depreciate nature. To raise oneself to God, it is not enough to de-
> preciate the world . . . [People] believe that, because they have not the
> strength (and the grace) to belong to nature, they belong to grace. They
> believe that, because they lack temporal courage, they have passed the
> threshold of the eternal. They believe that, because they have not the
> boldness to be worldly, they are godly; not brave enough to be on
> man's side, they believe they are on God's side; not belonging to man,
> they think they belong to God. Because they love nobody, they believe
> that they love God.
> And yet Jesus Christ was a man.[23]

The requirement of transcendence concerns, not the actual discharge of one's service, but the spirit that animates it. It is a matter of respecting in all that we have the quality of its being something belonging to one of God's children, a member of his family and of Christ's mystical body: being ours, it is yet not altogether ours, it belongs to God and to all our brethren. The Christian's kingly condition is such that he not only owns things, he dominates them and looks on them as a service or an oppor- tunity for service. That is the concrete programme of that spiritual king- ship—so close to inward priesthood—whereby we rule by offering and giving: and that is a thing we have to learn to do properly, just as we have to learn technical competence. There are the words of Jesus, "What shall it profit a man if he gain the whole world, and lose his soul? Or what shall a man give as a price for his soul?" and the other places where he emphasizes the importance of "being" over "having", of the person made to love and serve by love over the individual who is slave of a selfish affection (Matt. 6. 19–21, 25; 18. 8–9, etc.). And after the Master, his apostles: "All things are lawful to me, but to nothing will I become enslaved" (1 Cor. 6. 12); "By whatsoever thing a man is overcome, to that same is he made a slave" (2 Pet. 2. 19). Surely these considerations on Christian freedom and spiritual kingship give a concrete meaning to some rather enigmatical sentences earlier in this chapter: Having as having not, weeping as weeping not, and, in contemporary terms, finding life hard yet being assured, worried for our children yet full of trust. . . . We can now see how those whose vocation keeps them "in the world" can still answer the call addressed to all believers in the person of their father Abraham, "Go forth out of thy country and from thy kindred and out of thy father's house." Go forth as not going forth, use as not using—in other words, not to let oneself be tyrannized over by the very things through which we are called to work and serve God with our whole heart.

Engagement and responsibility. God's will, vocation to service, engage- ment, feeling of responsibility—these are firmly linked with one another. There is a logic as living as it is sound in the fact that, while our era has

[23] *Œuvres complètes,* vol. ix, pp. 180, 181.

taken up the idea of the lay condition as a question of Christian situation and sanctification, it is at the same time particularly drawn to an apostolic (missionary) engagement and shows itself alive to a duty to "take charge" of this or that corner of the field wherein one is called to work. We have seen that these aspirations would appear to have been given providential encouragement by certain canonizations and other examples of holiness, as well as by pastoral pronouncements. Every generation has its master words. The mind of the Middle Ages answered to "unity" and "order"; during the first third of the sixteenth century, everybody was stirred by "the Gospel" and "Christian freedom"; the eighteenth century was all for Reason, Nature, the Sublime; today we hear on all sides "engagement" or "committed", "mission", "community", "taking responsibility".

These are not simply fine Christian words: they express searching realities, of which the essence is that every person has been given a task and talents for which he will have to account, and that they are given for the benefit of the whole family of God's children. Each person is responsible for something to somebody, namely, to the authority who gave the charge in respect of which he is accountable. So in a last analysis we are responsible to God in person, for all authority comes from him. But it must not be overlooked that between God and us there is mediation through the order of things in which he has put us, and this mediation, if it be authentic, partakes of the absolute character of his authority. That is why it is not ridiculous to hold oneself responsible before Society, the World, Mankind, History, or to write those words with capital initials—they designate so many faces of God, since they represent so many orders of his will. Unless withdrawn from them by a higher order, every person is pledged to these general orders as to God himself.

One's obligation to these universal orders is sacred. It is not only found in such general duties as speaking the truth or doing a fair day's work for a fair day's pay, but in occasional happenings in which a man finds himself involved, whether he is bound by any express law or not. If we see a child in danger we know we are bound to help; if we know something about an accident or a crime, we feel bound to say so: to do nothing would be to betray something towards which we are responsible. If I do not do it, it will not be done; if I slip away, something will be lost, and I feel a responsibility is on me; if I avoid it, I betray the best in myself. The human person, and still more the Christian person, is not free in Sartre's sense of freedom: he is free and bound, both at once. St Paul wrote: "Ye were called to freedom, brethren; only let not your freedom be an occasion for the flesh; rather be ye slaves one of another by charity" (Gal. 5. 13). It is written into the structure of his personality that man has a relationship to universal and absolute goods, whose nature is determined for each one by the circumstances in which he is.

Dostoevsky wrote in a book that we are responsible (and we may be to blame) for everything and everybody. It is not a matter of books. Many Christians—and non-Christians too—live it. When they see that something they value will not be done if they do not do it, they feel personally called by a higher power; and at God's word they voluntarily add other responsibilities to those already incumbent on them. A household, for example, or group of households, takes charge of the religious upbringing of neglected children, or an individual undertakes to represent Christians in some political or social organization or a trade union. Free vocations? Yes, but they feel *bound* to undertake them, because each is responsible for all and all for each, the circumstances, external and internal, of every man determining his obligations, as we have said of apostleship.

Engagement, mission and the rest are indeed great Christian words, and moreover they deliver us from that vapid vocabulary which is so embarrassing to an adult. One has to be gradually initiated into all these things by a process of education, and the words accordingly stand for values which are those of adult life. Engagement, to be committed, is at the same time a means to and an indication and fruit of "growing up"; maturity of personality is both a result and an expression of it. An adult is he who takes full responsibility for what he does and who realizes—in both senses of the word, "understands" and "effects"—the part he is called on to take in the little world of his daily life, and perhaps on the bigger stage of society and history. He is a man fully born into the world: not the birth to separate physical life after a few months of gestation, but a gradual birth through a slow personal acquiring of the capital of cultivated life garnered by mankind, through difficulties successively overcome and stages reached and passed one after the other; a birth which brings him into the world of action and history, that he may take his place in it and in his turn do the work of creation according to his measure.

To shoulder responsibility means first of all to take a stand: in the home, at work, in economic and political matters, in social life; in the matter of personal witness, too, in parish affairs, perhaps in Catholic Action. To take a stand means to come into collision with differing choices and elements, and so to have opponents: it means a state of strife. That is a test of character, for "to have character" means to uphold one's convictions in one's own life and to maintain them in face of things, however murky or difficult they may be. To take on responsibility for something often leads to setting bounds to the accepted commitment and to laying down its conditions. A true sense of responsibility is not consistent with an attitude of all-round acceptance; passive obedience kills the psychological and moral roots of responsibility. Authorities who are tempted to abuse their power would do well to reflect on the way God acts: so great is his respect for our freedom that his own mastery gives way before it, as H. Gohde has so well said (*Der Achte Tag*, Innsbruck, 1950, p. 242).

But above all, responsibility or engagement means personal judgement and making choices. Those who always have a habit of asking for answers and directions ready-made, who are always afraid of taking an initiative on their own, run the risk of becoming infantile, poor-spirited, ineffectual and at last of drawing back altogether from any new undertaking that requires decision and wholeheartedness. Many have written about the harm done by legalism with its cut and dried answers, and by the habit of living and thinking as it were by proxy, which makes it impossible to produce a laity up to the requirements of the present day.[24] There is much that needs doing to cure lay people of their mania for looking for directions that dispense them from thinking out their own problems, and to dissuade the clergy from their habit of deciding and prescribing for everything. It would be a good thing were the excellent thomist theology of prudence again to find its place among theologians and in manuals for clerical students, and then to be propounded to the faithful and livingly applied to the needs of contemporary consciences. Something has been done in this line[25]; but St Thomas's lofty and delicate treatment of the subject is far from being really understood by all the doctors in Israel, and therefore far from being properly put to the confused consciences of today.

This is one of the reasons why some people can see no way out of "moralism", or no alternative to plain obedience to the dictation of cut and dried determinations tempered by casuistry, except in a *mystique* of evangelical freedom or in a pure "ethic of the situation". For the first of these, conscience at every moment is given its rule of action according to love; for the second, each situation, often full of insoluble contradictions, is to be judged simply in a spirit of loyalty to oneself and of obedience to God's immediate will. There are several factors drawing people in this direction, real factors, but some of them regrettable. They are, in Father K. Rahner's opinion, the following: the superseding of a hierarchized and stable world by a moving, changing world, full of revolutions and disasters, in which man is confronted by unprecedented, complex and often tragic situations in which it is very difficult for him to know what he ought to do; the influence of Existentialism, of Kierkegaard, and of some Protestant pronouncements, with their suspicion of all metaphysic of essences and of all "morality" of general rules, and their insistence on the individual's obedience to a positive willing and an immediate call by God, recognized as such in his conscience[26]; and the feeling of insoluble antinomies, aggravated by the difficulties of existence and by the loss of clear and ordered objective certainties. To these factors two others must be added, at any rate in France: the renewed appreciation of religious and mystical values over "morality", and the return to the Bible. In this last, the rediscovery of the Old Testament has been very important: from beginning to end it shows that man's good is what God wants him to do; its conception of the religious situation is hardly at all essentialist or

---

[24] In addition to the writings of Mgr Guardini, Father Doncoeur and Charles Péguy, there may be mentioned among many others M. de la Bedoyère, *Christianity in the Market Place* and *The Layman in the Church*; E. Mounier, *L'affrontement chrétien* (Neuchatel, 1945), pp. 70 ff.; and R. Egenter, *Von der Freiheit der Kinder Gottes* (Freiburg i. B., 1948), pp. 132 ff., 216 ff. Among many references in *La Vie spirituelle*, see especially the issue of Oct. 1951 and May of the same year, supplement, "Loi et Amour".

[25] See G. Leclercq, *La conscience du chrétien* ... (Paris, 1947); A. Gardeil, *La vraie vie chrétienne* (Paris, 1934); the Cahier de la Vie spirituelle, *Prudence chrétienne* (Paris, 1948); T. Deman's French translation of the treatise in the *Summa*; and the writings of Canon J. Leclercq, Fr H. D. Noble and Dr J. Pieper (in German).

[26] Protestant writers often prefer to speak of "ethic" rather than of "morality", ethic envisaging Christian behaviour in conformity with God's will, morality considering the objective content of man's works and deeds. Protestant theology rejects (in principle) distinction between sins and appreciation of their gravity according to their matter or object.

sapiential, but is determined by the willing and action of God.[27] There can be no doubt that that has moved people's minds in the direction of a "situation ethic": not that it has led them to substitute the magisterium of conscience for the magisterium of objective laws; but in the sense that, beyond objective laws and general principles, people are ready to refer themselves to what God asks of them *hic et nunc*, to what he wants as perceived in a conscience that is possessed by the desire to make loving obedient response to his will.

Our own opinion, formed in the school of Holy Scripture, is that there is some truth in this point of view of a "situation ethic". It can be seen against the background of Christian life in the work of the world, with its series of God's holy and hallowing will—→vocation—→service—→engagement and responsibility. God's will is a daily bread, given from on high—Christian conduct in its truth is to be ceaselessly formed through a progressive deepening of the subject himself confronted by God. "Be ye transformed by the renewing of your mind, so that ye find out what is the will of God, the good and the well-pleasing and the perfect" (Rom. 12. 2); "We have never ceased praying for you, asking that ye may be filled with the full knowledge of God's will in all wisdom and spiritual insight. Thus may ye walk worthily of the Lord and in all ways please him . . . , increasing in the full knowledge of God" (Col. 1. 9–10).

But it is quite clear that St Paul thought the will of God to be known to us firstly in the commandments he has given, and that there is an imprescriptible objective law of actions by which he is pleased or displeased: Father Rahner rightly invokes the list in 1 Cor. 6. 9 ff. (and compare Gal. 5. 18–21), as well as the texts where St Paul presents law-abidingness as the condition of life, plainly echoing the formal teaching of our Lord himself.[28] It can scarcely be denied that any "situation ethic"—or rather, as we should prefer to call it, "ethic of the immediate will of God"—must *in the first place and always* be an ethic of obedience to God's will objectively expressed in the commandments, on which Christian tradition, itself elucidated by the apostolic magisterium, is like a living commentary. There is not simply an "ethic", there is a true "morality" (cf. note 26 above); and at the edge of a science of objective moral laws there is a legitimate discussion of cases wherein the truth of these laws is applied to more complex objective situations: why, St Paul himself uses a certain "casuistry". . . .[29]

[27] It is no matter for surprise that the best exegete among the Fathers, St John Chrysostom, wrote that a reputedly wicked deed is good if God wills it, and inversely: "it is not the nature of things but God's decision that makes an action good or bad" (*Adv. Judaeos*, 5; P.G., xlviii, 873). He refers to the examples of Ahab (3 Kings 20. 32 ff.) and Phineas (Numbers 25. 6 ff.); he could have added Abraham's sacrifice (Gen. 22), Osee's marriage (Osee 1), and others. For the explanation of such cases in classical theology, see, e.g., T. Deman, *Le mal et Dieu* (Paris, 1943), pp. 49–50; A. D. Sertillanges, *Le problème du mal*, vol. ii (Paris, 1951), p. 39.

[28] Matt. 19. 17; John 14. 15, 21; Rom. 2. 13; Gal. 3. 12; etc.

[29] A. Adam, *Spannungen und Harmonie* . . . (Nuremberg, 1948), pp. 111–15, refers to 1 Cor. 7 and 10. 27 ff., and shows how Paul's "casuistry" does not stop at a sort of "prudent dosing"; it takes the cases of conscience seriously, and in each one shows the principle, drawn from the heart of Christian existence itself, from which the faithful soul can and must himself form a conscientious judgement: in the end, this principle is always charity, which "builds up". Cf. R. Egenter, *op. cit.*, note 24. It was after these pages were written that Pope Pius XII pointed out the exaggerations in the *Situationsethik* and the errors to which it can give rise (*A.A.S.*, 1952, pp. 270–8, 413–19; *Doc. cath.*, cc. 449–56, 589–96).

We are convinced that the authentic demands of an ethic of God's immediate will (or "situation ethic") are met by the thomist theology of action, with its enlightening ideas in the practical order, of prudence and of the gifts of the Holy Spirit. Prudence according to St Thomas is something quite other than an inclination towards "how much or how little" and mediocrity generally: it is a virtue—that is, an energy—of commitment and effectiveness arising from a conviction about ends in view; it is not at all a collection of recipes or ready-made opinions, nor is it a passive submission to utterances of some acceptable official origin, after the manner of the childish mob in Dostoevsky's Legend of the Grand Inquisitor. Prudence is a virtue, a living adaptation of the subject to his existence in the sense of Good; a moral virtue of the practical understanding, in which the vital right-ordering in respect of Good is of moment to the perception of truth and concerns a sphere wherein truth is *to be made* and built up by the subject himself: a very different thing from copying it line for line from the pattern in some elementary textbook of design. Accordingly, the job of priests with respect to lay people is not to make them the *longa manus* of the clergy, telling them what they've got to do; but to make them believing men and women, adult Christians, leaving them to meet and fulfil the concrete demands of their Christianity on their own responsibility and in accordance with their own consciences.

Prudence is, moreover, an intellectual virtue, which means that the person will inform and cultivate himself for his own enlightening, that he will use all his knowledge, and that he will turn to advisers when necessary. But advisers should never, even where children are concerned, become dictators, making unnecessary the living movement of a conscience animated by enthusiasm for its ends and by the will to serve them. It is right and proper that the priest should come into the picture, and he will be the faithful mouthpiece of the Church's teaching; but he will do all he can to enter into people's problems and to help them to think *practically*, with God's eye upon them. That can all be done only in an atmosphere of prayer, and of habitual submissiveness to God and to the best in oneself. In these conditions, the virtue of prudence, with all its human limitations, is helped by the gifts of the Holy Spirit, especially wisdom and counsel. These gifts represent openness of the soul to God's comings and to what they call for: openness, then, to the "event", and submissiveness to the Lord's immediate and positive will. St Thomas sees the field of the gifts as coextensive with the whole spiritual life, as one of the conditions of Christian existence.

It is desirable that this context of morals should be affirmed anew. The problems set by lay engagement and a spirituality dominated by the will of God can thus be solved without falling into the *in pace* of subjection to the cut-and-dried or embarking on the venture of a purely "situation ethic".

Meaning of the Mass:
The Mass and the Church*

Joseph A. Jungmann, S.J.

IF we put together such meanings as we derive from the names of the Mass we glean nothing more than a very superficial sketch. The Mass is a celebration for which the Church assembles, a celebration which occupies the centre of her charge and service, a celebration which is dedicated to the Lord. It is a celebration which presents God with a thanksgiving, an offering, indeed a sacrifice. And it is a celebration which reacts with blessings upon those who gather for it. Other essential features have been revealed to us by the course of history, for we have learnt the various aspects which were given special prominence as time went by. But we must now inquire what the Church herself has said in her formal pronouncements, whether by direct teaching or in theological discussion, regarding the meaning and the essence of this celebration.

It will not be out of place to present this question in a book which has as its primary subject-matter the variety of forms that the Christian celebration possesses. For the discussion should serve not only to establish or prove this variety but also to understand it in its development and growth from its roots, from the very core of its nature. So it is necessary, first of all, to have this essential core before our eyes to see what it is. Naturally it is not our task to excerpt and to rewrite the pertinent treatise in dogmatic theology as an isolated and self-contained chapter or even one related to the full-rounded theological structure or more particularly to the doctrine of the Sacraments. We must rather realize the liturgical connotations of the problem, and try to pose the questions and construct the answers with an eye to religious life and ecclesiastical service.

Let us first orient ourselves with regard to the liturgical facts hitherto established, making them the starting point for a broader excursion into the field of theology. These facts show that we cannot make the notion of sacrifice a basis absolutely and exclusively, otherwise we would leave no room for many other important and essential features. We must start off from one of the broader and more general ideas which find an application in an examination of the essence of the Mass solemnity. Such a notion is the one by which our Lord himself indicated the meaning of what he instituted: "Do this for a commemoration of me." The Mass is a solemnity dedicated to the memory of Christ; it is *dominicum*. And further, it is not merely a remembrance of his person, but a recollection of his work—according to the word of the Apostle: "For as often as you shall eat this bread and drink the cup, you proclaim the death of the Lord, until he comes" (1 Cor. 11. 25).

The consideration of the Mass must therefore commence with the mystery of our Lord's Passion and death. This is what is continually

* From *The Mass of the Roman Rite*; see p. x above.

being made present and actual—in the institution of the Last Supper. However, neither can this mystery be exhausted with one simple idea. In this mystery our Lord sealed with his blood his testimony to truth (John 18. 37), to the Kingdom of God which had come in his own person, and thus had "borne witness to the great claim" (1 Tim. 6. 13). With a heroic obedience that was steadfast even to the death of the Cross (Phil. 2. 8), he had in this mystery fulfilled the will of his Father against whom the first Adam had set himself with defiant disobedience. With free resolve our Lord had put himself into the hands of his enemies, silently, making no use of his wondrous might, and had offered up his life as "a ransom for many" (Mark 10. 45). He had taken up the warfare against the invisible enemy who held mankind imprisoned in sin, and as one who is stronger still, he had been victorious (Luke 11. 22): he had cast out the prince of this world (John 12. 31). He took his place at the head of mankind, striding forward through suffering and death, thus entering into his glory (Luke 24. 26). As high priest he has offered up in the Holy Spirit the perfect sacrifice; with his own blood he has entered the sanctuary and set a seal upon the new and eternal covenant (Heb. 9. 11 ff.). He himself became the Paschal Lamb, whose blood procured our ransom out of the land of bondage, whose slaughter inaugurated our joyous Easter feast (1 Cor. 5. 7 ff.), the Lamb that was slain and yet lives, the Lamb for whose wedding feast the bride has clothed herself (Apoc. 5. 6 ff.; 19. 7 ff.).

By all these notions, by all these pictures the attempt is made in the writings of the New Testament to circumscribe and to illustrate the great occurrence by means of which Jesus Christ effected the re-establishment of mankind.

All that is characteristic of the redeeming death of Jesus is clearly contained in some way in the institution of the Last Supper. There, in a manner that is full of mystery, this suffering is made present, this suffering that is at once testimony and obedience and atonement and struggle and victory and stainless sacrifice. It is made present under the signs of bread and wine, the elements of a simple meal, which are transformed by the hallowing words into Jesus' Body and Blood, and thus changed, are enjoyed by all who partake of them. But what is the more precise meaning of the Presence that is consummated day after day in a hundred thousand places? Does that meaning rest in the very Presence as such?

When Christ on the Cross cried out his *Consummatum est*, few were the men who noticed it, fewer still the men who perceived that this phrase announced a turning-point for mankind, that this death opened into everlasting life gates through which, from that moment on, all the peoples of earth would pass. Now, to meet the expectant longing of mankind, this great event is arrested and, through Christ's institution, held fast for these coming generations so that they might be conscious witnesses of that event even in the latest centuries and amongst the remotest nations, and might look up to it in holy rapture.

The Middle Ages actually did turn to this side of the eucharistic mystery with special predilection. What takes place on the altar is above all the *memoria passionis*. The suffering of Christ was seen represented in the breaking of the bread, in its distribution to the faithful, in the partaking of the Chalice whereby the Blood of the Lord is poured into the mouth of the faithful. From this obvious symbolism the step to an allegorical interpretation of the whole rite was easily made; particularly after the ninth century the whole Mass was explained in a comprehensive representation of the Passion of Jesus. In the action of the assisting clerics, who step back at the start of the preface, is seen the flight of the disciples. In the celebrant's extended hands our Lord is seen agonizing on the Cross with arms outstretched. In the commingling of the species is seen his glorious Resurrection. In fact, the whole life of Christ, the whole history of Redemption is seen represented in the Mass. The sacred action at the altar becomes a play, in which drama and reality are intermixed most mysteriously. How strong an impression this viewpoint made can perhaps be gauged by the fact that even today we use the expression "to hear Mass", as if we were an audience.

We must perceive that even in these explanations of the medieval interpreters, a primary essential trait of Christ's institution is given expression; this institution is a memorial ceremony, a sacred action which recalls into the midst of the congregation a redemptive work which occurred long ago, a "mystery-action".

Another aspect of Christ's institution which was prominent from the very outset and which in earlier times was made visible through its liturgical form, was the fact that a holy meal was being held—a meal and a memorial. The Eucharist is a memorial instituted by our Lord for a remembrance of himself. A table is set; it is the Lord's table. For a long time Christian speech avoided—or at least refrained from using—the term for altar derived from pre-Christian religion and even today still employs the simple name *mensa*, ἄγια τράπεζα.

At this table the faithful community is gathered in holy society. Here the Lord himself is given them as nourishment, his Body and his Blood handed to them under the species of bread and wine, as a spiritual food, a spiritual drink (cf. 1 Cor. 10. 3 ff.).

Thus the eucharistic institution does more than commemorate our Saviour. In it the communion and society of the faithful with their Lord is continually renewed. The meal is a sufficiently striking proof of that. And we can therefore safely say that, aside from the external activity, the meal is still in our own time the basic form of the eucharistic celebration. However, even in the biblical sources, this meal is distinguished as a sacrificial meal. The table of the Lord which is prepared in the church in Corinth is contrasted to the tables of the demons, the tables at which the meat offered up to the heathen gods is eaten. Already in the primitive Church it was recognized that in the celebration of the Eucharist a sacrifice was offered up, and that therein was fulfilled the prophecy of Malachias who foretold a clean oblation which would be offered up in all places. The thought of a sacrifice, of an oblation to God, taking place in the Eucharist, occurs time after time in the works of the Fathers. That thought has definitely figured in every text of the eucharistic celebration which is known to us.

The Middle Ages, too, whose devotion to the celebration of the Mass had drawn the remembrance of the Passion so much into the foreground, did not on that account lose sight of the idea of oblation and sacrifice.

In fact the later medieval period did so much to emphasize the sacrificial aspect and stressed in so many forms and fashions the value of the Mass for gaining God's grace and favour for the living and the dead, that not only did the Reformation find herein a subject for its immoderate indictment but even Church authorities, both before and after the storm, found reasons for making certain corrections.

The Council of Trent, therefore, was careful to clarify this very phase of the eucharistic mystery. The Council stressed the doctrine that the Mass is not a mere meal nor only a memorial service recalling a sacrifice that had taken place of yore, but is itself a sacrifice possessing its own power of atonement and petition. Christ had offered this sacrifice at the Last Supper and had given his Apostles and their successors the commission to offer it. Indeed he himself makes the offering through their ministry. Thus he left to his beloved spouse, the Church, a visible sacrifice. The Mass is therefore a sacrifice which is made by Christ and at the same time by the recipients of his commission; it is the *sacrifice of Christ* and the *sacrifice of the Church*. In our liturgical study we may not treat the sacrifice of the Church as a matter of secondary moment.

In the theological controversies of the Reformation period and in subsequent theology, the sacrificial notion did indeed stand out as central, but the Church's sacrifice played only a minor role. For the main concern was over a much deeper presupposition, whether the Mass was a sacrifice at all, and—opposing Calvin especially—whether believing that it was, contradicted the teaching of the Epistle to the Hebrews regarding the *one* sacrifice of Christ. Thus, above all else, the Mass had to be safeguarded as the sacrifice of Christ.

But when apologetic interests receded and the question once more arose as to what is the meaning and the purpose of the Mass in the organization of ecclesiastical life, it was precisely this point, the sacrifice of the Church, which came to the fore. The liturgies themselves are quite emphatic in the matter. One has only to scan the text of the Roman Mass, or of any other Mass-liturgy for that matter, to see that there is nothing plainer than the thought that in the Mass the Church, the people of Christ, the congregation here assembled offers up the sacrifice to Almighty God. What is happening at the altar is called, in one of the most venerable texts of our liturgy, an *oblatio servitutis nostræ, sed et cunctæ familiæ tuæ*. And, corresponding exactly to this, there are the phrases to be read right after the words of consecration, at the very climax of the whole action: *nos famuli tui, sed et plebs tua sancta ... offerimus præclaræ maiestati tuæ*—and the gift mentioned is the *hostia pura*, the sacred Bread and the Chalice of salvation. The same notion finds expression in a phrase incorporated into the Mass some thousand years later, when the priest speaks of *meum ac vestrum sacrificium* which should be acceptable to God. That the Mass is also the sacrifice of Christ is, in the Roman Mass *ordo*, only assumed, but never directly expressed.

There is actually a definite contrast between this language of the liturgy and the language we are used to nowadays in sermons, catechisms and other religious writings. We prefer to insist on the fact that on our altars Christ renews his Passion and death in an unbloody manner. We talk about the renewal of the sacrifice of the Cross, about an oblation in

which Christ gives himself to his heavenly Father. But it is only in very
general terms that we mention the sacrifice of the Church, and for this
reason even our theological textbooks in discussing the ensuing problem
as to precisely where Christ consummates his sacrifice, refer without much
reflection to his presence in the sacred Host.

If, by way of contrast, we skim through the pertinent writings of the
Fathers even casually, we are surprised to note that they use similar
terms in reference to Christ's oblation in the Eucharist and in reference
to our own. They emphasize with equal stress the fact that we (or the
Church or the priest) offer up the Passion of the Lord, indeed that we
offer up Christ himself. This is likewise true of the pre-Scholastic Middle
Ages. Seldom, it is true, do they use words of their own to express the
traditional teaching, but when they do they are especially clear in pointing out that it is the priest at the altar, who, in place of Christ, offers up
our Lord's Body, that in so doing he is the *coadiutor Redemptionis* and
vicarius eius. And at the same time they declare that the Church offers
up the sacrifice through the ministry of the priest. Even the theologians
of earlier Scholasticism and the great teachers of the flourishing schools
of the thirteenth century use the same language, without, however, going
into any deeper discussion of the topic. Only Duns Scotus lays any great
emphasis on the sacrifice of the Church. The Eucharist, he says, is
accepted by God, not because Christ is contained in it, but because he is
offered up in it, offered up by the Church. The theologians of the de-
clining Middle Ages stress the activity of the Church with such one-
sidedness and partiality that the sacerdotal function of Christ himself is
to some extent obscured.

Even the Council of Trent itself pointed out, as we already remarked,
that it was our Lord's intention at the Last Supper to leave "to his beloved Spouse, the Church, as human nature requires, a visible sacrifice".
The Church, therefore, was to have this sacrifice, and through it was to
be able to satisfy the desire of human nature to honour God by means of
sacrifice. For any theological view which would also do justice to liturgical
reality, this statement of fact is fundamental.

Our next question therefore follows along this direction. We want to
know *how* Christ's institution is to be understood as a sacrifice of the
Church, in what relation it stands to the life of the Church in all its
fullness, and especially what principles of liturgical formation are taken
for granted in it.

To be more precise, how is this sacrifice which the Church is supposed
to offer up—how is it brought about? By the fact that the Church joins
in the sacrifice of her Lord and Master, so that his oblation becomes her
oblation. Therefore, in the Mass the one sacrifice of Christ, the one
oblation of Golgotha by which he redeemed the world, is in mysterious
fashion made present. Because of St Paul's letter to the Hebrews, the
oneness of the sacrifice of Christ is a matter which cannot be assailed.

But how is this presence of the sacrifice of Christ to be understood?
There must be something more here than just a representation of the
oblation that took place once upon a time, something more than the
memoria passionis as we see it commonly exhibited by the separate
presentation of the Body and the Blood of Christ. On the altar a sacrifice

truly takes place, but it is a sacrifice which in many respects coincides with the sacrifice of the Cross. For the Council of Trent says of it: "There is the same oblation, and the same Person who now makes the oblation through the ministry of the priests and who once had made an oblation of himself on the Cross. Only the manner of offering is different." It is here that the speculations of theologians take their start; the result has been a variety of explanations which, since the sixteenth century, have continued to multiply.

The simplest solution seems to be one that was not proposed till our own day. According to this explanation the *memoria passionis* is intensified into an objective remembrance in the sense of a *Mysteriengegenwart* —a mystical presence. In the celebration of the Eucharist not only Christ himself but his one-time act of redemption are made present under cloak of the rite, "in the mystery". The past happening, Christ's Passion and Resurrection, is re-enacted in time, not indeed in its historical course but "in the Sacrament". So, from the very nature of the case, there is present an oblation—the same oblation which once took place. This, however, is a supposition which is not found in tradition in the precise form it here takes, but is rather the result of reasoning from tradition, a deduction which must enlist the aid of certain hypotheses which are themselves quite questionable. According to this theory the one oblation of Christ achieves simply a new presence by means of the consecration. The disparity of the actual oblation would thus be reduced to the barest possible minimum, so small that it is hard to see how there could be any new *ratio offerendi* or how the Eucharist could still be called *our* sacrifice, or how we would be linked to Christ's oblation in any relationship except a very external one.

The older explanations, on the contrary, generally sought to find the new and "different" manner of offering, of which the Council speaks, in the act of consecration itself. By means of the consecration, the Body immolated on the Cross and the Blood shed thereon are presented to the Father once again at this point of time and space. In this re-presentation which Christ fulfils through the priest—*ministerio sacerdotum*, says Trent—we have the oblation in which, according to the testimony of Christian tradition, the great high-priest offers himself at every Mass. This new offering is necessarily also a sacrifice in its own right, but not one that has independent redemptive value, since it is nothing else than a sacramental extension of the one and only redemptive sacrifice on Calvary which the Epistle to the Hebrews had in view.

There appeared to be only one difficulty. This re-presentation is indeed some sort of offering (*offerre*), but is not properly a sacrificial offering (*sacrificari*), an *immolation*. Pre-Tridentine theology was not at all agitated over this distinction, the sacrificial character of the Mass being supplied by the *oblatio* which took place in it. But the pressure of controversy seemed to demand a search for the precise sacrificial act within the Mass. And especially in view of the sacrifices of the Old Testament, it seemed necessary to acknowledge that a destruction of the gift was essentially required, so that, in the case of a living thing it had to be killed (destruction theory), just as Christ himself consummated his redemptive sacrifice by his death. The post-Tridentine Mass theories are concerned for the most part with demonstrating this "destructive" sacrificial activity in the Mass. However, no agreement over the solution has ever been reached.

Some theologians wanted to substitute for this destruction a mere alteration of the gifts, which, added to the offering, would suffice for a sacrificial act. Others finally thought they could ignore any special act of immolation that would require the destruction or alteration of the gift, and following the lead of pre-Tridentine tradition they explained that the simple presentation of the gifts was sufficient. Christ, they declared, is made present under the species which by their separation are a sign of his bloody sacrifice of old; thus he presents himself anew to the Father. There could not, of course, be any thought of an oblation of Christ that takes place here and now if this presentation were to consist simply in the interior resignation, in Christ's sacrificial sentiment which is present in this moment of time and space (because enclosed in the sacramental presence) and enduring (because also retained permanently in heaven). For an interior sacrificial sentiment, the will to sacrifice is not itself a sacrifice. Sacrifice demands some sort of action which moreover must be expressed in an external sign. Those who hold this opinion are therefore forced to assume that Christ in heaven makes a sacrifice which fulfils these conditions, and which is made present in the consecration—an assumption which cannot easily be confirmed.

Christ does, however, make the presentation of his one-time sacrifice before the fact of God in an externally perceptible action, namely in the consecration which he performs through his priests. The consecration not only stems from Christ, in so far as the commission and powers are derived from him, but it is in its very performance his work in the first degree, a work of his priestly office. And it is a work which—unlike the other sacraments, aimed in the first place at the sanctification of souls—is directed immediately to the glorification of the Father. It is a presentation or offering to the heavenly Father in the very here and now, in an act which enshrines in itself the core of every sacrificial activity: *dedication.*

This dedication is consummated upon a thing which is still profane, still the world, is in fact the world and human life in the intensest sense, since men prolong their life through it; but it is altered and transformed into the holiest thing between heaven and earth, into the sacrificial gift offered up on Golgotha, an image of which is set forth in the species after the transubstantiation. In the "holy and venerable" hands of the Lord the earthly gift has become a heavenly gift in the very act of giving. Thus the oblation of Christ is again on our altars, and as an oblation which he himself performs anew before our very eyes. But he does not perform it in order to present us a drama, but in order to include us and his Church everywhere on earth and in every century in his *pascha,* his passage out of this world to his Father. His sacrifice becomes each time *the sacrifice of the Church.*

Our Lord offered up the sacrifice on the Cross not for its own sake but that he might therein give his life as "a ransom for many" (Matt. 20. 28). In this way he concluded for us that everlasting covenant with God which was promised in the prophets (Is. 61. 8; Jer. 33. 20 f.; Bar. 2. 35), that covenant by which God receives mankind into his favour so that he no longer remembers their misdeeds (Jer. 31. 31–34; cf. 33. 8), but rather wishes them every good (Jer. 32. 40), in the hope that the destined heirs obtain, for ever, their promised inheritance (Heb. 9. 15). But because it is a covenant, a compact, obedience and fidelity are expected also on our part. It was at the very time of its institution, at the Last Supper, that Christ spoke of the covenant. He speaks of his body "which is to be given up for you" (1 Cor. 11. 24; Luke 22. 19). He designates his blood as "my blood of the new Testament, which is to be shed for many" (Mark 14. 24; Matt. 26. 28), and points to the chalice as "the new testament in my blood" (1 Cor. 11. 25; Luke 22. 20). As if to say, this institution has a special meaning within that testament, and in the commission to do this perpetually as a memorial, something more is intended than merely a theoretical commemoration in connection with the repetition of this transubstantiation. Much more is accomplished than that. In it is created an opportunity for all the faithful of all times to ratify in conscious manner this covenant which he had concluded in their name. At Baptism we are already taken up into this covenant and its goods are portioned out to us, without our having to do anything except receive them. In the Eucharist, Christ sets before us the Passion by means of which he inaugurated this covenant; now it is up to us to step forward with a willing "yes" to protest our adherence to the law of Christendom. His sacrifice should become our sacrifice, the Church's sacrifice, so that it might be offered up in her hands "from the rising of the sun to its going down" and the name of the Lord of hosts "be made great amongst all the peoples" (Mal. 1. 10 ff.).

The Church received a sacrifice from Christ because it is in man's very nature to honour God by sacrifice. More especially is this true where all religion is not to be limited to the inwardness of the individual, that is to say in a social union like the Church, in the divine service of the community. Here the need to glorify God by outward gift, by the visible emblem of an interior subjection or an internal giving of oneself to God —this need naturally arises of its own accord. The inner thought has to be the starting-point and the driving force of every sacrificial service if this service is not to be turned to mere pharisaism, for sacrifice is and must always remain only the symbol and sign of something else, an indication of what the soul intends.

But why could not a simpler gift suffice to express this intention? Because this intention, this inner sentiment towards God, is in Christianity a species all its own, at least as an ideal to which our striving is constantly pointed. The Sermon on the Mount, the Gospels, all the books of the New Testament speak of it. It is plainly put in St Paul's *Hoc sentite in vobis quod et in Christo Jesu* (Phil. 2. 5). It means entering into the thoughts of Jesus, rising to his mind and sentiment. In the life of our Lord himself the peak and triumph of that sentiment was reached on the Cross—a Cross which was erected as the wood of shame, and which our Lord willingly embraced in order to give himself wholly to his Father and at the same time to stretch out his arms over all the world and mercifully bring it back to the grace of God. The great commandment on which the Law depends and the Prophets, to love God with one's whole heart and soul and strength, and one's neighbour as one's self, this commandment of which he gave the living model, he also exemplified in death. That is the height to which he beckons his disciples. That is the fullness, the maturity of Christ to which they must grow.

So it is understandable—and yet remains a mystery!—that our Lord should choose as the token of his followers' glorification of God the very last and greatest thing that he himself had to give God the Father—his body that was offered and his blood that was shed. But this sacrificial gift is presented in such a way that each time it actually grows out of his followers' own gift, out of the produce of their own clay and sweat, out of a tiny piece of bread and a sip of wine by which they live. And it actually grows out thus by their own doing, by the words of consecration which someone from their midst is empowered to utter. So the Church is able not only to join in some extrinsic fashion in Christ's oblation which is made present in her midst, but she actually offers it as her own gift, as a gift which, in its natural state, is expressive of her own life and leads that life back to God, along with all that God's creative hand apportions to it along the way. This gift in its supernatural state manifests and confesses what the Church has become by God's grace and what she knows she is called to be. Thus the Church is enabled truly to offer up her very self; as St Augustine says, she learns to sacrifice herself in his sacrifice. This self-oblation of the Church is the precise object which the eucharistic mystery serves. Never is the Church so closely bound to her Master, never is she so completely Christ's spouse as when, together with him, she offers God this sacrifice.

By the term "Church" is here meant—as everything we have said goes to show—not only the Church Universal and the priest representing her at the altar, but likewise the assembly of the faithful gathered around the priest at each celebration of the Mass. That the faithful offer the sacrifice was taken for granted in the more ancient theological tradition. *Plebs tua* explicitly stands in juxtaposition to *servi tui* in the Roman canon. Now, as an understanding of the priesthood of the faithful reawakens, the thought once more comes consciously to the fore. It is announced with complete clarity in the great encyclicals of Pope Pius XII.

And now, looking at it more closely, how is this self-oblation of the Church accomplished? The action which brings this about precisely is—again—the consecration. The same act which realizes the sacrifice of Christ also realizes the sacrifice of the Church, but with this difference, that the Church's sacrifice begins to take shape from the very start of the Mass and then receives the divine seal and acceptance when at the consecration Christ takes it in hand and, after richly ennobling it, offers it to his heavenly Father as his own. For the priest who performs the consecration in Christ's name and with Christ's power is always at the same time acting on commission from the Church. This commission he received at his ordination, for it was the Church that appointed him and ordained him as a priest of Christ. And he receives this commission for this precise situation by his office or at least by the fact that, in his celebration of the Eucharist, he fits himself into the Church's pattern and thus places himself at the head of the faithful who, as a portion of the Church Universal, have here and now gathered round him. As their representative he stands at the altar. He consecrates the bread and the chalice to present Golgotha's sacrifice to almighty God as their own. And since all through the course of the Mass he acts and speaks not simply in his own name but on commission from the Church, this authorization does not cease at the moment of transubstantiation merely because Christ's commission is superimposed, for it is the Church that calls on him to accept this second commission so that she, as the Bride of Christ, might once more enter into his sacrifice.

This sacrifice is present on the altar under the form of gifts which are emblems of our life-support and are at the same time manifestations of unity, of the combining of many into one. The ancient Church was vitally conscious of this symbolism of the eucharist species to which even St Paul had already alluded: "As this broken bread was scattered upon the mountain tops and then, being harvested, became one", as the wine has flowed out of many grapes into this chalice, so the faithful should, through this sacrament, become one in Christ.

Another thing. This oblation was instituted with the express determination that the participants be fed with it: "Take and eat." The sacrificial meal is not something plainly included in the notion of sacrifice. There were sacrifices in the Old Testament which were entirely consumed in the fire, with nothing remaining for the offerers to eat—the sin-offerings, for instance; the offerers were not worthy to enter into so close a community with God. But the sacrifice of the New Covenant is essentially constituted as a meal, so that the offerers might gather around the sacrificial table, the table of the Lord, to eat. They are in communion with Christ who had undergone his sufferings and is now exalted; they become anew one body with him.

This element of the symbolism of the species, which is emphasized in the words of consecration—this element above all must be taken in earnest. Every sacrament serves to develop in us the image of Christ according to a specified pattern which the sacramental sign indicates. Here the pattern is plainly shown in the double formation of the Eucharist; we are to be drawn into the sacrifice of our Lord on the Cross. We are to take part in his dying, and through his dying are to merit a share in his life. What we here find anchored fast in the deepest centre of the Mass-sacrifice is nothing else than that ideal of moral conduct to which the teaching of Christ in the Gospel soars; the challenge to an imitation of him that does not shrink at sight of the Cross: a following after him that is ready to lose its life in order to win it: the challenge to follow him even, if need be, in his agony of suffering and his path of death, which are here in this mystery so manifestly set before us.

If the Church's gift of homage to God is thus changed by the priest's words into the immolated Body and the spilled Blood of our Lord, and if the Church, firm and unafraid, then offers it to God, she thereby stamps her "yes" upon the chalice which her Master has drunk and upon the baptism which he experienced. And by that same oblation which she bears in her hands, she is dedicated and sealed for the same road that he travelled on his entrance into glory (Luke 24. 26). The sacrifice of Christ is renewed sacramentally not only *in* his Church but *upon* the Church, and is renewed daily because it is daily demanded of

her (Luke 9. 23). The Mass-sacrifice is not only a presentation of the
redemptive Passion and, with it, of the whole collection of Christian
doctrine on salvation. It is also an epitome of Christian life and conduct.
The height on which Christ lived and died comes before our gaze each
time as an ideal, admonishing and alluring, as a towering peak which we
can only reach by tremendous trying, along the ascent of Christian
asceticism. All this puts Communion in a new light. Communion, too,
is stamped with the Cross and the death of the Lord.

At the consecration, the Church as a society affirms the oblation of
Christ and makes it her very own, but the individual Christian might
feel satisfied to follow from afar, more of an onlooker than an actor in
the sacred drama. In Communion, however, it is the individual partici-
pant who really wants to co-celebrate the Mass—it is his word that
counts. Everyone must be seized with the impulse to be swallowed up in
the mystery of Christ's Passion. Thus and only thus can the partakers
hope to meet him who had already entered into his glory; thus and
only thus can they be embraced by him and hallowed by the fire of his
godhead.

Just as the participation of the Church in Christ's oblation at the
consecration is a sacramental proceeding, so too the completed incorporation of the individual in Communion is a sacramental proceeding. The
recipients of the Eucharist become participants in the oblation *ex opere
operato*. But it is somewhat different with sacrifice as such. Since this
is a moral activity, a free and humble homage before God, a genuine
and essential consummation of the sacrifice cannot be produced in the
mere reception of a divine operation, as is the case with the sacraments
in which God sanctifies man. Therefore the sacrifice, in so far as it is the
oblation of the Church, is not completely concluded with an *opus
operatum*; the *opus operantis* must join in, and not merely as an addition
to the completed work, but as a requisite belonging to the very structure
at least as an integrating part. True, Mass is not simply man's good work
—as Luther pretended to explain Catholic teaching on the subject—but
neither is it simply the result of God's activity, as, for instance, Baptism
is. The Church is not drawn into Christ's Passion under compulsion, but
enters into it freely, consciously, deliberately. That is the Mass.

In a higher measure and in another way than in the sacraments, therefore, there is required beside the passive moment also an active one.
Were Mass only the *mysterium* of Christ's Passion or only a memorial
meal, then—with the addition perhaps of a consentient anamnesis to
cast a glance at the redeeming sufferings—the account of the Last Supper,
with the consecrating words over bread and wine, and the reception of
the Sacrament would suffice. Mass, however, is also and primarily an
immolation to God, an expression of the self-offering of the Church.
The Church does not wait for the redemptive grace that pours down on
her anew; having long ago obtained the favour of her Lord, she takes
the initiative, she sets out on her own to offer God her gift which, at the
height of her ascent, is changed for her into the oblation of Christ.

We therefore find that it is a common phenomenon in the history of
the Mass-liturgies that some action of the Church precedes the consecration, a movement toward God which gains its essential utterance in the

great prayer of thanksgiving but which is also expressed in many customs that, even during the preparation of the elements, suggest the προσ-φέρειν the presentation, the *oblatio*, the gift, just as they continue to express the same thoughts after the transubstantiation. According to its essence, therefore, Mass-liturgy is accomplished in three steps—not very sharply defined: the submissive and laudatory approach to God, the sacramental performance of Christ's sacrifice, and the reception of the sanctified gift.

The institution of Christ thus once more implies that the Church realizes this active moment of the sacrificial proceeding not only in her official representative who stands at the altar but also in the participating congregation. The "we" in the priest's prayers and the spatial assemblage of the participants around the officiating priest already tend in this direction. It follows that an interior immolation is required of the participants, at least to the extent of readiness to obey the law of God in its seriously obligatory commandments, unless this participation is to be nothing more than an outward appearance. A participation that is right and justified in its essentials should, of course, involve the desire to tread again the pathway of the Master and to make progress on it. To such an interior attitude, however, corresponds an exterior expression which exhibits a connection with the essentially significant sacrificial proceedings by means of tokens or words that have the presence of the participants as their starting-point. All the liturgies have developed for this a wealth of expressive elements, but of these only a portion have stayed in living practice. The ideal condition would be if the sacred activity conducted by the priest would evolve from the ordered activity of the congregation and all its members, just as it does evolve from their will.

Since the Mass is a sacrifice of the Church, it normally presumes a larger or smaller assembly of the people. The different types of this assembly gave rise, in the course of history, to a principle of formation; it will be our task in the next few chapters to study the development of this principle more closely. In its most complete development we have the assembly of all the people in the place; in early times this occurred mostly under the leadership of the bishop, while later on the priest, especially the pastor, was appointed for this. The bishop's Mass and the priest's Mass, therefore, form two of the basic ties of the Mass. But the assembly can also shrink to just a few persons, and finally—as an irreducible limit—to the single person of the celebrating priest, who, indeed, can also offer up the Mass in his own name. However, we find the Church constantly trying to avoid this extreme case, to such an extent in fact that in none of the rites, either East or West, did any form of Mass develop in which at least the external outlines of community participation were left out. The forms of private Mass are always only diluted forms of public celebration.

The Foundation*

Rudolf Schwarz

THE ALTAR was called "Christ" in former times, just as many other things were called "Christ" or "the body of Christ": the congregation or the house in which it gathered or, very generally, the earth. This was meant so literally that the individual parts of the house were compared to the individual limbs of his body, the nave with the trunk, the transept with the outspread arms and the choir with the head. Thus Christ hung perpetually on the cross, and because he bowed his head in death, as the Gospel relates, the choir was sometimes built at an angle to the nave. And so within this image—which was far more than a comparison—it would be fitting to call the altar the head or the heart of the Lord. And this was surely the intention.

It is hard for modern men to take such ideas seriously. Usually it is objected that they were based on false concepts of life, that the levels were confused, that reality and image were not kept distinct. There may be some truth in this. Still it must be retorted that the medieval concept of life was not a naïve one and that, in the assertion that this or that "is" the body, the little word "is" remains completely open and is ready to exist at the most varied levels. The decisive reason for the modern objection cannot lie here.

Now it is certain that the Middle Ages knew how to build churches and that their churches were true churches. In this respect we have not surpassed them in the least. And so it is well to assume that their theoretical concepts cannot have been entirely false either.

Actually what separates us from these early teachings is not so much their content as the difference of language. Today we no longer connect the same images with the words and we put a new meaning into the old terms. When men spoke of the "body" or of the "body of Christ" in earlier times, they probably meant something quite different from what we mean when we speak about our body. And so to begin with we must try to make clear to ourselves what medieval men saw as "body".

This can be quite readily recognized in the early pictures which show the body in its holiness. The bodies are shown as something radiant and all the most brilliant colours are used for them, all the colours of glowing, burning things. And the head is enveloped in the "halo" as if in a radiant sun.

There is a hierarchy of colours in these pictures, culminating in the brightest white, and the gold is then the eternal light in which the saints are bathed.

The pictures also show the body condemned and rejected, usually in the form of an animal: it has taken on claws and beaks and the like or has been completely transformed into a monster. There is an order of the condemned colours, too, ending in a flame, the flame of an evil,

* From *The Church Incarnate*; see p. x above.

inwardly-burning fire. And the abysmal darkness into which all this is sunk is the darkness of damnation, not the blackness of the sheltering night about the babe in the manger.

These pictures clearly showed that the holy body is something luminous, something star-like, and it is obvious that an eternal meaning was ascribed to the colours—in the mandorla of colour the true essence found expression. And people believed that the luminous power of the body could be perverted and turned into its evil opposite. Here we are reminded that the Scripture tells us similar things, for instance when it relates that the Lord's face "shone" or Stephen's—in the latter's case it adds the explanation that he was looking up into the "wide open heaven".

In the Strasbourg tympanum, where the death of the Virgin is represented, the likeness of her dying body is escaping out of it and the Lord already holds this likeness in his hand. This is what is lasting: the body of the soul or the soul of the body. It is exactly like the corpse itself except that it is much smaller—but this does not mean that it is unimportant or only a leftover: it means that this is the intrinsic reality, the essence of body which, although it is not bound to any particular size, is indeed bound to the structural laws of bodily form and bodily growth.

The magnificent portal at Autun depicts the Last Judgement. The Lord is of mighty stature and is seated between heaven and earth to separate the living from the dead. Mary is also very large and the angels are only slightly smaller. These great angels are raising the people out of their graves, and the people are so small that it is hard to believe that all this is for them and their judgement. But the "souls" or the "spirits" are not depicted, for that would have been against the belief in the resurrection of the flesh. These are real men with real bodies who are climbing out of their graves, and this is the real Lord, the Lord whose incarnation in the flesh and in history the Christians have always taken so terribly literally. But if the Lord appears tremendous and mighty this can only mean that he has a mighty body and men a modest one.

There are many such representations of sacred history and they should be taken seriously. What they show is not meant as a landscape of the soul nor as an artistic interpretation—it is meant to be genuine history. Apparently in the course of this no one reflected on the fact that all the people should actually be shown with bodies of approximately the same size. The painters saw history from the centre point of an absolute perspective, similar to the way in which God sees it, and within this perspective of very essence the differences in size arose by themselves. When, later on, the school of historical painting developed, the early art of painting history was lost. Painting continued to be done in perspective, but this new perspective was developed from a completely accidental standpoint and all the things were given in relation to it. The thing which happened to lie right next to this accidental point, were it only the tail-end of a horse, became immense. The school of historical painting moved the centre of history out of God, but it did not transfer it to a great and important person, to a king, for instance, or to the leader in a battle—it simply moved it anywhere, into the arbitrary. Historical painting lost the centre of history and then disintegrated into idle gossip. This is a comfortable art; or perhaps we should call it a highly difficult un-art, since it presupposes a singular and complex disturbance which no longer even sees what the pagan mythologies could see: that the great are great and the lesser small. (How splendidly the Edda builds a world for itself out of a few figures and their great works —a few men, a tree, a wolf, a snake, a bridge and the like. And is not a city such as Mycaenae similarly designed, with its few glorious elements, the grave, the gateway, the street, the hall?)

In earlier times men must have seen the community itself like this.

Troubetzkoy, who speaks so beautifully about the holy fire burning in the ancient icons, speaks, too, about the old Russian cities. The "onion dome" has nothing to do with either an onion or a dome. It is the flame, he says, and when one sees such an old city, lying with her many churches sunlit upon the open plain, the earth is afire. The city is a sea of flame.

The structure of our own cities in Europe was little different. The houses were small and were consumed in the flames of the great spires.

If we gather a large number of such things out of art, out of the lives of the saints and also out of the teachings—for instance the teaching about the transfigured body—then we gradually gain some idea of what it was that people vividly connected with the word "body" in those days. Namely two things.

First and foremost they took the body seriously. They thought its every detail terribly important and they took it literally. They accepted it in a way which we are no longer capable of today. Even the comparison of the church building with the Lord's body would have been unthinkable without this absolute earnestness about the body's structure. The human form was for them a representation of absolute form. The body had not grown together out of a series of accidents but had been given by the Creator in accordance with the sacred plan. To them this real body of everyday reality in its everyday structure was created "in the image of God". In it, God had imparted his own form, first on the sixth day of the creation, as Genesis described it, and then once more when the word became flesh. In the Saviour, in his holy body and in that which visibly befell him and in what he did, the first revelation was clarified, surmounted and founded anew. And ever since then all true growth and all sacred life had imitated this revelation which had happened in form and in history—for in the body of the Lord the eternal had become visible. The Middle Ages certainly did not simply imagine their conception of the body. To be sure, much of their knowledge was superficial. What lay inside the body could only be guessed at: anatomy was unknown since it was thought that even cutting into the structure of the dead body was forbidden to men. This led to lacks in the teachings and in the work, for many of these conjectures were utterly false. But even the renunciation of anatomy and of the living model prove how serious a matter the real body was to these people and with what great awe they experienced the sacred connection between its structure and the holy chastity of its life.

But—this is the second thing—the body which was seen with such realism was not a rigid pattern. The very nature of its appearance which they took so seriously was the fundamental articulation for the wealth of forms in a free and radiant life. Body was both given and ever effected anew. The body could transform everything. Body was bound to no definite size and to no definite form and yet it possessed an eternal structure; it could assume this form and later on another and yet through all this remain true to itself. Body was a work to be continually accomplished between God and the Soul, ever new interpretation into living freedom. Even the fact that the saints were often hard on it did not at bottom mean a mortification of the body but rather its sacred interpretation. Had the body not meant anything to them they would not have treated it as they did.

These, then, are the approximate premises for the assertion that the congregation or the church building itself are the mighty holy body of the Lord. He who says this believes that the Lord's body is so rich that it can assume all these forms. And at the same time he believes that the body's structure is the form of the eternal, so that wherever the eternal takes on body this articulation becomes visible. The great churches and cathedrals are for him a whole cosmos, a revelation of eternal structure, objective form set before God.

Personally we believe that the sacred objectivity of these old concepts is true and that we will ourselves have to be converted to it. The times have erred far away from it. Sacred structure is no longer understood as that which it actually is: as structure, as the dogmatics of eternity. Rather is it understood in the same way in which historical painting understands history. Idle folk run about within it and seek their own private viewpoints, have their private pleasure and write them down in private books. Even photography was invented at the right moment for them, for by means of it reality can be deprived of all form and can be misinterpreted in every way; and at all events it put the movable standpoint in the place of the gloriously objective structural plan. Assuredly the medieval master who taught that "the beautiful is that which is pleasing to see" seemed to acknowledge them to be right. But what a lot of misunderstandings! How distorted the meaning of each of these few words! That old "beauty" was the final witness to the truth, the "laughter of the universe" which simply became itself, child in the Father's hand. And "to please", *"placet"* was the "yes" of the creature, its final, consummate consent; "seeing" was acceptance and response through a believing pair of eyes.

But the total con-version and re-version of the building art must come to pass wholly out of what is genuine.

We cannot return to the early cathedrals and take up their interrupted discipline once more. This was the error of the historicists. Even the tools, our "technology", would fail us. It would of course be possible to copy the deep doorways and the mighty pillars of the Romanesque or the pointed arches of the Gothic. But it would not be true. For us the wall is no longer heavy masonry but rather a taut membrane, we know the great tensile strength of steel and with it we have conquered the vault. For us the building materials are something different from what they were to the old masters. We know their inner structure, the positions of their atoms, the course of their inner tensions. And we build in the knowledge of all this—it is irrevocable. The old, heavy forms would turn into theatrical trappings in our hands and the people would see that they were an empty wrapping. They would draw premature conclusions about the matter which is served by these empty forms.

But in a far profounder sense we cannot return to the Middle Ages. The great realities of the cathedral are no longer real to us. This does not mean that "in themselves" they are no longer true. No, they are as true to us as on their first day and they move us deeply. What a "spire" is and proclaims, the procession of "pillars" and "arches", the crowd of "pinnacles" and "responders"—these are valid for all times, as valid as a painting by Lochner or the sculptures of Bamberg. But even so we can no longer build these things because life has gone on and the reality which is our task and which is given into our hands possesses completely different, perhaps poorer, form. Deep in our hearts we know what the solemn words of the old cathedrals mean, and still it is not given to us to realize them as that which they once were. We know what a Gothic spire was but our own spire is something very different. For us the old words no longer name the same living reality. Here we are not speaking as historians or theorists whose only question is "how it actually was at that time", regardless of whether or not that past reality can still be brought into living consummation today. We speak rather as creating men, as masters of building who are supposed to make out, not with what may be theoretically "right", but rather with what is at hand, with what is real, here and now. There is a great difference between an abstract truth and an architectural reality. For the master builder, what proves true is true, real what realizes. In his bare workshop the things are worth only as much as they can perform. When he perseveres in the genuine he does what God wants of him, even if this genuine thing be poor. We should not fall upon his work and demand realizations of theoretical truths which he cannot provide, for then nonentities may arise, unproved fabrications and faithless sacrality—and along with these weeds the people may throw away the seed out of which the genuine might grow. It is easy to say that we can no longer build in the medieval manner and yet it is difficult to hold out where we are, to make out with what is given us and to avoid that historical doing which uses only the historical things and not the historical forms.

On the other hand, it does not suffice to work honestly with the means and forms of our own time. It is only out of sacred reality that sacred building can grow. What begets sacred works is not the life of the world but the life of faith—the faith, however, of our own time. This is the third thing: that sacred substance out of which churches can be built must be alive and real to us. It would be simple to go back to the old teaching and to say that we should build the "body of Christ"—it would even be modern. Today people again recall the old terms and like to use them. They speak of the body of the Lord and relate the word to the individual, to the community and even to the works of their hands. Or they say that man was created in the "image of God", and once again they call the church service "God's work". The old words awaken in them memories and hopes. But people no longer combine any clear conceptions with them; they use them in Latin, solemnly, like ancient conceits of a holy theology but they do not use them to name something which they see in each detail of outline, form and colour. At the time when these words were discovered they named straightforwardly that which was seen and experienced; but when we repeat them today we express at best a feeling. Nowadays we no longer see the body as people formerly saw it, with luminous head, tall, radiant and buoyant. Our body is inert and heavy, bound to the spot. And so it is that when we speak of the sacred body our only possibility is to think either completely honestly of this our body as we see it, exercise it, heal it every day, as our science has investigated it, as it now is—admittedly a needy premise for theology—or to think of something generally solemn. He who calls the church a "work of God" either means precisely what is meant today by the word "work", or he means something completely vague, which means that he doesn't think at all but only has feelings. The old words named a very definite and particular sight. And since we today are no longer capable of seeing this sight at all, we have found a strange way out: the sacred is invisible and the old words referred to miracles. Historicism exists in the realm of the sacred, too, and it has little prospect of standing the test of time.

This, then, is our task:

To build churches out of that reality which we experience and verify every day; to take this our own reality so seriously and to recognize it to be so holy that it may be able to enter in before God. To renew the old teachings concerning sacred work by trying to recognize the body, even as it is real to us today, as creature and as revelation, and by trying to render it so; to reinstitute the body in its dignity and to do our work so well that this body may prove to be "sacred body". And beyond all this to guard ourselves against repeating the old word when for us no living content is connected with them.

In the following we will attempt to show, in the two examples of the eye and the hand, that it is possible to believe in the body as we know it today as a creature; then we will attempt to show that our work as we practise it today is good and that it could well be made into "God's work". And finally we shall try to show in what respects this work must be differentiated from our daily work.

THE EYE

How beautiful is our knowledge of the human eye! How it waits to be rightly understood! As eye, the body sees the light which is in the world. The light comes to it over the things but goes forth from the stars.

"Star"—that is primary streaming light. Three things make up its form:

the generating centre: a shining point;
the rays of light: the paths which go out from the centre in all directions;
the sphere of light: the growing ball to which the centre expands.

These three elements together make up the star-form. Each one of them is the expression and the transformation of the others and each is un-thinkable without them—the form is wholly unified. Centre expands into sphere, rays spring from the centre point and beget the surrounding ball. He who names one part names the whole. The star is primary form.

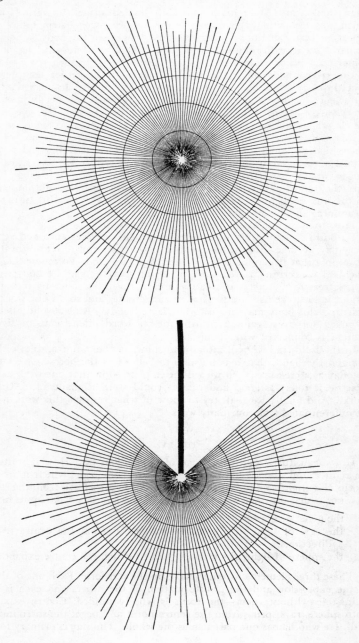

The light beats a path through the space, irradiates it and takes it up into the star-image. At last the light strikes a thing and then this thing in turn begins to shine. Since, however, the light and the star are one and the same, it is in reality the star which reaches this thing on the rays of light and which is united with it. In the course of this process the shining object takes a part of the light, now changed to darkness, into itself. The rest it passes on and in so doing the thing itself becomes a star. At each point on its shining surface the star-form is formed once again and coloured light streams out in all directions.

But these countless new stars on the radiant thing have no independent existence. Their sphere of light exists only as long as they continue to be fed from the primary light. Hanging from it by the bridge of rays, they "de-pend" upon it.

The first star is the only one which really unfolds, welling forth out of its own centre. All the later ones are "open stars". They, too, are composed of centre, rays and sphere but their centre does not itself generate. Inwardly, the centre depends on the primary star. The primary star sends out a beam to this centre which then transforms it into the star-image. The centre is not source but turning-point—it "mediates" the primal light. "Open stars" denote those places where the first light founds its settlements in the world.

Such open stars are made whole only in the primary star, for it is the primary star which closes their openness. They stand open to it through a "window", through an inner opening. Nor do they pass on the full light. Their light is "broken", for one part of the original light, now transformed to darkness, has sunk into the depths of the things. The strained-out light which remains goes on as colour. Therefore it is not quite accurate to say that the essence of the things finds expression in their colour, since the light which passes to the inside and is consumed there is exactly complementary to the colour of the object. Indeed the light which passes to the inside is just what would fill out the colour to make up the original light. More correctly we would have to say that the colour is the reply to the inside of the thing, and as reply it is also of course a key to the inside. We recognize the things in their coloured shadows. Colour is light which has united with an object. The surface of the things is clothed with "open stars"—open toward the sun—or with "open sockets", and in this latter connection it makes sense to say that the things of the world are covered with eyes.

When his eye sees, the human being becomes open for the light. It enters through a window. Once inside, it comes together at the focal point, whence it shines, again a star, on to the horizon of the retina. Thus the star-image comes into being for a third time in the eye.

The light comes as a ray from the outside to the star in the eye, too, and this second star is "open" in the direction of the bridge of rays. If the eye closes, the star is extinguished. The star in the eye lasts only as long as it hangs, through the window, on the seen thing. Therefore the star in the eye is not a rebirth of the thing in the world but only its subordinate dwelling. This object reaches into the eye over the bridge of rays. Actually, of course, it is not the object which enters the eye, for the object itself is in turn dependent on the primary star—the object's

sphere of light exists only as long as it "de-pends" on the original light.
Thus a chain of connections develops, the first light is passed on again
and again and each time it produces a star. The eye is complete only in
the sun, and so actually we see nothing except the sun and the things
as shadows in it.

Even of the colourful surface of the world we·see only the side turned
toward us, and this, too, we see in an apparent coherence which does
not exist at all "in reality". The eye cannot see the backs of the things,
their depths and furrows, the things which are disguised or turned away
from it. The eye is easily deceived and easily led astray and therefore it
has often been accused of being a poor instrument. Extensive theories
have been built up about the "optical illusion", but these theories are in
themselves an optical illusion since they are deluded as to the eye and
its meaning. The eye is not an apparatus for the purpose of recognizing
the things. Rather is it man's profound and open answer to streaming
light. The eye sees the star without illusion and in the star it can see
the things, but only in so far as they themselves are star. In them it
recognizes the star-image, nothing more, for in the star everything is
arching smoothness without furrows or depths. The eye alters the world
according to the plan of the star, and the eye itself is built according to
this plan, in order that the world may enter into it. When we look at
the world it becomes a star to which the eye replies—an open star in
which one segment is lacking, an open star which is made whole in the
sun.

This is approximately what we know today about seeing. It was not
known formerly and it is glorious. Only one thing is lacking here: that
warm and good understanding which finds meaning and form in all
these things.

Does not to behold something mean to choose one particular thing
out of the world and to move it into the centre of the eye? Does it not
mean to place this chosen thing as the only sun in a new universe, to
make oneself, one's own body, into the sphere of this shining thing? To
form one's own body into a dark world arching about the new central
sun of the seen thing? Does it not mean to establish across and beyond
this thing a relationship with the primal star, to make oneself "dependent" upon it, to nourish oneself from it and to unite oneself with it?

And all this has a form.

The eye is form, beautifully and wisely built in accordance with the
design of the star-image. It is the answering body which sees the light and
is inwardly enriched by it. Thus this is the way the body looks when it
gives answer to the stars; the body's meeting with the light "looks like"
this.

The open eye is a valid image of the body and hence of the human
being; its open shell-like form is a genuine symbol. This sign stands for
the human being and we may designate the human being with it since
we did not invent it: the body itself created this form. We can learn
from this primal sign that the body is built on encounter, that it is
answer to light, that the human being is an "open form"; that we recognize the world only as shadow in the light and that we never possess it
completely; and that consequently the human being is not a microcosmos

but rather a deficient being, needful of completion. Or far more, that by making himself into an open form, thus repeating inwardly the openness of the universe and its dependence on light, the human being may renew within himself the structure of the world.

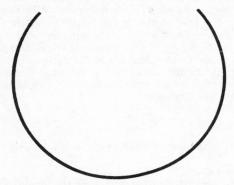

Only that eye which could look at the world on all sides and which could surround the world on the outside with its own horizon would see the world completely. And only those things, which stars are, are complete. The world disposes itself around them as perfect eye. But the horizon of the retina remains open, the human being clings to the distant light—and the constellation of the things are open, too.

The eye, then, is not a star, as is so often said, but rather answer to it. It is circumference, dark, hollow and in readiness. But the star is centre which gives itself forth in shining radiance. Eye and star hold dialogues, their forms complete one another. Here we see that there are certain forms which are based on one another—forms which find their meaning only when they meet, forms which become whole in each other. And we see that the forms of the living body are significant because they have meaning in discourse and dialogue.

Whether the eye is capable of action?

Our language thinks so, for it speaks of "casting" a glance, of shining eyes, and it says that we see the things, whereas to be optically correct we would have to say that the things look at us. Our feelings think so too, for they know that the things are changed by the way our eyes rest upon them, that the things can become little and grey, even evil, or that they can rise up to smile at us, that they can grow and radiate under our glance. Our feelings know that eyes can enchant or encourage, command or obliterate. The eye can make the things so trusting that they advance to meet us. Obviously all this means more than simply the outward ability to avoid a meeting, to cast down the eyes, to close them; more, too, than the ability to turn the eyes in a particular direction and to focus them at a particular distance. Actually all this says that through our eyes we may yield ourselves.

Here our present knowledge helps us no further, the question has not been investigated. But it seems to us that a dark counter-current must be assumed which flows toward the things when we look at them, a sort of influence in which inner being is communicated to the being of the things. For clearly the creatures on which our eyes rest are addressed in their very depths, are comprehended and changed. Everything which is asserted and believed about the effects of seeing concerns the whole, never the details; it is as if a dark power, utterly without contour, streamed out through the eye. This meeting would be consummated in all purity where one pair of eyes looks deep into another, where darkness enters into darkness and where, from being to being, purest concord happens. Perhaps the figure of the seeing eye could be read backward: then the nerves would be the channels of the dark current which enters space at the retina. In the act of seeing the things, the light current from the outside and the dark from the inside would unite and together they would create the "image".

THE HAND

How beautiful is the hand! How much it can do and how beautiful its function!

The hand can radiate.

The arm rises, the fist clenches and over the single pointing finger the gathered power discharges—the hand becomes radiating point. But when it opens, stretching all fingers outward from the palm, it is an open star at the end of the arm.

The hand can hollow itself.

The fingers come together to form a bowl, empty and open in the movement of holding. In the cupping motion the two hands come together to make up one single bowl.

The hand which we offer is both "active" star-image and receptive, empty form.

The hand can touch.

The farthest finger-tip softly touches a thing, the gentlest power of communication flows out to it and slowly, softly it reveals itself.

With the first gentle touch the reaching movement is reversed: surrender to the thing becomes submersion in it. Quietly the hand rests on the thing and fingers it. The hand can reassure, love and bless. Here being surrenders to being. Here is healing. What happens in the laying-on of hands may be compared to the communication of intrinsic being which occurs when the eyes rest on a thing. Both eye and hand work changes deep within. The mysterious meeting of one pair of eyes in another corresponds lastly with the clasping of two hands whose streams of being are exchanged and become one. (And the eye also possesses that second movement of folding one's own hands: it is the movement of closing the lids.)

The hand can feel.

The hand which yields itself to a thing assumes the form of the thing. Yet it does this in such a way that where the thing protrudes the hand is concave and where the thing is concave the hand is pliable. Thus the hand is "answer" to the formed-ness of the things and in this it is like the eye which sees. The hand runs over the surface provingly and this movement is at once feeling and communicating, moulding and a calm stroking, a sort of silent conversing.

In many ways the hand understands the world better than the eye. It "sees" the world from all sides. The hand can grasp. Its fingers close around the thing, forming a vault. The power of the hand to radiate streams back into itself and in a dark current this power flows about the clasped thing, awakening the answer within. Thus the thing is taken up completely into the circulation of the body; it is buried in the hollow of the hand; the hand can conceal—and this the eye cannot do either, since for it the world is always open. The hand can take a piece of the world completely into itself and contain it wholly; it can grasp the thing from all sides. The hand makes an entire world, it notices the backs of the things, too, the indentations, the dissimulations. But the hand's world is not large—it cannot reach very far and its capacity is small. The hand is built for what is nearby, for the limited, for the things themselves while the eye is in reality built for the sun.

Eye and hand are sister and brother for both apprehend the surfaces—that is, the ex-pressions of the things, the utterances through which they speak. But where the hand itself possesses depth and inner structure it opens up for itself a part of the world which is closed to the eye: the inner space of the things. With a testing push or pull it explores the mass. The "grasping" hand strains the material until it begins to grow soft. The resistance of the mass is expressed in the increasing tension of sinews and muscles, in the growing pressure within the bony structure. The hand creates an answer to the insides of the things within its own inner structure; and with the same instrument it can form them and also weigh them.

If we want to test the weight of a thing we must lift it, hold it suspended against the force of gravity. This happens through the hand. The hand passes its inner stress on into the arm which in turn passes this stress into the body. Hidden within the body is a system of tension running over sinews, muscles and bones, through arm, spine and legs, from the weighted object down to the earth. A sort of pathway is formed between the earth and the thing, a course which passes over the body as the bearing bridge. Thus we may say that as the seeing eye is related to the sun high overhead, so is the grasping, weighing hand related to the depths of the earth.

It is not by becoming mass itself but rather by translating mass into buoyance that the body perceives the inner nature of the world, its dull, massive heaviness. Body which apprehends the heavy things is not weight but response to weight. Its answer to the heavy compactness of the world's matter reads "Column" and "cable". Mass is expanding, unformed, roomy; the body's answer is linear, slender, articulate. Mass is fullness. The body replies with the "skeleton", a delicate fabric of curves in space. Therefore it is false to accuse the body of being earth-bound or to contrast it with the supposed lightness of some "spiritual" principle. By its very nature, the body brings into its encounter with the heavy earth the will to transform dull massiveness into buoyant power. The body is not primarily weight, but lightness—"power" which interlaces space on linear paths.

We experience Mass in the growing tension of ligaments, which is to say that we experience it lineally. This very simple circumstance reveals its relationship to numbers and to the lineal law of their growth which we find expressed in the curve. The experience of mass can be "reckoned", it can be delineated in the movement of numbers, it can be represented in curves. During the last few centuries this fact has largely determined our picture of the world and also our work itself. The experience of what lies within the things came late and when it came it was overwhelming. For a long time hardly anything else counted. Afterward the "grasping" hand was bitterly attacked—the hand which saw only the massiveness and weight in the things and which discovered in them only their function. And when, at last, the eye and the "world of forms" were given their rightful place beside the grasping hand—and with them the outlines of the things, their shapes and colours and the timbre which is in the world—all this was felt to be a liberation.

We do not contradict this. By itself the hand obviously provides a contribution to the recognition of the real world—but again, only as an organ for the depths of the world's matter. If this aspect remains isolated, the image of the world is distorted and the work even more. But we may not now replace the "haptics" of the grasping hand with the "optics" of the seeing eye lest a new distortion arise. The liberation must lead from the part to the whole, it must place the eye, the ear, the whole body, next to the hand so that once again we may achieve total works and so that the world may become whole once more. The hand itself must become whole again, too, "feeling" must enter in next to "grasping", the hand must once more become "eye"—and like the eye it must come to stand for the whole body since like the eye the hand, too, is a little human being, is the image, the body of man. ("Manu" means "little man".) Within this whole, however, a very high place is owed to the "concept", to the grasping hand. It is not true that concepts understand nothing of the essence of the things. The concept answers a particular part of the world through a wonderful fabric of curves. Here it achieves profoundest concord with the world. The concept and its works are lofty deeds of the mind.

We could continue to consider the body in this way; the image would grow ever richer but in essence it would remain the same. We found the body in ever changing form: as hollow ball in relation to light, as linear scaffold in relation to weight, as ray, star, surface, arch. And we found that the body is not ultimately bound to any form at all but is extraordinarily free. The world is filled with a great dialogue which passes back and forth between thing and thing, between form and form. The body is drawn into this great flow of speech. It is open to every invocation which comes to it from the forms and it replies to them with clear forms of its own, forms which it assumes for the moment and then relinquishes once more. This dialogue is not limited to the sound of words alone: it is exercised with the whole body and all its limbs. Thus the body is constantly formed and yet, beyond all transformation, it remains true to itself. If we observe only its material—which is now eye, now hand, now foot, now ray, now ball, then bowl, then ligament, then shaft—this material seems to be hardly more than a plastic mass out of which that something which imparts the answer kneads its forms of reply. If this "something" is the "soul" then the body is hardly more than its changing image, its message into the world—and also the soul is wedded to the body far more intimately than was previously supposed. But if it is the body which imparts one answer after the other, which gives one invocation after the other—and we are very inclined to this opinion—then the body is "really" something, and this something commands the material almost like a sovereign, playing with the forms and yet not losing itself in them. Then body also means faithfulness to one's own form; then it is not something-or-other, not some proteus-like fluid, but rather clear structure to which everything applies which we mean when we speak of "form". The body is consumed utterly in its momentary form and takes this form completely literally. However, it is not ultimately bound to this form. Rather it is prepared to answer all sorts of situations in the manner appropriate to the moment through forms which are ever different and ever clear, and yet beyond them all it remains itself. And so the body would be both potentiality and form: potentiality, which can take on almost all forms, and form, which, as it is, is serious and complete.

What we have said may not be exact in every detail. It is neither our task nor our field to provide an anthropological doctrine. Our concern is rather good guidance to true work. And since our work can be true work only if it grows out of what is real, we wanted to show that reality is not such a bad building material after all and that we could make out with it without fleeing into historisticism. What we have pointed out is not actually new. Children learn it in school. But we believe that it might be looked at for once as if it *were* new, as if we had just heard about it for the first time. We believe that we can accept reality understandingly, as being made up of things and processes which exist and which have a form whose meaning is reasonable and deductible—as things and processes whose form and meaning coincide. It must be possible for us to trust the body to be what it "looks like". And it must be possible to trust that the Creator meant something in giving it this form and no other.

Perhaps in this way we should arrive sooner at a comprehensible teaching about man, which indeed we all need so badly. It seems to us that at the present time no tremendous outlay of ceremonious metaphysics would be necessary in order to get to the root of what man actually is, and it seems to us, too, that no such difficult books need be written about it— books whose readers even at the end have still not found out how many legs are allotted to a man. Perhaps it would be better to look for once in awe at what is there, not with great learnedness but with the warm understanding of the good mother. She knows that it is the details which are the really important things about her little boy and she tends to base the proof for the divine origin of man on the fact that this little boy happens to be just as he is, with two feet, on each of them five toes; and she is convinced that she will one day be held accountable for having kept his ears clean, since she believes that these precise ears are a part of the particular revelation given in this little creature. But the philosophical mother, to whom these ears are not "of the essence", has little prospect of eternal life.

Would not this perhaps be even the more correct way of learning to see revelation in the body, too, and of learning to believe once more in the sacred body? A body ever effected as speech and answer would not be difficult to believe in as an image or a likeness or as an answer to the Creator's invocation. And it would be understandable that the body can become unutterably beautiful when it makes itself wholly into a loving answer under the eyes of God. The body constantly enacted or effected would be the most serious of tasks. And lastly it would even be more comprehensible to us that the body, giving answer anew to the voice of the Creator, can be restored in regenerate form. If it is true that man is something constantly effected, constantly regenerated, if it is true that he is a creature who ever "de-pends" on his Creator, a creature who is capable of hearing and of answering God's holy word and work, then he really is a likeness, and then God himself is not something-or-other but rather has a form, a form which is shown in man, not directly, but as that reply to God's own form which has been awakened in earthly matter.

PAINTING

How beautiful are the works of the creating body and how gloriously they reveal its innermost being!

When a painter paints his picture almost the same thing happens in the open as that which takes place in secret when the eye sees. It is not, as the ancient philosophers thought, and as has been repeated ever since, that this painter has a little picture in his head which he reproduces by covering a canvas with forms and colours, continually testing to see whether or not he has copied it exactly. It is rather that in the beginning he has only a seed within himself, and he takes care not to think this seed out into an "inner picture" (which he could easily do in every detail) because then he would do his own work ahead of time and afterward he would succeed only in making a tired reproduction—should he still have any desire to make the boring transcription. Far more does his picture grow under his hand as a young creature, and his eye, astonished and moved, reports to the inside what is taking place there on the outside. From time to time, then, the painter steps back and views the work with an appraising eye. The eye itself cannot actually paint. It is conceivable that it could. The motion picture projector gives an example of how a light can be shone through an exposed ground, which has been fixed and made transparent, so that the negative appears positive. Otherwise, however, this occurs as simple reflection and without any creative ingredient. This the eye cannot do. It can see pictures but it cannot produce them. Its radiance is dark and without outline. Therefore in painting the eye weds itself with the hand which is colour-blind. And hence what arises is not radiation (projection) but a giving forth, a birth (production). The eye rests encouragingly on the hand and what comes into being is neither a reflection of the world nor a reflection of what lies within, rather it is image. But now the spot where the image grows is not the inner retina but the external canvas. In painting it is almost as if the painter were to transpose his retina to the outside, as if he thus made the image objective and public and placed it where the visible world stood before.

SCULPTURE

Sculpture, too, is a work of the hands. The hand lays hold of a material and models out of it the image. The hand awakens it to speech. Flattening, testing and improving it moves over the surface and the eye watches, resting quietly on the busy hand. Here again the eye's contribution is purely feminine.

But sculpture is primarily the work of the feeling hand, not of the grasping hand. The sculptural form has its own true place on the surface: it is imposed form. What lies beneath should carry and support this form, and when really successful, it expresses itself through the surface.

Here there are two borderline cases. One case is where the sculptor chooses a material because it possesses the baser quality of sticking together and occupying space—here he can impose a form onto it, a form in which the material itself participates only in as far as it holds the shape and prevents it from immediately dissolving. This is the case of pure minting. A pure form is pressed into an impressionable material. Wax and soft clay are worked in this way. And this is also the case with casting: a liquid material is poured into a hollow form in which it hardens.

The other borderline case—here the sculptor literally carves out his image—is where the sculptor wins the form from his material. He lets the grain of the wood or the vein in a block of marble "speak", too. But this "speaking" is not real dialogue since the material does not understand the form which it should have but only contributes its accidental physical qualities or at most the form of its growth. Only dumbly does the stuff sense what is imposed upon it. In no case does the material take a greater part than this in sculptural work. It is dangerous to compare the educator or the politician to the sculptor, for the latter imposes his form on a dumb material.

In sculpture the hand reverses itself, as it were: its particular way of feeling becomes assertion. The hand which perceives a thing by feeling fingers the outside of it, thus noticing its external form, and through this form the hand can guess at what lies within. In a sculptural work, this act of feeling becomes utterance. The hand turns into a speaking form and places itself on the outside as a work. Thus this work's strange existence between the dimensions is explained. This work is spatial but its spatiality is that of an oft bent surface—and there is something else too, for this surface is given depth by the quiet submission of the sculptural mass. The way in which the depths of the sculpture participate here corresponds to the silent communication of the hand which rests softly on a thing. One is transposed into the other, the sculptor exchanges the world for his own hand, he puts his hand in the place of a thing in the world.

BUILDING

The art of building is not a genuine work of the hand since it is done with the whole body. The labourers lift up the materials, place them one on top of the other and join them together. They execute movements which correspond to the forms of the growing part of the building and they deposit these movements in the building materials. In this way the act of raising turns to upright structure. The workers go over the wall with the trowel, and out of their stroking motion comes a skin of colour or plaster. They saw and plane the wood, draw and forge the iron. Each limb of the body moves in its own particular way and all of them together create the building as a second body.

Nor is building the work of one man. Under the head foreman a whole ordered company of men takes part in the work on the building.

What then comes into being is first and foremost circumscribed space —shelter, living space, ceremonial space, a space which replaces the space of the world. We could almost say, and indeed it is true, that building is based on the inner spaciousness of the body, on the knowledge of its extent and the form of its growth, on the knowledge of its articulation and of its power to expand. Indeed it is with the body that we experience building, with the outstretched arms and the pacing feet, with the roving glance and with the ear, and above all else in breathing. Space is dancingly experienced. But the surroundings are the inversion of the dance: that space inside of which the dance extends itself, that space which stands ready for the body, is not, as is usually assumed, the outward radiating of the body but rather its inverted space—the body's space turned inside out and projected into the outer world. The body's space, however, forces itself outward whereas the space of the building forces itself inward so that its "skin" lies close to that of the dancing people. The "inside" of the structure overflows, the content of the space is larger than its "skin".

SHELL CONSTRUCTION

At its outer limit the building space is bordered by the walls. Here difficulties arise because this all-embracing construction has itself two sides, one turned toward the world, the other toward the inner space; and between them is again a mass, and this mass is itself a particular "work-body"; and, again, seen from the outside, the whole structure is sculpture. Thus the layers and processes of work interweave in many varied ways. It would be quite simple if the entire enclosing construction were only a membrane which spanned the space of the inner form. This is the case in the stereometrical body where the surface is the exact expression of the contents: in a ball, which has the greatest content in respect to space, the smallest expanse in respect to surface, and in which surface and content correspond exactly to each other, both signifying the same thing, each in its own way. If truthfulness consists in clear expression, then shell construction is the truest of all ways of building, for the shell adheres completely to the inner space, and it seems—none of these things can be proved—that the inner condition within such a shell, the static articulation of its stuff, is "contained without a remainder" in this "equation". When, in addition, the form of the people's ordering corresponds with the spatial form, we achieve a completely "unanimous" work in which the whole structure is permeated from the inside to the outside by the same form. Here would be realized that total architecture which is the dream of our new building art.

BUILDING AS SCULPTURE

We can also build in a completely different way.

Walls and construction may be regarded as a plastic theme and we may then allow space and walls to orchestrate the structure contrapuntally. Then, like the material of a statue, that which happens within the walls themselves participates only softly through their "skin". The construction contributes little to the form—its task is hardly more than to provide a stiffening for it. The most magnificent example of this type of building is provided by the human body itself. The body hides the skeleton and the play of muscles, it reveals them only by intimation, making them as it were into the theme of a sculptural composition which plays freely and in many variations about what lies within. The Greeks built in this manner. Their building is not a form effecting the conquest of gravity as is the Gothic—rather do gravity and its conquest here become one single artistic theme. This form speaks in the Doric as it may speak in a statue. It would be senseless to call this sort of building untrue. It is conceived differently from the skeletal structure but in its own way it is honest. Even now it is not obsolete. In our own time we have an utterly new and genuine relationship to the block, to delicate and organic contour, to the succulent abundance of Doric capitals, to the melody of Ionic fluting. In the buildings of antiquity the space is obviously little more than that which plays round the contours of the sculpture, gathering itself in the hollows to run off in the fluting of the columns. It is significant that many of our own very beautiful new buildings of the sculptural type—for instance those of Mies—have almost no outer walls and are only "of necessity" closed by means of glass panes. In a higher sense they remain open.

SKELETAL CONSTRUCTION

Skeletal construction, the third way of building, comes from still another source.

This type of construction springs from a concept of the world in which matter gathers itself to a skeleton of slender arches of tension—a concept of the world which sees space shot through with powers. ("Dynamism" is a false name for this since the ancient δύναμις is dark and compact like a Doric capital.) This method of building is of recent origin—unless one believes it to have been prefigured in the wooden halls of our forefathers which disappeared long ago. This type of construction found its first great representation in the Gothic and it is consummated in our "technology". To be sure, the Gothic skeleton knows of practically no wrought members. It is limited to groups of slender, resistant columns and consequently it remains vaulting and upright structure—but as such it is formed completely of buoyancy. "Technology" brings for the first time the tensile strength of steel and with it the play of upright and cable. Seen from the vantage point of "technology" the Gothic method is antiquated. But "technology" had the misfortune not to be taken seriously and accusations have been made against it similar to those made against the grasping hand. It was born into a small-minded age.

TENT CONSTRUCTION

Actually the skeletal type of construction is spaceless also. For it, space is only the abstract means of orienting a curve, that something through which its powers pass. If we wish to win a living-space from this scaffold, we must span it. (This is obviously only an act of "self-defence" for the play of these interlacing members is at its most expressive when it weaves through free space, unspanned and uninhabitable, as in the tracery of a Gothic spire.)

Actually, where skeletal construction is used to provide living space, we must speak of tent construction. This is the form of transition to shell construction. And it would seem that we are now undergoing this transformation in our own time.

When, in skeletal construction, that power of the body which answers gravity is turned into a work, it can be compared to the hand which closes about a thing. Here, as in the hand, lines of force encircle the hidden content. Man has laid his own hand about himself as the content. It is immaterial whether the building art occurs as shell form, as sculpture, as skeletal or tent construction, for each time it is the "body" which turns about, which moves to the outside and which makes itself into its own shelter. That which made the body as the first answer given to the world, builds for it the house of architecture.

Thus the works of art would be closely related to the body which creates them. Not that they are "enlarged body"—this they are not. We receive them into ourselves with the body and this may have led us to mistake them for amplifications of the body, since the theories often confuse the means of perception with the work itself. Rather do they stand in an active reciprocal relation to the body, but again not within the simple dialogue of question and answer. The eye is hollow and dark, the light is shining abundance: eye and light converse. A painting, however, is coloured "image" just as much as the image on the retina, except that it lies outside of the body and can be looked at as if it were a coloured world. Sculpture is like the palm of the hand, but one can put one's hand upon it. Works are "other body". That something which addresses the world and replies to the world in the changing forms of the body here exchanges that which originally confronted it as world for something second in which the encounter is consummated. That which happens buried deep within the body is created here outside of it. Then body can live in its work, work can become the body's house. These two are sibling forms.

All these things are thoughts which occurred to us about our own work and much may be wrong or even false in them. It is neither our task nor our intention to invent a science of the arts—we trust the scholars will take care of that—and for the things which are going to be said in this book it is not necessary that our suppositions be perfect. The book stands on its own feet: we have not wished to set forth a theory and we shall not now proceed to a practical application. It is too bad that these things are always discussed scientifically—that is to say starting from observations and ending in definitions—and that they are never discussed for the architect, that is to say starting from creation and aiming at right doing and true works. And so, may these thoughts have the good quality that their goal is the doctrine of work—and we have found that they do help us onward. If they do prove true, then the works themselves are closely related to the body and almost all the things can be said about them which were said about the body: that they are an inexhaustible task, that they may turn out to be great or lowly, that there are whole hierarchies of works.

There are levels of doing. At the highest step in this order stands that work in which man spends himself utterly in order to consummate the world as sacred likeness. This work awakens the slumbering image and makes whole the creaturehood of the world. If you wish, this is the worship, the service of God, not service to the Godhead in becoming, as Scheler erred so terribly, but service to the image in becoming. The creative hand yields itself completely into the hand of God the Creator and God's guiding hand is placed upon it. God sees his world through the knowing eyes of his creatures. God lifts the heavy things which we lift, he places his two hands easingly under ours. Such work is holy work, blessed with an abundance of fruit—it is, if we wish, sacrament.

One thing it is not: it is not prayer. Work, even work in its noblest magnificence, is service to the world in whose fundament the sacred image rests. Prayer, however, is the clear, pure invocation of God. The man who prays does not busy himself with the things, he leaves them. He turns his eyes to God, opens his arms and hands and empties them before the Lord. Or he folds them and confesses his helplessness, he ties them and shows that their work is over. By this he does not mean to say that he has freed himself from the things, for this he cannot do nor may he attempt it. It is out of his eyes that the creature looks to the Lord and it is in his hands that the creature grows empty. Man takes God's creatures with him into his prayer. The mother, who has served God in her own holy way by the bearing and rearing of her children, places them beside her and puts both arms about them as she prays. With them she enters in before God. In the same way everyone brings that which is entrusted to him in love, opened, to the Lord and gives it back to him. In prayer the things are reversed—their pyramid whose summit was man turns into an empty form at whose very bottom the open human being stands.

Creation begins when God calls on man and names him. Man answers with his existence, his body, his work, and God blesses these things. But prayer begins when man calls out to God and awaits an answer. Worldly work is God's work with the world, praying work is the world's work with God, at first a work of helplessness and afterward a work rewarded by God. It is foolhardy to say that a man should make God into his answer or that man should bring him forth, and it is sacrilege when it means that God lies within man's power. But it becomes true when it is taken up into God's loving freedom: in his love it is his habit to answer his creature. He gives himself into his creature's hands and heart and his creature may move him.

IV

The Political Order

Politics and Moral Theology*

Don Luigi Sturzo

CONCEIVED as the art of governing or as the organization of society, politics cannot withdraw itself from the authority of natural morality nor, for the Christian, from that of theology. There is no dearth of studies on this subject; nevertheless, there is felt today more than ever the necessity of an extensive revision of positions already achieved dictated by the laicization of political power, its extension to all the personal and collective activity of citizens and its intrusion even into the domain of conscience. Neither the casuistic art of the past, nor purely theoretical casuistic, conducted without reference to the facts, have any power to meet the new demands. What is lacking above all is a synthesis which might serve as a moral guide in the swift evolution of politics.

The present study is offered as nothing more than a summary schema, a contribution toward a wider and deeper examination of these problems.

I

The first problem: it has always been said, and is still said today, that the Church makes no pronouncements on forms of government; and this remark is quite correct. This pronouncement may, however, appear academic, based on an abstract classification of the forms of government. In the concrete, there are no forms without *content*. This fact gives value to all reform effort. Today, it matters little whether a state assumes the *form* of a monarchy or of a republic; it is of greater interest to notice its *content*; to know whether a state be liberal or socialist, a totalitarianism of the right or left. Each of these types raises special problems which the moralist is under obligation to study closely in order to distinguish the ethical matter from the political element. A communist state creates characteristic situations which impose on a Christian moral attitudes unknown in liberal states, and *vice versa*. It is not enough to condemn the principles upon which a modern state (liberal, Nazi, bolshevist, fascist) may rest; it is necessary to examine to what point the conduct of Christians who belong to such states may be influenced.

One of the most absolute obligations of Christian morality is to avoid co-operating with evil. But to what degree can the concrete application of erroneous political principles (whether formally condemned by the Church or not), upon which modern states rest, be called co-operation with evil?

Economic liberalism is founded on the principle of *laisser faire, laisser passer* and on the principle of absolute concurrence—principles which lead inevitably to the oppression of the weak. If such a system is admitted to a country, may Catholic industrialists and business men take advantage of it? Under what conditions? And how are the injustices inherent in the system to be rectified?

* From *Les Guerres Modernes et la Pensée Catholique*; see p. x above.

The case of economic communism, whether open or disguised, today is the burning question. Devaluation, economic autarchy, state socialism involve experiences of communism. Can Catholics accept regimes of this type, profit by their advantages and acquiesce in them as definitive? At what cost must they refuse acquiescence? In Germany and Austria, in Italy and, at present, even in France, persecution of Jews for reasons of race has lifted its head; the momentary economic effects of this persecution are advantageous for non-Jewish doctors, professors and business men. How far is participation in such a measure legitimate?

II

The distinction of the political form from its *content* (liberal, socialist, totalitarian, etc.) suggests a re-examination in a new light of the problem of modern political regimes. Leo XIII had some time before counselled the French people to accept loyally the republican regime with the intention of co-operating with it for the common good, for the improvement of existing laws and the repeal of anti-Christian laws (February 1892); such a line of conduct could have practical effects only in a regime of opinion in which all the citizens are free to support the programme they judge best for the good of the country and to belong to the party which best conforms with their own point of view. However, could similar counsel be given to Catholic citizens of a totalitarian state (whether of the right or of the left) in which political nonconformism, even of a practical character, or any moral reservation, no matter how small, not only is not permitted but will of necessity be considered a crime of *lèse-patrie* or of *lèse-autorité*?

In 1938 the Austrian bishops invited the faithful to vote in the plebiscite of 10 April, in favour of union with the German *Reich*, but later it was made clear that the episcopal instructions were neither an order nor a counsel but signified only that *it was not contrary to Christian morality to participate in such a plebiscite and to vote "yes" while keeping intact the rights of God and of conscience.* As necessary as it was useless at this moment, this reservation was motivated by persecution on the part of the *Reich* and by the principle of race on which it was based. The same formula of tolerance "safeguarding the rights of God and conscience" is found in the encyclical *Non abbiamo bisogno* of 29 June 1931, with reference to the oath demanded by the fascist government of certain categories of citizens. The same encyclical obliged the faithful to make this reservation known in cases of necessity, to render testimony to the Catholic faith in order to avoid scandal.

The moral problem posed by the totalitarian state (of whatever kind) has not been studied sufficiently in our moral theology. The ecclesiastical documents (encyclicals, instructions of Sacred Congregations, episcopal letters) already form a considerable material basis for such a study. There is still lacking, however, the scientific elaboration on the part of philosophers and practical discussion by casuists in order to place in a clear light the complexity of the phenomenon in its ethico-religious implications.

The essential character of totalitarianism is such that the citizen finds it impossible to remain outside the system once established, since total politics penetrates his entire life: family, culture, religion, economy, external activity. In Italy, the very infants were given fascist membership cards; and they belonged to fascism until death. In certain cases the dying received the invitation (which was an obligation for their relatives) to don the black shirt as a final act of faith in fascism.

The praise, the flattery are part of the system: all must praise and applaud the dictators, even if they commit crimes. Who would have been able, in Germany, to criticize the executions of the night of 30 June 1934? In a parish bulletin in Vienna a simple priest (R. P. Brettle, OFM), a few days after Hitler's occupation, wrote these stupefying words, "During the days while the regime was changing, a great number of persons have asked me how, as a pastor of souls, I could reconcile with love of Christ the fact that Jews will be everywhere replaced in their employment. I answered that the idea of this replacement has always existed in the plan of divine providence. No one invited the Jews into the several parts of Europe. The Jewish question had not yet been resolved. Our leader, the Chancellor of the Reich, has now resolved it in radical fashion which at the same time brings release to both."

We do not wish to pass judgement on anyone, nor call their intentions into question: we remember that von Papen and Dollfuss together received communion from the hands of the Holy Father: this fact, when made public, was looked upon as earnest of a future of religious peace and moral renovation. And who does not remember the Catholic secretaries of van Papen, so mysteriously assassinated? The question arises: in what degree is it possible for a Catholic to collaborate with a totalitarian state? Collaboration implies liberty to differ and to withdraw. But at what price is this possible?

III

Several years ago Pius XI, receiving a delegation of young Belgians, told them that politics, well understood, is a form of charity. This principle is fundamental to moral theology: though it certainly is not such in human actions neither for those (sometimes the best) who, looking on politics as a contaminated thing, leave it to evil people (a fine gift to the community), nor for those who, taking part in it, no longer feel bound by the moral laws, because, within those laws it would be difficult to carry on political activity as everyone else does (that is, as "the world" carries it on).

But it would seem necessary to go deeper into the matter and to ask to what point does political activity become a duty in justice and when, more generally, it is imposed by charity.

Let us take a few preliminary examples. The members of the electorate believe that they alone have the right to vote and sometimes they neglect to do so, without much preoccupation. But there are no rights that do not carry obligations with them, even obligations in justice. Indeed, the electorate is the representative of those who do not vote; these latter must be protected in their moral, economic and political interest by those who do have the voting power. Nor is that enough; the voter, if he be Christian, has the duty of protecting the interests of religion, or moral education, and of the Church, interests which can be jeopardized by a false or inopportune tendency in politics: is this a duty of charity? of piety? of justice? The instances are numerous, with different characteristics and different motives.

The need to re-examine and clarify the idea of justice, not perhaps in its essence, but under its varied aspects and particularly in the context of human relations, is keenly felt today. Cardinal d'Annibale wrote in his *Summula Theologiae Moralis* (ed. 1902), "Right, understood in a wide sense, exhibits a triple order; that of the commonwealth toward its citizens, of citizens toward the commonwealth, of citizens, or better, of men, among themselves. The justice which governs the first is legal; the second, distributive, the third commutative. Legal justice, therefore, orders all virtues to the common good; distributive justice is concerned with public office, meting out rewards and punishments to citizens on the basis of what benefits the commonwealth; finally, commutative justice concerns what is due each one according to strict right; that is, with *mine* and *thine*. Legal justice scarcely merits the name, for it is, in fact, nothing but obedience to the written laws and popular institutions; wherefore, we may pass it by. The notion of distributive justice is clear. Consequently we have only to deal with commutative justice." In thirty years the opinion of moralists has changed, although the author cited at that time enjoyed a great reputation.

I have alluded to the opinion of P. Faidherbe on *distributive justice* conceived no longer as a potential element of the virtue of justice, but as a specific aspect of justice complete in itself which considers right and obligation defined by the very nature of the community. Distributive justice is not merely that of the relations of the state with its subjects; it also extends to all forms of the life of the community where the integrating action of leaders is necessary to distribute the social advantages and burdens, excepting those which are due in virtue of commutative justice. The question commonly called "social" finds its equitable solution in the widest possible application of distributive justice.

It does not seem to me that the moralists have, up to this point, reached sure conclusions in the instance of devaluation and revaluation of money (instances which frequently occur) in the light of the principles of distributive justice, given the changes which these involve for the economic situation of entire categories of citizens, to the harm of some and the profit of others. When in 1922 the German government cancelled all currency in use and all debts of the state to the bearers of interest bearing bonds, it assumed the power of stripping the thrifty and property-holders of their resources and in fact dispossessed these groups to the advantage of other groups of citizens. When the Italian government, a few years ago, assumed the debts of certain industrial firms to the banks— to the sum of seven milliards—it imposed by this action a new burden on the taxpayers, to the profit of the tycoons. The monetary problem is one of the gravest and most difficult to examine from the point of view of distributive justice. I do not remember ever having read any studies by moralists on the case of the destruction of goods (wheat, coffee, barley, cattle) in order to maintain prices, ordered by governments or by economic associations.

Passing to the notion of *legal justice* it is superfluous to say that it is confused with the virtue of justice in so far as it is adequation between law and action. "Law" here does not signify (as some seem to think) written positive law, but the moral law in general or the natural law as the "rule of reason". It is the objective concepts of *equality* and of *adequation* which import the quality of justice. It is by no convention that we are accustomed to call legal justice the relation of the citizen or of the association toward the community, as the inverse of distributive justice which embraces the relations of the community toward the citizen or association. It might be necessary to call it *communitative* justice to place in relief its specific nature to insure it the place in the manuals which it deserves and not to confuse it, as D'Annibale does, with obedience to written laws.

It is *communitative* justice, on the part of the taxpayer, to pay duties (as compensation for general and specific services), on the part of the voters to vote in elections, of deputies to sit in parliament, of the king or president of the republic to exercise their charges. There were at one time "corvées" to the profit of communities and of the state; it was a personal tax for the use of roads and canals. The concept of justice derives here from reciprocal relations of the community and its own members in an organic living adequation, and vice versa. The violation or alteration of an equitable adequation and the non-observation of duties which are born of reciprocal relations cannot fail to destroy that fundamental justice upon which society is based.

The idea of "politics" as the participation of the citizen in public life contains two elements: to co-operate for the common good in the measure of one's own powers (charity) and to fulfil the duty, the charge, the mandate with which one has been invested.

IV

With this point of departure: "the relations between citizens and communities are based on justice and charity", we profit from a more exact orientation in order to appreciate more clearly the nature of the *political community* and of the *authority which it exercises.*

We have become so accustomed to celebrate the state, to exalt its powers and to seek its intervention that it is no longer astonishing that, according to the current conception, the state is treated as a thing in itself like an entity endowed with personality and that people speak of it as a real being with a will and purposes of its own. Among Catholic sociologists and jurists those who uphold the thesis of the "state as a moral person" over and above its citizens do not realize, perhaps, what a concession they make to the myth of the state.

Since there is no society without individuals, nor individuals without society, we do not have to manufacture a self-existent entity. The community exists through a series of relations among individuals living together, in a permanent and organic form, for natural and necessary ends. The family, the social class, the commune, the state, the Church, are so many existent and co-existent communities, which assume a juridicial character in the specific organization of each on the basis of its liberty (*coexistentia multorum*) and of authority (*reductio ad unum*).

In this manner, we avoid the determinism underlying the formation of myths: state, nation, race, class, which from politics have insinuated themselves into sociology, and from sociology into ethics and in this way creep into the phraseology of certain sacred orators and sentimental moralists who speak readily of the cult of the nation, of obedience to the state and other similar things. We have read the *Landschreiben katholischer Deutschen an ihre Volks und Glaubensgenossen* published by Aschendorff, of Munster, in Westphalia in 1935, and written by Kuno Brombacher and Emil Ritter who there try to demonstrate, speaking for a group of Catholic theologians, the possibility of reconciling Nazism and Catholicism. Mgr Hudal, who at that time drew protestations from the Austrian bishops, also adhered to this thesis. Later, he amended his thesis of "Catholic Nazism" and in a lecture at Vienna spoke against Nietzschism, the basis of Nazism. A circular of the Roman Congregation of Seminaries and Universities of 13 April 1938 brought an end to this confusion. This circular invited the professors to refute eight propositions on the theories of racism and statism; the last of which is the foundation of Italian fascism. "Each man exists only through the state and for the state. All that he possesses by right comes solely from a concession of the state."

Let us return openly and courageously to the Christian idea of community, having at its basis truth and justice and inspired by a spirit of fraternal charity, of constant co-operation with the natural ends of the state, co-ordinated and subordinated (as the case demands) to the supernatural end of each individual, a human and Christian person, responsible and worthy of respect. There is nothing new in all this, it is two thousand years old, from the Gospels which restored the human person, breaking the carnal bonds of the family, clan and tribe, people or nation, so that each individual might experience in himself the divine vocation and follow it, separating himself, if need be, from mother, wife and children.

From this Christian conception there flows, consequently, the very modern need of recognizing the proper worth of the human personality both against liberal individualism which dissolves him in statism and against "gregarism", whether racist or national socialist, which results in state totalitarianism.

Among Catholic writers there are some, currently, who confuse state and authority. This is an error; the state is the political organization of the nation, it is not the nation nor the authority of the nation. Without authority, there is no state, but the state comprehends all the political and administrative machinery of the nation, of the electorate, with universal suffrage, even to the chief (king or president) of the army, the navy and the civil bureaucracy; the laws and the magistrature, and so forth. And if a state is transformed into a dictatorship, it does not follow that its citizens, subjects or comrades (as they say in Russia) lose their personal rights, for these do not derive from the state. In this case, instead of consecrating and guaranteeing these rights, the state minimizes them and deprives them of all juridical and political coherence. Nevertheless, the complex of these rights will persist in the conscience of the people and in the traditional spirit of the nation and no tyranny will ever be strong enough to erase it.

V

The preceding paragraph has had the purpose of dislodging the myth of the "state as sovereign entity", and to fix the true character of the "state as community". In this way, it will be possible for us better to define *political authority* on which moral theology bases the discipline of the common life.

Non est potestas, nisi a Deo: this is the fundamental principle of authority on earth by which *omnis anima potestatibus sublimioribus subdita sit* (Rom. 13). Some theologians have seen in the phrase which follows this (*quae autem sunt, a Deo ordinatae sunt*) a kind of divine investiture given to each individual to whom authority is entrusted, a preternatural communication of power from God to men. But, it seems to me, to give it this meaning is to strain the text. God is the author of nature. Everything in nature comes from God. St Paul, insisting forcefully that no power can come from any source but God, gave the precept of obedience a superior sense: it thus ennobles a society in its entirety and places it on its true foundations. On the other hand, he deprives authority of any absolute character by placing an *ethical limit*, which it would not suffer were God not the origin of all authority. St Paul affirms the ethical limit of authority as it affects both superior and inferior: man does not submit to man, but to God (the ethical value of submission); the superior holds authority not of himself but from God (ethical value of authority).

So long as states were governed by Christian monarchs, political authority recognized its limits in Christian morality, in principle, and, in practice, in the authority of the Church, bishops or the pope as the case might be, and in canon law, as the juridical-ecclesiastical basis of civil law. Even when it happened that a good number of monarchs violated the moral law as well as the precepts of the Church and conceived their own power as absolute, fundamentally they clung to the conception that power comes from God. Later this principle, twisted from its true significance and altered in its application, gave way to the theory of the divine right of kings (in opposition to the power of the Church).

But when the political authority became lay, either by the theory of natural right or by that of the sovereignty of the people, the ethical limit which bound it to God disappeared at least in theory, leaving only *juridical or political limits.* It is true that these theories did not lack a fundamental ethical value, deriving either from the concept of the human person as the subject of right, or of the will of the people as the expression of natural goodness; in fact, however, neither the one nor the other furnished efficacious ethical limits but only formal limits which issued from a positive morality. Thus it was that the search began for a statist ethic (the so-called lay morality) which would be, as it were, a self-limit on the power of the state.

The experience of two centuries—rendered interesting by the firm opposition of Christianity to the idea of a lay morality and of the ethical autonomy of the state—has served to show: (*a*) the impossibility of setting ethical limits to authority without a basis in religion; (*b*) the insufficiency of the simple organic limits of modern democracy such as the separation of powers, the time-limits of office, the political responsibility of governments (though these limits have nevertheless made it possible to have a mechanics of authority which eliminated extra-legal abuses); (*c*) the substitution for the true basis of authority (God), of the mysticism and the myth of the collective being (the state, the nation, the class, the race) and the abolition of all limits by the transposition of the idea of individuality from the person to the collective being.

The modern problem consists in the re-introduction of the idea and the practice of an *ethical limit* on authority. In a democratic regime, in which all the citizens co-operate, directly or indirectly, with authority and share in its power (Cicero says that liberty is certain participation in power) it is necessary that the citizens, who conceive politics as within the orbit of moral law, constantly affirm the value of the latter. What we have above recognized as characteristic of the citizen, namely, the duty of justice and charity toward the community, we here conceive as the *regular exercise of liberty limiting authority*. In the regimes of the past, the clergy, as such, exercised a moral and religious control (sometimes excessive) over the civil authority; today, the citizens, by exercising their civic rights, must accomplish this duty. Without constituting a party and without acting as a party, *Catholic Action* has the office of informing with its religious spirit and with its Christian apostolate, the atmosphere in which modern society must develop and in which political activity must be exercised. Political power, whose domain today is vast, can be limited only by the ethical reaction of the people who must re-evaluate all activity which transpires on the ground of political life.

The popes and the bishops have not failed to make their voices heard on the moral problems of contemporary political life. During the past century a wealth of documents have accumulated from the encyclical *Mirari vos* (1832) to the *Mit brennender Sorge* and the *Divini Redemptoris* (1937) and the allocutions of Pius XII on Peace and the New Order (1939-41). It would be of great help to bring these documents together in a number of available volumes. But it is the task of sincere, faithful, Catholic citizens to carry them on to the terrain of political action and to try to correct and to limit authority when it sins by excess and by default; there are no other political and juridical means in the modern state "de droit et d'opinion".

So far as concerns the formation of new types of totalitarian states, it is necessary to recognize that the responsibility of Catholics in this process has been considerable. In attenuation it might be said that they could not have foreseen either the development or the dangers in these formations. But what in the past was an attenuating circumstance is today no longer such. When a portion of the Catholic clergy and the citizenry (though not all) defended the thesis of an unconditional return of the Saar to the Reich, when it would have been possible to postpone such a decision five or ten years, can it be said that they could not have foreseen the dangers of German totalitarianism? And the Austrian Catholics who were philo-nazi or pangermanists, the same who helped prepare for the seizure of their country by Hitler, did they not understand the moral dangers of such an adventure? And the pro-rexist Catholics of Belgium, could they not foresee what lay in store for them?

It is said that Italy under fascism is in favourable moral and religious circumstances. To say so one had to blind oneself to a situation in which favours and persecutions alike depended on the will of one man; and when favours were abundant, consciences were enervated, and resistance ran the risk of becoming weaker on the very day when it might be necessary. One might spell out a long litany of abuses of power in the face of which no one affirmed the principle of a moral limit. When the militarization of youth—at the age of six the child had to be inscribed in the *Figli della Lupa*, at eight, had to undergo preliminary training (see the law of 31 December 1934 and of 11 April 1938)—there was no criticism and reservations.

The gravest matter, in these totalitarian states, was that of education by violence, the consecration of the principle of the supremacy of force over morality, and most of all, education in the hatred of his adversary, at the cost of his personal rights and even of his life. This vicious spirit, unchained in the world, in the name of the authority of the state and by the very governments of states, found only feeble opposition from Catholics, for opposition had become practically non-existent. Amid these excesses of power, there are persecutionary laws against political adversaries, against linguistic minorities and minorities of race, against subjects who through conviction reject party conformism. There is an excess of power in the network of espionage extending even into the schools, families, churches; in the institution of concentration camps at the will of those in authority and of the party leaders; in the use of torture in prisons, murder by agents of the police or of private squads, actions either willed or permitted by the party chiefs. When the fascist government, on assuming power in 1922, granted political amnesty to those accused and condemned under common law, for crimes which were declared to have been committed "for a national end", it was a scandal. Since that time, Europe has witnessed a recrudescence of these crimes "committed for a national end", which have been, not only pardoned, but rewarded. Have we not seen the assassins of Dollfuss declared national heroes?

All this may seem to have been merely a political excursus; but I ask, what were the reactions called forth by these facts in the domain of moral theology which ought to have faced up to the causes of the diffusion of this spirit of authorized hatred, ordered by authority? Moral theology ought to have inquired whether in a majority of these cases Christians did not have a right and a duty to oppose passive resistance in order to arrest this anti-Christian deviation.

Wherever there is still freedom of speech and of the press, the defence of the oppressed has been confined to a minimum; many professed to see there problems which are foreign to our conscience, lying beyond the orbit of our duties. Obedience and respect for authority were confused with acquiescence in and justification of the excesses of authority.

For such a state of soul to have taken form among Christians it was necessary that they undergo the influence of those currents which equivocally are called authoritarian, but which are better defined as totalitarian. The fundamental idea, that there is no authority without moral limits, that this limit is implicit in the very idea of authority, in such wise that, if this limit is violated, the value of that authority itself disappears (*obedire Deo oportet magis quam hominibus*), is realized in social life under two aspects: (*a*) personal resistance on the part of anyone to whom an immoral order is given, by a refusal to obey; (*b*) positive action on the part of those who are convinced of their duty so to act, in order to lead authority back within the natural limits which it has overstepped or has tried to overstep.

I have written a study on the right of revolt and its limits, to which I will take the liberty of referring those of my readers who are interested in my work.[1] The point which I would like to place in relief here is the following: the duty of citizens to make prevail, by their legitimate activity (whether legal or "preterlegal"), the moral limit of authority when those in power forget that limit or take no account of it. To this end it is necessary that the members of Catholic Action be well instructed on the force of such a limit and prepared to make it prevail by all licit means. We have been accustomed to defending moral and social values under a regime of a democracy "of opinion"; now we must become accustomed to do it to the best of our powers under totalitarian regimes, even if it becomes necessary to return to the life of the catacombs, and even at the risk of being thought conspirators and enemies of the state, of the nation, of the class and of humanity.

VI

The moral limit, essential to all authority, extends from the state to the *international community*. Without a doubt, the beginnings of a community of states exists from the moment when, by geographical proximity, by affinity of language and culture, and by reciprocal interests, peoples communicate. There has been no lack of efforts to provide organization of such a community. No one can deny the moral basis of all existing juridical constructions of international law, deriving historically from canon law and from the *Jus Gentium*.

Those who confuse (and they are numerous) right with positive law, and who make the essence of right (*juridicitas*) consist in coercive power, end up by destroying all the juridical value of international law. According to their view, there can exist no authority above that of the states; treaties and alliances derive their force only from the will of the contracting parties; recourse to force is the only means which can guarantee an international order, and international morality itself has no normative value.

There is no doubt that all moralists reject both the premises and the conclusions of such theory; but we shall never succeed in overcoming all the difficulties unless we have the courage of accepting, despite everything, the thesis of the limitation of the sovereignty of states in their international relations. The moralist must make the needs of international society prevail as of ethical right and submit to moral judgement everything which favours or impedes the formation of such a society. The eight theologians who gathered at Fribourg in Switzerland in October 1931 published their *Conclusiones conventus theologici Friburgensis de bello*, in which they affirm this principle, a bit timidly it is

[1] The reference is to *Politique et morale*, Paris: Bloud et Gay; English translation *Politics and Morality*, London, Burns Oates and Washbourne, 1938.

true: "Docent praedicti auctores (christiani philosophi) supremam Status auctoritatem *externam* non idem sonare ac independentiam inconditionatam, sed potius significare libertatem qua eligantur organisationis formae, techniae, artis methodi, juridicae disciplinae et politicae institutionis, quae ad bonum commune internationale instaurandam aptiores esse videantur."[2] It is necessary that Christian philosophers supply something more to the moralists so that they may arrive at the necessary point, that is to say, to make them accept the principle that states, simply as associated, acquire, in the matter which is specifically their own, an international co-sovereignty.

In this way questions of intervention may be either resolved or bypassed, as well as those of neutrality, of limitations of armaments and of collective security, of colonial law and mandates: a whole complex of institutions up to this time vascillating and uncertain, which, projected into the play of material forces, lose their fundamental ethical character. At the same time, in the light of a more Christian morality, one might re-examine the problems of *émigrés*, of refugees, of minorities, and of even more difficult questions, which are usually solved in an egoistic manner, such as those of a controlled economy (better called autarchy) of tariffs, of international prices, or money and other such questions.

Granted that a better international organization is to be hoped for and granted that certain political and juridical aspects of the S.D.N. (League of Nations) have been open to criticism, one still cannot draw the conclusion from this that we have been without a law and a society of states and that war is the final means of regulating international conflicts. Moral theology has always considered war as the exception, the last legitimate resource, if it be a just war, if it be ordered by competent authority, if it is proportionate to the purpose at stake and if it is necessary. To remain faithful to the theological tradition, we must today renew these criteria of *competence, justice, proportion* and *necessity*.

So far as *competence* is concerned, moral theology did not consider, before the present war, the clauses of the charter of the League of Nations which forbid member states to undertake war, before fulfilling the procedure laid down in view of possible international conflict. This is as much as to say that the authority of these states was not competent to declare war save in the four cases foreseen by the Covenant; excepting in these instances, and only when due procedure was observed, war was no longer legitimate. The condition of competence in the view of St Thomas and other scholastics and moralists of his time had reference to the feudal system, according to which the lord had to wait before having recourse to war upon authorization from his sovereign who might refuse it and call the litigation before his court. Today, there are other customs, other systems, but the criterion of the limit of competence remains constant.

So far as *justice* is concerned, theology must transcend the casuistic which was formulated in days when mercenary troops traded victories in

---

[2] "The above-mentioned authorities (the Christian philosophers) teach that the supreme external authority of the State does not mean the same as unconditioned independence but means rather freedom to choose the forms of organization, the methods and the political and juridical institutions which seem best for the formation of the international community."

order to limit the number of the dead and when impoverished monarchs engaged in ambushes and forays which were called battles. I do not mean to imply that wars were in those days a joke; but they do not stand comparison with modern wars in which forty million men can be called to arms and eleven million human lives be lost in a war of four years and three months duration. In 1914–18 aviation was in its infancy: today much progress has been made in the art of killing.

Concerning the Ethiopian War Pius XI, in his address of 28 August 1935, posed a dilemma when he said, "If there is a question of an aggressive war, that would be unjust; if there is question of a defensive war, it must not pass beyond the limits of moderation, if it is to remain just." In a word, the proportion between the right to be defended and the means employed in war contain within themselves the necessary criterion of justice. Given the character of modern warfare and the changed esteem assigned the honour of a king, who today would be able to accept Suarez' opinion when he said that if a prince "gives a grave affront to the status or honour" of another prince, that action might prove the cause of a just and proportioned war? Or again, is a war just and proportionate which has as its purpose the defence of commerce or of other common goods which are such on the basis of the *jus gentium* as Suarez thinks?

Coming then to the idea of necessity, one can today no longer call any war necessary, in the sense of an inevitable means of policy. In the present state of civilization, there are available to all agents means sufficient to safeguard their proper rights without recourse to war. Modern jurists call a war just when it is undertaken for interests vital to the state; consequently, in their view, one might consider just the Japanese war against China and the Italian war against Ethiopia. In the *Conclusiones* of Fribourg, already cited, such a criterion of necessity is expressly denied, and only the case of legitimate defence is admitted as a limit of necessity: "But this legitimate defence does not imply *ipso facto* any right to take punitive action against an aggressor nor to institute a social process of war such that, only by recourse to arms, may the conflict between the aggressor and his victim be solved."[3]

Against those pessimists who think that war is a fatal heritage of fallen humanity and that it is impossible for man to free himself of it, we must affirm that the power of Christianity has not been extinguished. If, among Christian peoples, slavery, polygamy, the vendetta among families have been vanquished, it is surely not against, but according to the spirit of Christ to try to conquer war, too. The statement of Benedict XV (1 August 1917) is the most important contribution of the papacy concerning a proper organization of states. What is possible is not the elimination of war as a fact (for one can find, even today, cases of slavery, polygamy and vendetta) but the elimination of war as a legitimate means, admitted and recognized as such by honourable people; that the fact of a war is characterized as a crime in the same way as slavery or the murder of a personal enemy.

All this presupposes not only an international law, but a juridical organization which would ensure the observance of this law by the means

[3] Cf. *Paix et Guerre*, Paris: Editions du Cerf, 1932.

best adopted to make it respected. Moralists are not called upon to establish such an organization, but to delineate its ethical form, to create opinion favourable to it, and to correct the errors of the type of mentality opposed to it. Immediately after the great war, despite notable oscillations, the orientation of moralists was in this direction. But, hardly had the wars of Ethiopia and Spain broken out, than a practical and even theoretical complication took place. This is not the place to criticize certain positions taken by certain Catholic reviews on the League of Nations and on these wars. This extraordinary phenomenon can be compared to that which took place in the sixteenth century in relation to slavery. At that time, due to the discovery of the New World, the practice of seizing and keeping slaves was renewed. There was no dearth of ecclesiastical writers to justify this practice. Las Casas was not the most renowned. In the last years preceding the present war, those who wrote against war and against the methods of modern war—among them the bombing of civilian populations and the use of poison gases, were no longer listened to—a sure sign of increasing decadence.

What has been most disquieting is the impotent resignation of Catholics in the face of massive propaganda in favour of war, of its material and spiritual preparation, of the conviction of its fatality. If the apostles of peace are to arise everywhere to free the world from this state of blindness into which it has fallen, the moralists must scrutinize the responsibility of those who have fomented the causes of war. It is necessary at this tragic moment to avoid the disorientation and the confusion of the moralists. The pontifical teachings and the theological tradition are strong enough to lead us back into the right road; the traditional philosophy and Catholic sociology are valuable instruments for the interpretation of present problems. What makes their task difficult is the smothering of Christian thought under the action of practical naturalism: this nefarious spirit has penetrated the modern mentality and little by little has formed a public incapable of understanding and listening to the voice of a higher morality which demands sacrifices, even in the domain of national and international politics.

Perhaps the tragic experience of our own day will give the necessary impetus to theological speculation and practical action on the part of moralists in the international domain.

The Democratic Charter*

Jacques Maritain

I. THE DEMOCRATIC SECULAR FAITH

IN the "sacral era" of the Middle Ages a great attempt was made to build the life of the earthly community and civilization on the foundation of the unity of theological faith and religious creed. This attempt succeeded for a certain number of centuries but failed in the course of time, after the Reformation and the Renaissance; and a return to the medieval sacral pattern is in no way conceivable. In proportion as the civil society, or the body politic, has become more perfectly distinguished from the spiritual realm of the Church—a process which was in itself but a development of the Gospel distinction between the things that are Caesar's and the things that are God's—the civil society has become grounded on a common good and a common task which are of an earthly, "temporal", or "secular" order, and in which citizens belonging to diverse spiritual groups or lineages share equally. Religious division among men is in itself a misfortune. But it is a fact that we must willy-nilly recognize.

In modern times an attempt was made to base the life of civilization and the earthly community on the foundation of mere reason—reason separated from religion and from the Gospel. This attempt fostered immense hopes in the last two centuries—and rapidly failed. Pure reason showed itself more incapable than faith of ensuring the spiritual unity of mankind, and the dream of a "scientific" creed, uniting men in peace and in common convictions about the aims and basic principles of human life and society, vanished in our contemporary catastrophes. In proportion as the tragic events of the last decades have given the lie to the bourgeois rationalism of the eighteenth and nineteenth centuries, we have been confronted with the fact that religion and metaphysics are an essential part of human culture, primary and indispensable incentives in the very life of society.

As a result, it seems likely that, if democracy enters its next historical stage with sufficient intelligence and vitality, a renewed democracy will not ignore religion, as the bourgeois nineteenth-century society, both individualist and "neutral", did; and that this renewed, "personalist" democracy will be of a *pluralistic* type.

Thus we would have—supposing that the people have regained their Christian faith, or at least recognized the value and sensibleness of the Christian conception of freedom, social progress, and the political establishment—we would have, on the one hand, a body politic Christianly inspired in its own political life. On the other hand, this personalist body politic would recognize that men belonging to most different philosophical or religious creeds and lineages could and should co-operate in the common task and for the common welfare, provided they similarly assent to the basic tenets of a society of free men. These common tenets,

* From *Man and the State*; see p. x above.

that is the subject matter which requests our attention and which I should like to discuss.

For a society of free men implies basic tenets which are at the core of its very existence. A genuine democracy implies a fundamental agreement between minds and wills on the bases of life in common; it is aware of itself and of its principles, and it must be capable of defending and promoting its own conception of social and political life; *it must bear within itself a common human creed, the creed of freedom.* The mistake of bourgeois liberalism has been to conceive democratic society to be a kind of lists or arena in which all the conceptions of the bases of common life, even those most destructive to freedom and law, meet with no more than the pure and simple indifference of the body politic, while they compete before public opinion in a kind of free market of the mother-ideas, healthy or poisoned, of political life. Nineteenth-century bourgeois democracy was *neutral* even with regard to freedom. Just as it had no real *common good*, it had no real *common thought*—no brains of its own, but a neutral, empty skull clad with mirrors: no wonder that before the Second World War, in countries that fascist, racist, or communist propaganda was to disturb or corrupt, it had become a society without any idea of itself and without faith in itself, without any *common faith* which could enable it to resist disintegration.

But the all-important point to be noted here is that this faith and inspiration, and the concept of itself which democracy needs—all these do not belong to the order of religious creed and eternal life, but to the temporal or secular order of earthly life, of culture or civilization. The *faith* in question is a *civic or secular* faith, not a religious one. Nor is it that philosophic substitute for religious faith, that adherence forced upon all by reason's demonstrations, which the eighteenth- and nineteenth-century philosophers sought in vain. A genuine democracy cannot impose on its citizens or demand from them, as a condition for their belonging to the city, any philosophic or any religious creed. This conception of the city was possible during the "sacral" period of our civilization, when communion in the Christian faith was a prerequisite for the constitution of the body politic. In our own day it has been able to produce only the inhuman counterfeit, whether hypocritical or violent, offered by the totalitarian States which lay claim to the faith, the obedience and the love of the religious man for his God; it has produced only their effort to impose their creed on the mind of the masses by the power of propaganda, lies and the police.

What is, then, the object of the *secular faith* that we are discussing? This object is merely a practical one, not a theoretical or dogmatic one. The secular faith in question deals with *practical* tenets which the human mind can try to justify—more or less successfully, that's another affair—from quite different philosophical outlooks, probably because they depend basically on simple, "natural" apperceptions, of which the human heart becomes capable with the progress of moral conscience, and which, as a matter of fact, have been awakened by the Gospel leaven fermenting in the obscure depths of human history. Thus it is that men possessing quite different, even opposite metaphysical or religious outlooks, can converge, not by virtue of any identity of doctrine, but by virtue of an analogical similitude in practical principles, toward the same practical conclusions, and can share in the same practical secular faith, provided that they similarly revere, perhaps for quite diverse reasons, truth and intelligence, human dignity, freedom, brotherly love and the absolute value of moral good.

We must therefore maintain a sharp and clear distinction between the human and temporal creed which lies at the root of common life and which is but a set of *practical conclusions* or of *practical points of convergence*—on the one hand; and on the other, the *theoretical justifications*, the conceptions of the world and of life, the philosophical or religious creeds which found, or claim to found, these practical conclusions in reason.

The body politic has the right and the duty to promote among its citizens, mainly through education, the human and temporal—and essentially practical—creed on which depend national communion and civil peace. It has no right, as a merely temporal or secular body, enclosed in the sphere where the modern State enjoys its autonomous authority, to impose on the citizens or to demand from them a rule of faith or a conformism of reason, a philosophical or religious creed which would present itself as the only possible justification of the practical charter through which the people's common secular faith expresses itself. The important thing for the body politic is that the democratic sense be in fact kept alive by the adherence of minds, however diverse, to this moral charter. The ways and the justifications by means of which this common adherence is brought about pertain to the freedom of minds and consciences.

Certainly, it is supremely important to the common good that the practical assertions which make up the charter in question be true in themselves. But the democratic State does not judge of that truth; it is born out of that truth, as recognized and asserted by the people—by each one of us, to the extent of his abilities.

What would be the content of the moral charter, the code of social and political morality which I am speaking about and the validity of which is implied by the fundamental compact of a society of free men? Such a charter would deal, for instance, with the following points: rights and liberties of the human person, political rights and liberties, social rights and social liberties, corresponding responsibilities; rights and duties of persons who are part of a family group, and liberties and obligations of the latter toward the body politic; mutual rights and duties of groups and the State; government of the people, by the people and for the people; functions of authority in a political and social democracy, moral obligation, binding in conscience, regarding just laws as well as the Constitution which guarantees the people's liberties; exclusion of the resort to political coups (*coup d'état*) in a society that is truly free and ruled by laws whose change and evolution depend on the popular majority; human equality, justice between persons and the body politic, justice between the body politic and persons, civil friendship and an ideal of fraternity, religious freedom, mutual tolerance and mutual respect between various spiritual communities and schools of thought, civic self-devotion and love of the motherland, reverence for its history and heritage and understanding of the various traditions that combine to create its unity; obligations of each person toward the common good of the body politic and obligations of each nation toward the common good of civilized society and the necessity of becoming aware of the unity of the world and of the existence of a community of peoples.

It is a fact that in democratic nations, which, like the United States and France, have a hard historic experience of the struggles of freedom, practically everybody would be ready to endorse all the tenets of such a charter. Given that virtue of universality with which the civilization inherited from Christianity is endowed, as Toynbee has shown in a persuasive manner, we have good reason to hope that in all nations of the world the people—I say the people, whatever their governments may be—would be able to put forward the same endorsement. I should like to add two remarks which do not deal directly with the issue that I just discussed, but rather with the problems that we shall consider in the next chapter.

First: as a matter of fact, the more the body politic—that is, the people—were imbued with Christian convictions and aware of the *religious* faith which inspires it, the more deeply it would adhere to the *secular* faith in the democratic charter; for, as a matter of fact, the latter has taken shape in human history as a result of the Gospel inspiration awakening the "naturally Christian" potentialities of common secular consciousness, even among the diversity of spiritual lineages and schools of thought opposed to each other, and sometimes warped by a vitiated ideology.

Second: to the extent that the body politic—that is, the people—were imbued with Christian convictions, to the same extent, as a matter of fact, the justification of the democratic charter offered by Christian philosophy would be recognized as the truest one—not at all as a result of any interference of the State but only as a result of the free adherence which larger parts of the people would have given to Christian faith and Christian philosophy in actual fact.

And of course no religious pressure would be exercised by the majority. Non-Christian citizens' freedom to found their democratic beliefs on grounds different from those more generally accepted would by no means be jeopardized. What the civil authority and the State would be concerned with is only the common secular faith in the common secular charter.

II. THE POLITICAL HERETICS

The fact must be realized that the body politic has its own heretics, as the Church has hers. Nay more, St Paul tells us that there must be heretics[1]—and they are probably still less inevitable in the State than in the Church. Did we not insist that there is a democratic charter, nay, a democratic creed? That there is a democratic secular faith? Well, everywhere where faith is, divine or human, religious or secular, there are also heretics who threaten the unity of the community, either religious or civil. In the sacral society of the Middle Ages the heretic was the breaker of religious unity. In a lay society of free men the heretic is the breaker

[1] 1 Cor. 11. 19.

of the "common democratic beliefs and practices", the one who takes a stand against freedom, or against the basic equality of men, or the dignity and rights of the human person, or the moral power or law.

People who remember the lessons of history know that a democratic society should not be an unarmed society, which the enemies of liberty may calmly lead to the slaughterhouse in the name of liberty. Precisely because it is a commonwealth of free men, it must defend itself with particular energy against those who, out of principle, refuse to accept, and who even work to destroy, the foundations of common life in such a regime, the foundations which are freedom and the practical secular faith expressed in the democratic charter.

When the political heretic embarks on *political activity*, he will be met with, and checked by, opposite political activity freely developed by citizens in a body politic sufficiently lively and alive. When he embarks on *illegal activity*, trying to use violence, he will be met with, and checked by, the authority of the State, which in a society of free men, is exercised against him only in granting him, in a real, not a fake manner, the institutional guarantees of justice and law. There is no problem here. The difficulty begins when it comes to the *speaking and writing activity* of the political heretic.

The question of the freedom of expression[2] is not a simple one. So

---

[2] See the important report, *A Free and Responsible Press*, published by the Commission of the Freedom of the Press under the chairmanship of Robert M. Hutchins (Chicago: University of Chicago Press, 1947).

I would like to recall in this note the various recommendations made by the commission.

I. As concerns government: (1) that the constitutional guarantees of the freedom of the press be recognized as including the radio and motion pictures. (2) That government facilitate new ventures in the communications industry, that it foster the introduction of new techniques, that it maintain competition among large units through the antitrust laws, but that those laws be sparingly used to break up such units, and that, where concentration is necessary in communications, the government endeavour to see to it that the public gets the benefit of such concentration. (3) As an alternative to the present remedy for libel, legislation by which the injured party might obtain a retraction or a restatement of the facts by the offender or an opportunity to reply. (4) The repeal of legislation prohibiting expressions in favour of revolutionary changes in our institutions where there is no clear and present danger that violence will result from the expressions. (5) That the government, through the media of mass communication, inform the public of the facts with respect to its policies and of the purposes underlying those policies and that, to the extent that private agencies of mass communication are unable or unwilling to supply such media to the government, the government itself may employ media of its own. Also that, where the private agencies of mass communication are unable or unwilling to supply information about this country to a particular foreign country or countries, the government employ mass-communication media of its own to supplement this deficiency.

II. As concerns the press and mass communication media: (1) That the agencies of mass communication accept the responsibilities of common carriers of information and discussion. (2) That they assume the responsibility of financing new, experimental activities in their fields. (3) That the members of the press engage in vigorous mutual criticism. (4) That the press use every means that can be devised to increase the competence, independence and effectiveness of its staff. (5) That the radio industry take control of its programmes and that it treat advertising as it is treated by the best newspapers.

III. As concerns the public: (1) That non-profit organizations help supply the variety, quantity and quality of press service required by the American people. (2) That academic-professional centres of advanced study, research and publication in the field of communications be created; and, further, that existing schools of journalism exploit the total resources of their universities to the end that their students may obtain the broadest and most liberal training. (3) That a new and independent agency be established to appraise and report annually upon the performance of the press.

reat is the confusion today that we see commonsense principles, which ave been ignored in the past by the worshippers of a false and deceiving berty, being now used in a false and deceiving manner in order to estroy true liberty. Those maxims—dealing with our obligations toward bjective truth and with the rights of the common good—which were randed as an outrage against human autonomy when the Catholic hurch set them forth to condemn theological liberalism, and which, by pposing unbridled, divinely unlimited freedom of expression, were of a ature to save freedom of expression—the Communist State is now trumeting them and perverting them in order simply to annihilate freedom f expression. A sad Time's revenge. And, for everybody, an opportunity or melancholy reflections.

In discussing freedom of expression we have to take into account a ariety of aspects. On the one hand, it is not true that every thought as uch, because of the mere fact that it was born in a human intellect, has ie right to be spread about in the body politic.[3]

On the other hand, not only censorship and police methods, but any irect restriction of freedom of expression, though unavoidable in cerin cases of necessity, are the worst way to ensure the rights of the body olitic to defend freedom and the common charter and common orality. Because any such restriction runs against the very spirit of a emocratic society: a democratic society knows that human subjectivity's iner energies, reason and conscience are the most valuable springs of olitical life. It also knows that it is no use fighting ideas with *cordons nitaires* and repressive measures (even totalitarian States know that; onsequently they simply kill their heretics, while using psychotechnical ieans to tame or corrupt ideas themselves).

Moreover we have seen that the common agreement expressed in demoatic faith is not of a doctrinal, but merely practical nature. As a result ie criterion for any interference of the State in the field of the expression f thought is also to be practical, not ideological: the more extraneous iis criterion is to the very content of thought, the better it will be. It is o much for the State, for instance, to judge whether a work of art is ossessed of an intrinsic quality of immorality (then it would condemn audelaire or Joyce); it is enough for it to judge whether an author or publisher plans to make money in selling obscenities. It is too much or the State to judge whether a political theory is heretical with regard the democratic faith; it is enough for it to judge—always with the

---

[3] In order to sum up the considerations presented in this section, I would say:

A. Freedom of expression is a human right, but this right is only a "substantially", it an "absolutely", inalienable right. There are limits to freedom of expression, hich are inevitably demanded both by the common good and by very freedom, that ould become self-destructive if it were made limitless.

B. The State is entitled to impose limitations of freedom of expression, in view of rticularly serious circumstances. But in actual fact it can do so in a manner beneficial a democratic society only in most obvious and externally palpable matters and with gard to those basic ingredients in the common good which are the simplest and the ost elementary.

C. When it comes to higher matters, in which freedom of inquiry and the inner lues of intelligence and conscience are involved, and with regard to the most vital d spiritual ingredients (which *in themselves* are the most important) in the common od, the factual limitations to be brought to bear on freedom of expression depend the constructive and regulative institutions, organs and agencies and the free tivities spontaneously developed in the body politic.

institutional guarantees of justice and law—whether a political heretic threatens the democratic charter by the tangible acts he undertakes or by receiving money from a foreign State to subsidize antidemocratic propaganda.

You will answer quite rightly: is not the intellectual corruption of human minds, is not the ruining of primary verities, exceedingly more detrimental to the common good of the body politic than any other work of corruption? Yes, it is. But the fact is that the State is not equipped to deal with matters of intelligence.

Each time the State disregards that basic truth, which depends on its own nature, intelligence is victimized. And since intelligence has always its revenge, it is the body politic which, in one way or another, is finally victimized. Only one society can deal with matters of intelligence—that is the Church, because she is a spiritual society. Yet she, who knows what's what, had in the past some sad experiences in giving an eye to such ideas as the movement of the earth, and she does not use without thoughtful misgivings her spiritual weapons against her own heretics.[4]

Do I mean to imply that even with regard to superior matters the democratic body politic is disarmed? I mean just the contrary. I mean that positive, constructive means are exceedingly more efficacious than are mere restrictions of freedom of expression. And there are in a living democracy innumerable means of such a nature. Let us consider especially the matter of political heretics: Groups and leagues of citizens could devote themselves to the progress of democratic philosophy, the enlightenment of people with regard to the common charter and the intellectual struggle against warped political trends. The State itself could have the people informed of the judgements passed upon anti-democratic ideologies by some special body made up of men whose intellectual wisdom and moral integrity would be universally recognized.[5] Still more important, the various organizations, freely starting from the bottom, which in a pluralist society would unite readers and listeners on the one hand, writers and speakers on the other, could develop, as regards the use of the media of mass communication a ceaseless process of self-regulation, as well as a growing sense of responsibility. Still more important, the body politic, with the sense of community which it normally entails, has at its disposal the spontaneous pressure of the common consciousness and public opinion, which spring from the national ethos when it is firmly established, and which are strong enough to keep political heretics out of leadership. First and foremost it has at its disposal the work of democratic education.

III. EDUCATION AND THE DEMOCRATIC CHARTER

Education is obviously the primary means to foster common secular faith in the democratic charter.

[4] The Church, of course, is entitled to bring limitations to bear on freedom of expression in her own spiritual realm, as regards matters of faith and morals and with respect to the common good of the Kingdom of God. The claim to limitless freedom of expression laid by theological liberalism was a direct challenge to that right of the Church.

[5] See also Recommendation I, 5, of the Commission on the Freedom of the Press (above, footnote 2).

Education depends first and foremost on the family. For the end of the family is not only to beget offspring—promiscuity would be enough for that—but to beget them as children of man or to bring them up spiritually as well as physically. Under various particular forms and patterns, everywhere and in every time, men have been aware of this requirement of natural law. So the function of the educational system and the educational function of the State are only auxiliary functions with regard to the family group—normal auxiliary functions, moreover, since the family group is unable to supply the youth with the full stock of knowledge needed for the formation of a man in civilized life. My point is that in exercising this normal auxiliary function, the educational system and the State have to provide the future citizens not only with a treasure of skills, knowledge and wisdom—liberal education for all[6]—but also with a genuine and reasoned-out belief in the common democratic charter, such as is required for the very unity of the body politic.

The educational system and the State have a duty to see to the teaching of that charter of common life, and thus to defend and promote the common good and the fundamental statute of the body politic even up to the common secular faith involved.

Yet the educational system and the State can do this only in the name of the common assent through which the charter in question is held true by the people, and in so far as it proceeds from that agreement between minds and wills which lies at the root of the political society. And thus —since in actual fact the body politic is divided in its fundamental theoretical conceptions, and since the democratic State, as we have seen, cannot impose a philosophical or a religious creed—the State and the educational system, in seeing to the teaching of the common charter, can and must cling only to the common practical recognition of the merely practical tenets upon which the people have agreed to live together, despite the diversity or the opposition between their spiritual traditions and schools of thought.

Nay more, there is no belief except in what is held to be intrinsically established in truth, nor any assent of the intellect without a theoretical foundation and justification: thus if the State and the educational system are to perform their duty and inculcate the democratic charter in a really efficacious way, they cannot help resorting—so that minds be put in possession of such a foundation and justification, and perceive as true what is taught them—to the philosophical or religious traditions and schools of thought which are spontaneously at work in the consciousness of the nation and which have contributed historically to its formation.

Adherence to one of these schools of thought or another rests with the freedom of each person. But it would be sheer illusion to think that the democratic charter could be efficiently taught if it were separated from the roots that give it consistence and vigour in the mind of each one, and if it were reduced to a mere series of abstract formulas—bookish, bloodless and cut off from life. Those who teach the democratic charter must *believe* in it with their whole hearts, and stake on it their personal convictions, their consciences and the depths of their moral life. They

[6] Cf. Robert M. Hutchins, *Education for Freedom* (Baton Rouge: Louisiana State University Press, 1943).

must therefore explain and justify its articles in the light of the philosophical or religious faith to which they cling and which quickens their belief in the common charter.

Now, if every teacher does thus put all his philosophical or religious convictions, his personal faith and his soul into the effort to confirm and vivify the moral charter of democracy, then it is clear that such a teaching demands a certain spontaneous adaptation between the one who gives and the one who receives, between the inspiration animating the teaching and the basic conceptions that the student holds from his home circle and his social milieu and that his family feels the duty of fostering and developing in him. In other words, this teaching should awaken in those who receive it the deep interest which depends on the moral beliefs already formed or started in them, and without which it would lose the greater part of its vital efficacy.

The conclusion is obvious. The goal aimed at by the educational system and the State is unity—unity in the common adherence to the democratic charter. But for the very sake of attaining this practical unity a sound pluralism must obtain in the means; inner differentiations must come into force in the structure of the educational system so as to afford an efficacious teaching of the democratic charter. On the one hand the State—or the groups and agencies in the body politic which are concerned with education, or the authorities that govern the education system—should see to it that the democratic charter be taught—and taught in a comprehensive, far-reaching and vitally convincing manner—in all the schools and educational institutions. On the other hand, and for the very sake of fostering the democratic faith in people's minds, the educational system should admit within itself *pluralistic* patterns enabling teachers to put their entire convictions and most personal inspiration in their teachings of the democratic charter.

* * *

These are quite general principles. When it comes to application, I am aware of the great diversity in educational systems between countries where schools are mainly supported by the State or mainly privately endowed.

As concerns the educational system mainly grounded, as in France, on State support and control, I have offered some suggestions of my own in an annex to the French edition of *Education at the Crossroads*.[7] The pluralism which I am advocating for public schools should relate, in my opinion, not to the curriculum, but to the various inspirations with which the common curriculum would be taught if the members of the teaching body were distributed and grouped in the various areas of a city, or of the whole country, according to their own wishes as well as to the moral geography of local communities and the requests of associations of parents—so that their own personal religious or philosophical convictions would roughly correspond to those which prevail in the social environment.

In educational systems grounded to a degree, as in the U.S.A., on

[7] *L'Éducation à la croisée des chemins* (Paris: Luf, 1947), Annexe: "Le Problème de l'école publique en France."

privately endowed schools, colleges and universities, pluralistic teaching of the democratic charter would still more easily come into force, if the denominational institutions were more aware of the impact of religious inspiration on the whole realm of intelligence, and if the secular institutions freed themselves of the secularist prejudices they have progressively developed despite their not infrequent religious origins.

I am not treating here of the problem of religious instruction with regard to the youth educated in secular schools and colleges and State institutions, and of the facilities for a serious religious education which should be offered to those children whose parents desired it. What I am discussing is the teaching of the democratic charter in these institutions.

The most rational solution, in tune with the pluralistic principle, would consist, to my mind, in having the teaching of the democratic charter given not by one, but by several teachers belonging to the main religious or philosophical traditions represented in the student population of a given school or college, each one of those teachers addressing the students of his own spiritual tradition. Yet as logical as it may be, such a solution has little chance, I am afraid, to appear feasible to our contemporaries. Something else should be carried into effect, in every country, to insure a real and efficient teaching of the democratic charter in public schools.

The idea is that a *new discipline* should be introduced in the curriculum: this new discipline would bring together such diverse branches of knowledge as National History and History of Civilization as a basic framework, and then Humanities, Social Science, Social Philosophy and Philosophy of Law, all these to be centred on the development and significance of the great ideas comprised in the common charter: so this charter would be taught in a concrete and comprehensive manner, in the light of the great poets and thinkers and heroes of mankind, and in connection with the historical life of the nation, seen as woven of deeds and truths always full of meaning and deservedly treasured. As to the teachers, those only would be put in charge of this new part of the curriculum who felt able to swear that they sincerely believe in all the tenets of the democratic charter; they would also swear that if some day they ceased to believe in it, then they would request to be shifted to the teaching of another part of the curriculum—full assurance being given them, moreover, that they would not incur for that any professional drawback.

As concerns the role of the State, I do not believe that it is difficult to determine, if only one keeps in mind the golden rule of the common good. The State (precisely because it is not a substitute for the body politic, but a special agency concerned with keeping *that which exists* in the body politic in line with the common good)—the State should not stand aloof from, it should help and encourage (I do not mean as concerns any financial subsidization of the schools themselves,[8] I mean as concerns

---

[8] As regards the very controversial issue dealing with the financial subsidizing of denominational schools by the State, the general principle to be considered could, in my opinion, be expressed as follows: Either the various religious inspirations traditional in the nation are integrated in the public school system, or they give rise to merely private schools.

In the first case the public school system admits of an inner pluralistic organization, according to the diversity of spiritual lineages in the nation (cf. the Dutch school

welfare services to all children and all students) the educational effort accomplished by the various privately-endowed institutions, either denominational or secular, which emanate from and correspond to the diverse spiritual lineages at work in the nation. And as to its own State-supported schools and colleges, not only should every extra-curricular facility be offered by them for religious instruction, but in their very teaching full recognition should be given to the essential role played by the Judeo-Christian tenets and inspiration in the birth and maintenance of the democratic charter. To ignore, on the plea of a "separation" between State and Church wrongly and anti-politically understood, the religious traditions and schools of thought which are part of the heritage of the body politic, would simply mean for democracy to separate itself, and democratic faith, from the deepest of its living sources.

IV. PROBLEMS CONCERNING AUTHORITY

I have treated of authority in democracy in another book. Yet it is necessary to sum up a few considerations of the subject in order to have our concept of the democratic charter sufficiently complete. I am not dissatisfied, moreover, to have an opportunity to make certain positions clearer and more definite—and truer, I hope—than in my previous essays.

Authority and Power are two different things: *Power* is the force by which you can oblige others to obey you. *Authority* is the *right* to direct and command, to be listened to or obeyed by others. Authority requests Power. Power without Authority is tyranny.

This authority means right. If, in the cosmos, a nature, such as human nature, can be preserved and developed only in a state of culture, and if the state of culture necessarily entails the existence in the social group of a function of commandment and government directed to the common good, then this function is demanded by Natural Law, and implies a *right* to command and govern.

Furthermore, if said function, which in direct democracy is exercised

---

system); and the denominational schools—or those sections of the public school system which correspond to them—are State-supported. But the denominational schools are no longer autonomous, they are subject to the general regulations of the public school system.

In the second case, the denominational schools are completely autonomous. But they are not State-supported.

Given the conditions and difficulties of our times, it seems that, at least in Europe, the most appropriate situation would obtain if the first solution were applied as a rule and the second in particular instances as a complement.

Now if the public school system refuses any kind of inner pluralism and sticks to a merely "neutral" or a religious common teaching, then a basically unsound situation occurs. For such a public school system claims to be a *public* service and *is not* in reality, since it does not meet the basic needs and requirements—which, in justice, should be equally satisfied—of the various categories of citizens which compose the nation. As a result of that fundamental, intrinsic self-contradiction, the unsound situation in question cannot be remedied: some lack of justice will block either one way out or the other. If the denominational schools are not subsidized by the State, some categories of citizens will be obliged to pay the same bill twice (first taxes for the public school system; second, financial support of their own private schools). If the denominational schools are subsidized by the State, public funds will be used for private aims. The drawback implied in the second part of the alternative might be regarded, it is true, as making up for the more serious drawback involved in a public service which is not public. But, as a matter of fact, if the State is unwilling to adapt the school system to the legitimate requirements of all categories of citizens, it will probably be still more unwilling to use public funds to compensate for this defect.

by the "multitude" or the people themselves, can be properly exercised, in larger and more differentiated societies, only on the condition that the people entrust it to certain men who will be henceforth especially concerned with the affairs of the whole, then those men, once put in charge of the direction of the community, have a *right* (received from and through the people) to be obeyed for the sake of the common good: in other words, the relation of authority among men proceeds from Natural Law. I mean here the relation of authority taken as yet indeterminately, and not in the sense that *some* in particular must command and *some* in particular must obey; but rather in the general sense that there must be people who command and people who obey, the mode of designation of those who shall command being a different matter to be determined later and according to reason.[9]

Finally, since authority means *right*, it has to be obeyed by reason of conscience, that is, in the manner in which free men obey, and for the sake of the common good.[10]

But by the same token there is not any authority where there is no justice. Unjust authority is not authority, as an unjust law is not law. At the origin of the democratic sense, there is not the desire to "obey only oneself", as Rousseau puts it, but rather the desire to obey only *because it is just*.

*   *   *

Whatever the regime of political life may be, authority, that is, the right to direct and to command, derives from the people, but has its primary source in the Author of nature. Authority derives from the will or *consensus* of the people, and from their basic right to govern themselves, as from a channel through which natures causes a body politic to be and to act.

These two statements, expressed as they are in the most general and still undetermined way, have been a matter of common agreement for a century-old tradition in political philosophy. But they have been understood in quite different and sharply opposed manners.

A first issue, dealing with the relationship between the people and God, has been: do the people receive from God the right to self-government and authority to rule themselves in a merely *transient and transitory* way? So that when they designate their rulers they act only as an *instrumental cause*[11] through which God alone (as principal agent) invests with authority the one or ones designated?

Or do the people receive from God the right to self-government and authority to rule themselves in an *inherent* manner? So that they are possessed of this right and this authority as a "principal agent" (though

---

[9] Cf. Suarez, *De legibus*, Lib. III, c. 4, n. 5: "Unde potestas regia formaliter ut talis est de jure humano."

[10] For a thorough discussion of the matter see Yves Simon, *Nature and Functions of Authority* (Milwaukee: Marquette University Press, 1940); and *Philosophy of Democratic Government* (University of Chicago Press, 1951). Professor Yves Simon has rightly stressed the fact that the basic problem of authority (as a right of the people as a whole) comes prior to the problem of the necessity for having authority entrusted to a distinct governing personnel.

[11] Instrumental, not with respect to the choice or designation made, but with respect to the transmission of authority.

"secondary" or subordinate with respect to the Primary Cause) which through its own causal power—acting, as everything acts, in the virtue of God's universal activation—invests with authority the one or ones designated?[12] It is this second part of the alternative which has proved to be the true one.

And a second issue, dealing with the relationship between the people and their rulers, has been: do the people, when they invest certain men with authority, *divest themselves* of their right to self-government and their authority to rule themselves (whatever the way may be—transient or inherent—in which they have received these rights from God)? So that once the ruler or rulers have been put in charge, the people *lose* their right to self-government and their authority to rule themselves, which have been transferred to the ruler or rulers and are henceforth possessed by them alone?

Or do the people, when they invest certain men with authority, *keep* their right to self-government and their authority to rule themselves? So that they possess these rights, not only *inherently* with respect to the manner in which they receive them from God, but also *permanently* with respect to the manner in which they convey them to their rulers?

In modern history the age of the absolute kings, as we have seen in discussing Sovereignty, has answered affirmatively the first part of this alternative, negatively the second. Yet the right answer is *No* to the first part of the alternative, and *Yes* to the second. The realization of this basic verity (long ago pointed out by some great Schoolmen) has been a conquest of democratic philosophy. In this connection, whatever the political *regime* may be, monarchical, aristocratic or democratic, democratic *philosophy* appears as the only true political philosophy.

The trouble has been that from the very moment when it took the upper hand, this philosophy was imperilled by a counterfeit ideology, the ideology of Sovereignty. Instead of getting clear of the concept of Sovereignty (which implies *transcendent* or *separate* supreme power, supreme power *from above*), Rousseau transferred to the people the Sovereignty of the absolute monarch conceived in the most absolute manner; in other terms he made a mythical people—the people as the monadic subject of the indivisible General Will—into a sovereign Person separated from the real people (the multitude) and ruling them from above. As a result, since a figment of the imagination cannot really rule, it is to the State—to the State which, in genuine democratic philosophy, should be supervised and controlled by the people—that, as a matter of fact, Sovereignty, indivisible and not-accountable Sovereignty, was to be transferred. On the other hand, Sovereignty cannot be shared in; consequently, the people, or the Sovereign Person, could not invest any official with authority over them; only the people as a whole could make laws, and the men elected by them did not hold any real authority or right to command. The elected of the people were only passive instru-

---

[12] Thus this authority comes from God as Primary Source and Primary Cause, even comes from him "immediately", in the sense that human nature, naturally demanding what is necessarily implied in social life, immediately proceeds from God. Cf. Josephus Gredt, O.S.B., *Elementa philosophiae Aristotelico-Thomisticae* (St Louis: Herder, 1946), t. II, n. 1029, 4: "Auctoritas politica immediate est a Deo naturaliter ad societatem ordinata."

ments, not representatives. As a matter of principle, the very concept of representative of the people was to be wiped away.

This concept, however, is absolutely essential to genuine democratic philosophy. It is on the notion of representation or vicariousness, by virtue of which the very right of the people to rule themselves is exercised by the officials whom the people have chosen, that all the theory of power in democratic society rests. As I shall emphasize further, the representatives of the people are "sent", missioned or commissioned, by the people to exercise authority because they are made by the people participants, to some given extent, in the very authority of the people, in other words because they are made by the people *images* of and *deputies* for the people.

Those who represent the people are not the image of God. The Pope in the Church, being the vicar of Christ, is the image of Christ. The Prince in political society, being the vicar of the people, is the image of the people. A great deal of confusion occurred in this regard in the age of absolutism, because the authority of the king was often conceived of on the pattern of the authority of the Pope, that is to say, as coming down from above, whereas in reality it came up from below. For another reason a great deal of confusion had previously occurred in the Middle Ages: because the solemn anointing or coronation of the king, by sanctioning from the sacred heights of the supernatural order his right to command in the natural order, conveyed to him, as servant or secular arm of the Church, a reflection of the supernatural royal virtues, bounty, justice and the paternal love of Christ, Head of the Church. From this point of view the Middle Ages might regard the king as the image of Christ.[13] But in the natural order, which is the order of political life, he was not the image of Christ, he was the image of the people. Theologians, especially in the Thomist lineage, were able clearly to make that distinction. But medieval common consciousness remained enmeshed in an ambivalent idea of the Prince.

The civil power bears the impress of majesty: this is not because it represents God. It is because it represents the people, the whole multitude and its common will to live together. And by the same token, since it represents the people, the civil power holds its authority, through the people, from the Primary Cause of Nature and of human society.[14] St Paul teaches that "There is no authority that is not from God" and that those who bear the sword are "God's ministers" or "functionaries of God", "appointed by God" (let us understand, through the people) "to inflict his wrathful vengeance upon him that doth wrong".[15] Never did he teach that they were the image of God. What essentially constituted, in its own temporal or political order, the majesty of the king is the same as what the majesty of the President of a democratic nation consists of, especially when he is invested with such constitutional powers as those in the

[13] Cf. this passage from Bracton's *De rerum divisione*, quoted by Richard O'Sullivan in his Introduction to *Under God and the Law: Papers Read to the Thomas More Society of London, Second Series* (Oxford: Blackwell, 1949): The king "ought to be under the law since he is God's vicar, as evidently appears after the likeness of Jesus Christ whose representative he is on earth" (cujus vices gerit in terris).

[14] And in a sense—a theologian would add—from Christ's universal kingship. But this no more makes him a representative of Christ than an image of God.

[15] Rom. 13. 1–7.

U.S.A. For the President, just as the king, can be a quite ordinary man deprived of any personal prestige; yet look at him when he acts in his capacity of supreme chief of the body politic: millions of citizens, with their collective power, their hopes, their trust, their century-old heritage of suffering and glory, their prospective collective destiny, their collective calling in mankind's history, are there, in his person, as in a sign which makes them present to our eyes. Here is majesty, here is the essence of his political majesty. Not because he is a Sovereign! since in the political domain there is no such thing as sovereignty. But because he is the image of the people, and the topmost deputy of the people. And behind this majesty, as its supreme foundation, there is the eternal Law of the primary cause of being, source of the authority which is in the people and in which the vicar of the people participates. And if the man is righteous and faithful to his mission, there is reason to believe that, when the common good of the people is at stake, and when he acts in communion with the people, he may somehow receive, in whatever obscure or even tortuous way, some particular inspiration (*grâce d'état*, aid called for by one's vocational duty) from the One who is the supreme governor of human history.

The majesty of which I am speaking exists also (in the European parliamentary regimes it exists mainly) in the assemblies composed of the representatives of the people, in so far as they are a collective image of the people and a collective deputy for the people. (They should be conscious of that; when they themselves lose the sense of their inherent majesty, and behave like a throng of irresponsible schoolboys or clan fighters at feud, this is a bad sign for democracy.) And in each one of these representatives separately taken, as deputy for a fragment of the people, part of that very majesty, broken so to speak into pieces, still really exists.

*　　　*　　　*

Thus, in a democratic regime, the fundamental truth, recognized by democratic philosophy, that authority in the rulers derives from the right to rule themselves inherent in the people and permanent in them, is given a particular and particularly appropriate expression in the typical structural law of the body politic. Then authority deriving from the people rises from the base to the summit of the structure of the body politic. Power is exercised by men in whom authority, within certain fixed limits, is brought periodically to reside through the designation of the people, and whose management is controlled by the people: and this very fact is a sign of the continued possession, by the people, of that very right to govern themselves, the exercise of which has entitled the men in question to be in command—in political command—of other men, in the virtue of the primary Source of all authority. I mean that the supremely just establishment of Uncreated Reason, which gives force of law, or of a just ordinance, to what is necessary for the very existence and common good of nature and society, causes the governing function of those men chosen by the people to be held *by right*, and, by the same token obedience to them within the limits of their powers to be *required in justice*.

To understand these things correctly, we need, it seems to me, to sharpen the philosophical concepts traditionally used in this matter. In other words, I think that in order to bring to its full significance the political theory of Thomas Aquinas, which has been developed in so valuable a manner by Cajetan,[16] Bellarmine[17] and Suarez[18] in the sixteenth and early seventeenth centuries, we have still to add certain further clarifications, the principle of which is to be found in the very notion of vicariousness, as used by St Thomas himself with respect to the Prince "vicar of the multitude",[19] and elaborated by him in quite another field, namely the theory of the sign as "vicar" of the thing signified.[20]

Then two main points of doctrine, to which our preceding remarks have already alluded, would be clearly brought out. The first relates to the fact that in investing rulers with authority the people lose in no way possession of their basic right to self-government. The second relates to the fact that the representatives of the people are not mere instruments, but rulers invested with real authority, or right to command.

When I possess a material good, I cannot give it to another without losing by the very fact my possession of it. Conceiving things in that way has been the trouble with the classical theories of political power, especially, as we have seen, with the misleading theory of Sovereignty.[21] But when it is a question of a moral or spiritual quality, such as a right is, I can invest another man with a right of mine without myself losing possession of it, if this man receives this right in a vicarious manner—as a vicar of myself. Then he is made into an image of myself, and it is in this capacity that he participates in the very same right which is mine by essence. (Similarly, the disciple *as such* participates in the very same science which is in his teacher, and if he teaches in his turn—I mean in his mere capacity as a disciple, conveying the science of another—he will teach as a vicar, or an image of his teacher, and as a deputy for him;—and for all that, his teacher will not have divested himself of any bit of his own science.) The people are possessed of their right to govern themselves in an inherent and permanent manner. And the rulers, because they have been made into the vicars of the people, or into an image of them, are invested *per participationem*—to the extent of their powers—with the *very same* right and authority to govern which exists in the people *per essentiam*, as given them by the Author of nature and

[16] Cf. Cajetan, *Com. on Sum. theol.* i-ii, 90, 3; *De comparatione auctoritatis papae et concilii* (Romae: Apud Institutum Angelicum, 1936), c. 1, 12; c. 11, 190; c. 24, 359; c. 27, 415; *Apologia ejusdem tractatus* (in the same volume), c. 1, 449–50; c. 8, 533; c. 9, 550, 557–64, 572, 590; c. 16, 801.

[17] Cf. Bellarmine, *Controversiarum de membris Ecclesiae liber tertius, De laicis sive secularibus,* c. 6; *Opera omnia* (Paris: Vives, 1870), III, 10–12. English translation by Kathleen E. Murphy, *De Laicis or the Treatise on Civil Government* (New York: Fordham University Press, 1928).

[18] Cf. Suarez, *Defensio fidei catholicae et apostolicae adversus anglicanae sectae errores,* Lib. III: *De summi pontificis supra temporales reges excellentia, et potestate,* c. 2; *Opera* (Venetiis, 1749) fols. 114 ff.; *De legibus.* Lib. III, c. 4.

[19] "Vicem gerens multitudinis" (*Sum. theol.* i-ii, 90, 3).

[20] Cf. our chapter "Sign and Symbol", in *Ransoming the Time* (New York: Charles Scribner's Sons, 1941).

[21] I am afraid such a concept remains in the background of some current Scholasticist views, which would finally reduce the democratic process to a moment of free choice, by the people, of their masters (just as Rousseau fancied that the representative system acted, when he condemned it). Cf. Gredt, *op. cit.,* t. 11, nn. 1932, 1033.

grounded upon his transcendent, uncreated authority. The people, by designating their representatives, do not lose or give up possession of their own authority to govern themselves and of their right to supreme autonomy.

Now there is a distinction between the *possession* of a right and the *exercise* of it. It is the very exercise of the people's right to self-government which causes the rulers chosen by the people to be invested with authority, according to the duration of the office, and to the measure and the degree of their attributions: the very exercise of the right of the people to self-government restricts therefore to that extent, not this right itself, but the further *exercise* of it (in other words, the "power" of the people) —since the right of the people to self-government cannot be exercised in actual fact (except in the smallest groups or in the particular case of popular *referendum*) without placing certain men in public service, and, by the same token, having them invested with genuine authority. There is no lack of similar examples, where the very exercise of a right (for instance the right to choose one's vocation or state of life) restricts further exercise without causing to end, or lessening in any way, the possession of that right itself.

Thus we come to the second point. The representatives of the people are possessed of authority in a vicarious manner, in their capacity as vicars or images of the people, and deputies for them. But they are a living and active, not a dead image of the people, an image which is a human person, endowed with reason, free will and responsibility. And they cannot *exercise* the vicarious authority of which they are possessed if not as human persons and free agents, whose personal conscience is committed in the performance of their mission. So the authority they exercise which is the very same authority of the people participated in to some given extent and within certain given limits, is a vicarious but a genuine authority, held, like all authority of the people, in the virtue of the primary Source of all authority; they really hold a right to command and to be obeyed. They are not mere instruments of a mythical general will, they are actual rulers of the people; they have to make their decisions conformably to the dictates of their conscience, to the laws of that specific branch of Ethics which is political Ethics, to the judgement of their virtues (if they have any) of political prudence, and to what they see required by the common good—even if by so doing they incur the displeasure of the people.

The fact remains that they are accountable to the people, and that their management has to be supervised and controlled by the people. The fact also remains that, since their authority is but the authority of the people vicariously participated in, they have to rule, not as *separated* from the people (except as regards the existential conditions for exercising authority), but as *united* with the people in their very essence of deputies for them. Here is a difficult question, which I should like to try to make clear. I just said that the representatives of the people must be ready to incur the displeasure of the people, if their conscience demands it. Now I am saying that they must carry out their obligations in communion with the people. Are these two statements contradictory? They are not, on the condition that this expression "in communion with the people" be correctly understood.

In what can be called the common psyche of the people there is a huge variety of levels and degrees. At the most superficial level there are the momentary trends of opinion, as transient as the waves on the sea, and subjected to all winds of anxiety, fear, particular passions or particular interests. At deeper levels, there are the real needs of the multitude. At the deepest level, there is the will to live together, and the obscure consciousness of a common destiny and vocation, and finally the natural trend of the human will, considered in its essence, toward the good. Furthermore—this is a point we shall meet in the next section—people are ordinarily distracted from their most capital aspirations and interests, as a people, by each one's everyday business and suffering. Under such circumstances, to rule in communion with the people means on the one hand educating and awakening the people in the very process of governing them, so as to demand of them, at each progressive step, what they themselves have been made aware of and eager for (I am thinking of a real work of education, grounded on respect for them and trust in them, and in which they are the "principal agent"[22]—just the contrary to selling them ideas through sheer propaganda and advertising techniques). It means on the other hand, being intent on what is deep and lasting, and most really worthy of man, in the aspirations and psyche of the people. Thus it is that in incurring the disfavour of the people a ruler can still act in communion with the people, in the truest sense of this expression. And if he is a great ruler, he will perhaps make that disfavour into a renewed and more profound trust. In any case there is nothing in common between despotically imposing one's own will on the people —as a ruler from above separated from them—and resisting the people, or becoming hated and rejected by them, while being united with them in one's inmost intentions, and heedful of keeping communion with their deepest human will, that they ignore.

If this question is intricate, it is because no relation is more complex and mysterious than the relation between a man and the multitude for whose common good he is responsible, precisely because the authority he possesses is a vicarious authority, ultimately grounded in God, which he exercises as a free and responsible agent, image of the multitude and deputy for it. If we are looking for the most significant—though too transcendent for our purposes—type of a Legislator, let us think of Moses and his relation with the Jewish People. But the rulers of our political societies are not prophets directly commissioned by God, and this makes their case a little more simple.

At this point it would perhaps be appropriate to use the distinction, which I have emphasized in another essay, between a *law* and a *decree*. "Law and decree belong to two specifically distinct spheres: law, to the sphere of the *structural forms* of authority; decree, to the sphere of the *existential exercise* of authority. . . . A law is a general and lasting rule (general, that is to say, which determines in the social body a certain *functional relation*; lasting, that is to say, which is directed to something

[22] Cf. our book, *Education at the Crossroads* (New Haven: Yale University Press, 1943), pp. 29–31.

beyond the present moment or circumstance, and *calculated not to change*). A decree is a particular ordinance, determining a *point of fact* in the framework of the law, and confronted with a given circumstance for a given time."[23] Then I would say that a decree can without too much drawback be promulgated contrary to the trends prevalent at the moment in the people, and forced upon a reluctant public opinion. But a law should normally be laid down (always supposing that it be just) in accordance with the common consciousness of the people as expressed in the mores or in the collective needs and requests of organic groups of the population, or in spontaneous social and public service regulations in the making. Here could be saved the element of truth in Duguit's theory, unacceptable in itself, of "objective law". Contrary to this theory, the law is and will always remain a work of the reason of those who are in charge of the common good: but this same reason of the Legislator has to give shape to, or to express in a formed "word", an achieved "verbum", what exists in the common mind in an inchoate, unformulated manner.

V. THE PROPHETIC SHOCK-MINORITIES

The last issue to be discussed no longer deals with the *people*, but with —how shall I designate them?—well, with the *inspired servants or prophets of the people*.

What I mean is that it is not enough to define a democratic society by its legal structure. Another element plays also a basic part, namely the dynamic leaven or energy which fosters political *movement*, and which cannot be inscribed in any constitution or embodied in any institution, since it is both personal and contingent in nature, and rooted in free initiative. I should like to call that existential factor a prophetic factor. Democracy cannot do without it. The people need prophets.

And those servants or prophets of the people are not—not necessarily —elected representatives of the people. Their mission starts in their own hearts and consciousness. In this sense they are self-appointed prophets. They are needed in the normal functioning of a democratic society. They are needed equally in periods of crisis, birth or basic renewal of a democratic society.

Truly speaking, something similar is to be found in every political regime. The kings of past ages were surrounded with *grands commis*, great stewards, favourite counsellors or ministers, in ruthless competition with one another; each one of them believed that his own views and endeavours expressed the hidden *real* will of the king. They took a risk. When they were mistaken, they were broken by the king, sometimes they were sent into exile or they were hanged. The same story takes place in totalitarian States with rival high officials and political cliques in the bosom of the party.

In democratic societies the people play the part of the king, and the inspired servants of the people that of the great counsellors. As a rule they are prophets of emancipation—national, political or social emancipation.

[23] *Principes d'une politique humaniste*, Annexe to chap. ii, "Pouvoir législatif et pouvoir exécutif."

In the normal functioning of a democratic society the political animation thus proceeds from men who, feeling themselves designated for a vocation of leadership, follow the usual channels of political activity—they will become chiefs of political parties, they will come to power through the legal machinery of elections. The happiest circumstance for the body politic obtains when the top men in the state are at the same time genuine prophets of the people. I think that in a renewed democracy the vocation of leadership which I just mentioned, a sinister image of which is offered us by the *unique Party* of the totalitarian States—should normally be exercised by small dynamic groups freely organized and multiple in nature, which would not be concerned with electoral success but with devoting themselves entirely to a great social and political idea, and which would act as a ferment either inside or outside the political parties.[24]

But it is in periods of crisis, birth or basic transformation that the role of the inspired servants, the prophets of the people, takes on full importance. Let us think, for example, of the fathers of the French Revolution or of the American Constitution, of men like Tom Paine or Thomas Jefferson; or of that John Brown—still a criminal for Southerners, a hero for Northerners—who was convinced he had a divine commission to destroy slavery by the force of arms, and who captured the arsenal of Harper's Ferry, to be hanged some months later, in December of 1859:

> John Brown's body lies a-mouldering in the grave,
> But his soul goes marching on.

Or of the originators of the Italian Risorgimento,[25] or of the liberation of Ireland; let us think of Gandhi once again, or of the pioneers of unionism and the labour movement. The primary work of the inspired servant of the people is to *awaken* the people, to awaken them to something better than everyone's daily business, to the sense of a supra-individual task to be performed.

That is a quite vital and necessary social phenomenon. And it is a quite dangerous phenomenon. For where there is inspiration and prophecy, there are false prophets and true prophets; thieves aiming to dominate men and servants aiming to set them free; inspiration from dark instincts and inspiration from genuine love. And nothing is more difficult than what is called "discrimination between spirits". It is easy to mistake impure inspiration for unsullied inspiration; nay more, it is easy to slip from genuine inspiration to a corrupt one. And we know that *optimi corruptio pessima*, corruption of what is best is what is worst.

The political problem we are confronted with at this point is the problem of the prophetic pioneering minorities or shock-minorities—I say shock-minorities as one says shock-troops—a problem which any theory of democracy should frankly face.

The people are to be awakened—that means that the people are asleep. People as a rule prefer to sleep. Awakenings are always bitter. In so far as their daily interests are involved, what people would like is business as usual: everyday misery and humiliation as usual. People would like to

[24] Cf. *True Humanism* (New York: Charles Scribner's Sons, 1938), pp. 162 ff.
[25] Cf. Carlo Rosselli, *Socialisme libéral* (Paris, 1930), pp. 47 ff.

ignore that they are *the* people. It is a fact that, for good or evil, the great historical changes in political societies have been brought about by a few, who were convinced that they embodied the real will—to be awakened—of the people, as contrasting with the people's wish to sleep. At the time of the Risorgimento, the great majority of Italians surely preferred not to be set free from the Austrian yoke. If a popular poll had been taken at the time of Samuel Adams, we may wonder whether the majority would have voted for the war of Independence. If a popular poll had been taken in France in 1940, it is highly probable that the majority would have voted for Marshal Pétain—they believed he hated collaboration with the Germans as they did. In all these cases, the majority went wrong, and the shock-minorities were right. Well, but we have also been able to contemplate how the makers of totalitarian States have used the power of vanguard insurgent minorities.

The question is: are the people to be *awakened* or to be *used*? to be awakened like men or to be whipped and driven like cattle? The prophetic minorities say *we the people* when in actual fact they alone, not the people, are speaking. Only the final decision of the people can prove whether that figure of speech was right or wrong. But each time a part speaks in the name of the whole, that part is tempted to believe that *it is* the whole. As a result the part will endeavour to substitute itself for the whole, or rather to oblige the whole to be "really" the whole, that is, what the part wills the whole to be. Thus the entire process will become rotten, and instead of awakening the people to freedom, as they believed or pretended they were doing, that prophetic shock-minority will dominate the people and make them more enslaved than they had been.

During the course of the nineteenth century a dreadful ambiguity existed in this regard in democratic ideology; concepts and trends inspired from spurious democratic philosophy and would-be dictatorial, mistaken devotion to the people were mixed up with concepts and trends inspired from genuine devotion to the people and genuine democratic philosophy. There were men who believed that, as Jean-Jacques Rousseau put it, they should *force* the people *to be free*.[26] I say they were betrayers of the people. For they treated the people like sick children while they were clamouring for the rights and freedom of the people. Those who distrust the people while appealing to the highest feelings and to the blood of the people cheat and betray the people. The first axiom and precept in democracy is to trust the people. Trust the people, respect the people, trust them even and first of all while awakening them, that is, while putting yourself at the service of their human dignity.

The actual contempt for and distrust of the people involved in the principle "to force the people to be free" was to impair in some places the democratic mind and to develop a spurious philosophy of the mission of the self-styled enlightened minorities.

Let us summarize that spurious philosophy in the three following points. First, since the action of what I just called a prophetic shock-minority results in a showdown, and since only the fact, the event, can

[26] Cf. *Contrat social*, Book I, chap. vii: "Quiconque refusera d'obéir à la volonté générale y sera contraint par tout le corps: ce qui ne signifie autre chose sinon qu'on le forcera d'être libre."

decide whether they were right or wrong in offering themselves as the personification of the people, then there is only one way to make good the risk that such a minority is taking, namely, *the out and out use of violence*, in order to succeed at any cost and by any means.

Second, once they have succeeded, they have to use *terror* to wipe out any possible opponent.

Third, given on the one hand the congenital dullness and infirmity of the people, on the other hand the indispensable role of prophetic shock-minorities in human history, the deep trend toward emancipation which is at work in that history requires *breaking of the law* as a perpetual and necessary condition of progress, and blossoms forth into the messianic myth of *the Revolution*. Thus the basic tenets of democratic faith were denied in the very name of democracy; and the myth of the Revolution, with a capital R, was to bring to naught the real changes of structure, let us say the particular revolutions (without a capital R) which could be possibly needed at certain given moments in human history, and which will be needed in actual fact as long as human history lasts.

How could we be surprised at seeing such spurious philosophy end up in totalitarianism, and the principle: *to force the people to be free*, reach its logical conclusion in the totalitarian dream: to force the people to be obedient in order that the State be free and all-powerful, or in order to make the people happy despite themselves, as Dostoievsky expressed it in his Legend of the Great Inquisitor?

The above-mentioned remarks, as well as the consideration of the present plight of the world, oblige us to take a serious view of the issue involved, and to ask from democratic philosophy a clear restatement of the theory of the role of prophetic shock-minorities. Such a restatement, as I see it, would emphasize the three following points, in accordance with the democratic charter.

First, the recourse to illegal activity is in itself *an exception*, not a rule, and should always remain exceptional; and it is only justified—as a lesser evil—when a prophetic shock-minority is confronted with a situation in which law has been already broken or suspended, that is, when it is confronted with some form of *tyrannical power*.

Second, just as exceptional as illegal activity, the use of force, or of hard measures of coercion, may be needed in such circumstances; but *justice* must always hold sway. The use of terror striking the innocent and the guilty indiscriminately is always a crime. Innocent persons can indirectly suffer from just public measures directed to the social group in which they belong; but no innocent person should ever be punished, put into captivity, put to death.

Third, it is true that only the fact, the event, can decide whether a prophetic shock-minority was right or wrong in offering itself as the personification of the people, but the only success which is to provide that test is the *free approval by the people*, as soon as the people can express their will. This means on the one hand that the use of force should always be provisional as well as exceptional, and the free consultation of the people always intended as an urgent, unpostponable aim; on the other hand, that the risk that a prophetic shock-minority is taking must be fairly taken, that this minority would betray itself as well as the people if it clung to power by any means whatever, and that it must be ready to lose the game if the people say so.

Finally, what can be the weapons of the people to protect themselves and the body politic either against false servants of the people and spurious prophetic shock-minorities or against the corruption of true servants of the people and genuine prophetic shock-minorities shifting from the struggle for freedom to the struggle for domination? Nothing can replace in this connection the strength of the common ethos, the inner energy of democratic faith and civil morality in the people themselves, the enjoyment by them of real freedom in their everyday life and of a truly human standard of living, and the active participation of them in political life from the bottom up. If these conditions are lacking, the door is open to deception.

Yet there is in any case a weapon which they should particularly treasure as a bulwark of their political liberties, namely, the freedom of expression and criticism. That's a new reason to confirm what has been said in this chapter about the vital necessity in democracy for the freedom of the press and of the means of expression of thought, even at the price of great risks—still less great than the loss of liberty. A free people needs a free press, I mean free from the State, and free also from economic bondage and the power of money.

*   *   *

I have said that democracy cannot do without the prophetic factor, and that the people need prophets. I should like to conclude that this is a sad necessity; or, rather, that in a democracy which has come of age, in a society of free men, expert in the virtues of freedom and just in its fundamental structures, the prophetic function should be integrated in the normal and regular life of the body politic, and spring forth from the people themselves, whose inspiration would rise in the body politic from the starting point of their free common activity in their most elementary, most humble local communities; and who, by choosing their leaders, at that most elementary level, through a natural and experiential process, as fellow-men personally known to them and deserving their trust in the minor affairs of the community, would be prepared in a truly consciousness-awakening manner to choose their leaders, at the level of the common good of the body politic, with true political awareness and as genuine deputies for them.

The Essential Functions of Authority*

Yves Simon

AUTHORITY AS CAUSE OF UNITED ACTION

THROUGHOUT the preceding exposition we emphasized the substitutional character of paternal authority. We now have to consider whether authority has essential functions. That it has no essential function at all is a proposition current among liberal writers.

Let us bear in mind the picture of a society made exclusively of clever and virtuous persons. If such a picture were necessarily utopian, it might still satisfy the conditions of a mental experiment. In fact, it is not unreal; e.g., a man and his wife make up a society; both of them may be virtuous and enlightened. There exist societies whose members are all perfectly good; but these societies are very small. We want to know whether such societies need authority. If they do, authority is not devoid of essential function.

Even in the smallest and most closely united community, unity of action cannot be taken for granted; it has to be caused, and, if it is to be steady, it has to be assured by a steady cause. Here are a man and his wife—both are good and clever, but one thinks that the summer vacation should be spent on the seashore, and the other would rather spend it in the hills. If they remain divided, one goes to the seashore, the other to the hills, and common life ceases temporarily. It would come to an end if a similar divergence concerned an issue of lasting significance.

Now unity of action depends upon unity of judgement, and unity of judgement can be procured either by way of unanimity or by way of authority; no third possibility is conceivable. Either we all think that we should act in a certain way, or it is understood among us that, no matter how diverse our preferences, we shall all assent to one judgement and follow the line of action that it prescribes. Whether this judgement is uttered by a leading person or by the majority or by a majority within a leading minority makes, at this point, little difference. But to submit myself to a judgement which does not, or at least may not, express my own view of what should be done is to obey authority. Thus authority is needed to assure unity of action if, and only if, unanimity is uncertain. The question is whether unanimity can be established in better than casual fashion among the perfectly clever and well-intentioned members of a society which is, by hypothesis, free from deficiencies.

In science, lack of unanimity always has the character of an accident, and there is something scandalous about it; people spontaneously trace it to failure, for science is supposed to proceed by way of demonstration and demonstration is held to communicate knowledge with necessity. What is taught and learned in our courses and treatises under the name of science contains a large amount of opinions and beliefs; but it also contains an inconspicuous, though all-important, nucleus of propositions

* From *The Philosophy of Democratic Government*; see p. x above.

possessing certainty, universality and clarity, which satisfy all requirements for steady communicability. *De jure*, it is always possible to
necessitate unanimous assent to a scientific proposition; unfolding the
demonstration is all that needs to be done. Let it be said that a genuinely
scientific proposition is, *de jure*, communicable without limits. Yet, when
a proposition fails to win assent beyond the boundaries of a group of
kindred minds, one should not infer, from this sheer fact, that it is devoid
of scientific character. A proposition may be *de jure*, communicable without any limit, though its *de facto* communicability proves narrowly
limited. That a discrepance should take place between *de jure* and *de
facto* possibilities is a common occurrence in this world of contingency.
The propositions of positive science are incomparably more communicable, in fact, than those of philosophy; yet some philosophic propositions
are fully demonstrated and consequently possess the objective foundation
of unlimited communicability; their relative incommunicability is purely
factual. It is by accident that only a few people can understand the terms
out of which they are made, know what the question is all about, master
the prerequisites to the demonstration and follow the demonstration
itself.

Thus, in the field of scientific thought, unanimity is guaranteed, *de
jure*, by a process of rational communication whose possibility results
necessarily from the nature of scientific objects. Faultless scientific minds,
no matter how many, would be unanimous with regard to scientific truth.
The problem with which we are now concerned is whether what holds
for scientific propositions holds also for those practical propositions which
rule the action of a multitude: Do they possess the power of commanding
unanimous assent, as least when conditions are entirely normal?

The theory of practical certainty and of practical truth, worked out by
Aristotelianism, is a first step toward an answer. The very exacting definition of science in the *Posterior Analytics* seems to make hopeless the case
of certainty in practical matters. If the certainty of science demands that
the scientific object should possess the kind and degree of necessity that
is found in universal essences alone, it seems that practical knowledge
admits of no certainty, for human practice takes place in the universe of
the things that can be otherwise than they are.[1] Events constantly give the
lie to our prudence. After careful deliberation we conclude that this
course of action is the right one; but it turns out to lead to a catastrophe.
The head of a family, for instance, decides, after having conscientiously
weighed advantages and disadvantages, that a certain trip would be a
good thing for his family. A train wreck occurs. A child is killed. Yet this
honest man had a right to believe in the course of action that he selected.

Such a simple example is all we need to perceive the twofold meaning
of a practical proposition. "This trip is going to be a good thing"—this
proposition is given the lie by the train wreck; it is found at variance
with facts; between it and the real, there turns out to be no relation of
conformity; it happens to be false, it never was certain. However, and no
matter what happens, it will remain everlastingly true that the proposi-

---

[1] On the theory of prudence, see Aristotle, *Ethics*, 6; Thomas Aquinas, *Sum. theol.*,
i–ii, 57, 4, 5, 6; 58, 4, 5; 65, 2; ii–ii, 47–56; John of St Thomas, *Cursus theologicus*, i–ii,
disp. 16, a. 4, 5 ([Paris: Vives, 1885], VI, 466 ff.): disp. 17, a. 2 (VI, 534 ff.).

tion "this trip is going to be a good thing" was the right conclusion of a properly conducted deliberation. No one could do better. Our calculations are not supposed to be infallible. This proposition was what it was supposed to be. It was what good will and loving devotion wanted it to be. Its agreement with the real was but probable, for the operation of a railroad line is subject to accidents; but its agreement with the demands of a good will was certain. Such agreement is a kind of truth, and the train wreck is no ground for charging the man with lack of judgement. He judged well, inasmuch as his judgement was what it was supposed to be. The conformity of a practical proposition with the real cannot be perfectly established; but such conformity is absolute truth, theoretical truth; it is not the truth that belongs to the practical proposition qua practical. Practical truth is a relation of conformity between a judgement or a proposition and the requirements of an honest will.[2] When a decision is what honesty demands that it should be, this decision is true in a practical sense, and its practical truth is certain and unqualified. The uncertainty of our qualifications entails painful consequences, but it does not affect the possession of practical truth, which retains its firmness amid ruins.

So far as its cause is concerned, the judgement possessed with practical certainty must be described as a particularly clean and familiar case of *affective* knowledge. In rational knowledge, a judgement which is not self-justified owes its justification to antecedent cognitions and ultimately to self-justified or obvious cognitions. The dispositions of the will and the heart have nothing to do with the determination of knowledge; they concern only its exercise. It is not by being docile to the inclinations of our heart that we shall ever *establish* the true answer to a question of theoretical science. On the contrary, when I am concerned with the question "What do I have to do, here and now, in the midst of this unique, unprecedented and unrenewable congeries of circumstances, in order to make a good use of my freedom, in order to preserve the good of virtue?" I know that no deduction, no induction, no argumentation, can supply the final answer. The science of ethics, i.e., the rational knowledge of morality, would supply an initial answer but not the final one. Between the last rationally established conclusion and the entirely concrete rule that action demands, there is a gap that no argumentation can bridge. Doubt cripples action, or an uncertain rule is issued, unless the will and the heart are so dedicated to the good of virtue that their inclinations can be relied upon. The ethical man may be unable to explain why, ultimately, he comes to such and such a decision; he may have nothing to say, beyond mentioning an inclination to act in this way and an insuperable repugnance to act in the opposite way. That is all he needs to direct his action, but more would be needed to bring about conviction in the mind of his neighbour. Unlike scientific judgement, practical judgement, for the very reason that it is ultimately determined by the obscure forces of the appetite, does not admit of rational communication. It is, so to say, a secret.

[2] On practical truth, see Aristotle, *Ethics*, 6, 2, 1139, a. 21; *Com. of St Thomas*, les. 2; *Sum. theol.*, i–ii, 57, 5 ad 3, and Cajetan's commentary on this text.

Let these propositions be exemplified briefly. When a teacher of ethics shows that the right of private ownership is suspended in case of extreme necessity, so that a starving person may use things which under ordinary circumstances belong to his neighbour, some listener inevitably raises the following question (which constitutes, in this listener's mind, an insuperable objection): "But who is going to decide whether or not I do find myself in the state of extreme necessity?" The only possible answer is calculated to discourage those who expect of the science of ethics things that no science can ever procure. Let the answer be that everyone has to make such decisions for himself and that the conditions to be satisfied, if such decisions are to be made safely, are extremely costly. In order to know for sure whether I find myself in the state of extreme necessity, I must possess the virtue of justice; by it I shall be inclined away from my neighbour's property and prevented from using goods that do not belong to me until my want is actually extreme. But unruly desires would interfere with the operation of justice; thus temperance also is required. And so is fortitude, for a coward would act too early, out of fear of a danger, or too late, out of fear of another danger. In short, practical wisdom or prudence, the virtue whose act is certain knowledge of practical truth, presupposes all moral virtues.

In an early writing on the subject of authority I stated that, on account of the incommunicability of the prudential judgement, unanimity in practical matters is always precarious or casual.[3] I wish to criticize this view, in which I now recognize a serious error.

Consider a group of persons confronted with a duty of united action for the common good. We assume that they are all virtuous; by their virtues they are properly related to the common good as end. We assume also that they are all enlightened and that no ignorance or illusion interferes with their ability to determine the proper means. Unanimity cannot be brought about by demonstration, for the proposition that such and such a course of action ought to be followed is not demonstrable. Attempts at its rational establishment, no matter how sound and helpful, will fall short of necessitating the assent of the minds. Let an example be that of a nation threatened in its freedom and existence by an ambitious competitor. A time comes when survival demands war-readiness, and a time comes when nothing but fighting can preserve the common good. Yet it is never possible to demonstrate that whoever loves the common good must support a policy of war and that whoever opposes such a policy is wrong. Who knows? Decisive factors often are extremely unobvious. A policy of abstention may not bring about the calamities whose unfolding is considered evident by some. And war is a risky enterprise. The dialogue goes on, though the situation imperatively demands that all should contribute full measure of devotion, with all their minds and hearts, to a uniquely determined policy. The question is whether such disagreement can take place among citizens that are both good and enlightened.

One thing is plain: if unanimity can be achieved in non-fortuitous

[3] *Nature and Functions of Authority* (Milwaukee: Marquette University Press, 1940). For the correction of this error, as well as for countless greater blessings, I am indebted to Professor Maritain.

fashion, it is not by way of necessitating argumentation and rational communication. But the analysis of practical judgement, which rules out rational communication as a steady cause of unanimity in these matters, shows also that a steady cause of unanimity is found in the inclination of the appetite, whenever the means to the common good is uniquely determined. If, and only if, there is only one means to the common good the proposition enunciating this means is the only one that admits of practical truth. It is the only one that conforms to the requirements of a properly disposed appetite, and a properly disposed appetite cannot make any other proposition win assent. The community of the end and the unique determination of the means bring about a situation distinguished by happy simplicity.

The proper mystery of practical wisdom (prudence) has been so commonly ignored by philosophers that its rediscovery is not unlikely to cause some sort of intoxication. In sharp contrast to the youthful ideal of a science-like knowledge of action, the theory of prudence describes a universe of normally and necessarily different judgements, each of which, on close examination, turns out to bear a mark of secrecy. Two brothers, for instance, would govern their families in strikingly different ways, and each of them may be unable to understand why the other one uses what seems to him queer and irrational methods. Unless they answer similar problems in similar fashions, should it not be said that one of them is wrong, or both? But the situations of two individuals are really dissimilar whenever the unique implications of individual history play a part in the statement of the problem. A feeling for the mysterious operation of individual history in the regulation of individual conduct is a most important element of practical wisdom. When such a feeling has just awakened in our souls, we come to imagine the ethical destinies of individual men as a multitude of universes governed by so many unique and incommunicable rules of action. But all at once the spirit of rebellion endangers the universality of the law and the unity of common action. Indeed, diversities resulting from the uniqueness of individual situations never can supply a ground for dispensing with the law, for it is within the unity of the law that they take place. As to the necessary unity of common action, how could it be affected by the diversity of our individual histories? When there is a question of common action for the common good, such diversity no longer matters; the only history that matters is that of the community. In the case of two individuals who pursue individual goods belonging to the same genus, duality on the part of the good intended and duality on the part of the agent supply grounds for possible divergencies regarding the rule of action. In the case of a community in quest of its common good, the good intended is one and the intending agent is one; the only just ground for divergent opinion is the diversity of the means capable of leading the same collective agent to the same common good. Whenever there is only one means, there ought to be unanimity, and failure to achieve unanimous agreement is traceable to some deficiency.

Consider, again, the case of a nation whose salvation, in justice, demands that war be fought. What about dissenters? They may be ill-intentioned citizens, who do not love the common good but wish for the enemy's victory or who place above everything else the specific pleasures that attach to obstinacy. They may be well-intentioned citizens but lack intelligence; or they may have intelligence and good will but lack information and, by accident, be fooled into believing that they have all the information needed for the uttering of a fully determinate judgement as to what the country should do. From our present viewpoint, whether or not these erring citizens retain their respectability does not matter. What matters is that their error is definite and traceable to a deficiency, which may or may not involve guilt.

In the daily life of small communities—I refer principally to the couple and the family—unanimity plays a great part as a factor of unified action. When the means to the common good is uniquely determined—the only case in which there is a firm foundation for unanimity—it is not infrequently recognized and assented to in unanimous fashion. In large societies—state, nation—the astonishing thing is not that complete unanimity is never realized but rather that situations closely resembling unanimity, so far as most practical purposes are concerned, arise not rarely when the threat to the common good is dire. Notice that a situation resembling unanimity does not necessarily imply overwhelming majority; a substantial majority within the part of the nation—perhaps a minority—which is actively interested suffices. If no such situation is produced, in spite of the seriousness of the common predicament, salvation becomes uncertain, and a doubt appears whether there still is anything to be saved. For it can be wondered whether a multitude incapable of achieving some kind of unanimity in the hour of extreme peril retains the character of a community; disintegration may be too far advanced. The hopeless plight of a society that is no longer capable of achieving an approximation to unanimity bears witness to the absolutely normal character of unanimous assent to the uniquely determined means of common salvation.

To sum up: When the means to the common good is uniquely determined, affective community supplies an essential foundation for unanimous assent; unanimity is, then, the only normal situation, and, if everything is normal, authority is not needed to bring about unified action. Unity of action requires authority in so far as not everything is normal, in so far as wills are weak or perverse and intellects ignorant or blinded. The function of authority remains substitutional.

But when, on the other hand, there is more than one means of procuring the common good, there is no foundation whatsoever for unanimity. Anyone may disagree without there being anything wrong either with his intentions or with his judgement. It is only by chance that unanimity can be achieved, for it has no essential cause. Even in a very small society it will partake of the unsteadiness of the fortuitous and fail to assure unity of action; yet unity of action may be indispensable and all-important in spite of the plurality of the means leading to the common good. Shall we drive on the left side of the road, as in Great Britain, or on the right side, as in most countries? The common good, i.e., order and safety, admits of either method, and prior to the establishment of definite habits it seems that neither method enjoys any superiority. Here the rule of action is entirely optional. But it is all-important that one and the same rule should govern the behaviour of all drivers; lack of unity of action, in such a simple case, would entail catastrophes. The common good does not demand that we should drive on the right side, and it does not demand that we should drive on the left side; but it does demand that all should drive on the same side. Of the two opposite judgements (drive right, drive left), it does not make either one mandatory, but it demands that one of them should become mandatory and be obeyed by all, regardless of their preference. In other words, the common good demands that a problem of united action which cannot be solved by way of unanimity should be solved by way of authority.

Considering, thus, the function that authority plays as an indispensable principle of united action when there are several means to the common good, let the question be asked whether this function is essential or substitutional. Since the need for authority, here, is properly caused by the plurality of the means, the real question is whether this plurality of means is itself caused by a deficiency or by the good nature of things; in the latter case alone will the function under consideration prove to be an essential one.

Without being stated in these very terms, this question was often examined and was given a definite answer by various schools of scientific anarchism. Ever since the awakening, early in the nineteenth century, of a rationalistic enthusiasm for the possibilities of social science, it has been a current belief that the indetermination of the means, which makes unification by way of authority necessary, is but an appearance due to our inability to identify the appropriate means. The situation could be described as follows: on the basis of our incomplete information, a, b and c seem to be so many adequate means to the good that we are aiming at. United action, if needed, has to be procured by the decision of authority. But if we knew more about a, b, c . . . , there would be no need for such decision; for we would realize that only one course of action is really appropriate and to this uniquely determined course of action honest and clever people would give unanimous assent. In other words, our ignorance opens a phase of indetermination that authority, in blind fashion, closes. Better knowledge would eliminate the phase of indetermination and its unenlightened ending. Authority substitutes for a determinate knowledge of a situation which is really determinate—its role remains substitutional.

In order to ascertain the real meaning of this argument, let us apply it to a simple example. Consider, again, the case of a family that is deliberating about the summer vacation: some would like to stay home, some would rather go to the hills, and some to the seashore. Let it be granted that these three are the only existent possibilities. According to the argument that we want to test, one of the three ways is right and the other two are wrong. But, as an effect of insuperable ignorance, these people, in spite of their good will, may remain divided, in which case unity will be brought about by authority.

Later developments, in fact, sometimes show that, out of several ways which all seemed proper, only one was really conducive to the good; we really had no choice, although we honestly believed that we had plenty of it. But the relevant question is this: Supposing that there is only one real means, what kind of factor causes it to be uniquely determined? And supposing that there is a plurality of genuine means, what kind of factor causes them to be several?

One obvious reason why a family should stay home during the summer is the high cost of a vacation in the hills or at the seashore. Thus poverty is a factor of unique determination. Wealth, on the contrary, makes for choice; this is what men of property know very well, and poor people still better. One obvious reason why a family should not stay home during the summer is the condition of the health of its members; if some of them, or all, are in such bad shape that, without a period of rest in the hills or at the seashore, they are likely to catch bad diseases next winter, then (all other things being equal) one possibility out of three is ruled out. If, on the contrary, all are in very good health, they can stand, without ill effect, a summer in town. Supposing that they leave home, one reason why they may have no choice between hills and seashore would be the nervousness of some or all, since nervous people tend to become sleepless and more nervous than ever at the seashore. It happens also that a family, in spite of financial strain, feels obliged to move to the country for a while, just because a young man is going through a period of moral uncertainty out of which he can be helped by a change in environment and by wholesome entertainment. If all the family, on the contrary, are robust persons, you can trust that they will fight their way through, regardless of whether they stay at home or go away. In short, wealth, health and strength are factors that cause independence from particular courses of action, dominating indifference, mastery over several means, freedom. Destitution, ill health, uncertainty, weakness, are factors that cause dependence upon certain means. Plenitude causes choice, poverty leaves no choice. Deficiency, such as lack of knowledge, may render the genuine means undistinguishable from the illusory one and thus make a plurality of means appear where there is really no more than one. But fullness, actuality, determination, achievement, accomplishment, power and greatness, knowledge and stability, produce or increase liberty in societies and individuals as well. A society enjoying a supremely high degree of enlightenment would, all other things being equal, enjoy much more choice than ignorant societies and have to choose among many more possibilities. It would not need authority to choose between two courses of action one of which is bound to lead to disaster, since, by hypothesis, knowledge would rule out illusory means. But it would need authority, *more than ever*, to procure united action, for, thanks to better lights, the plurality of the genuine means would have increased considerably. The function of authority with which we are concerned, i.e., that of procuring united action when the means to the common good are several, does not disappear but grows, as deficiencies are made up; it originates not in the defects of men and societies but in the nature of society. It is an essential function.

Doubts affecting this issue result from a general philosophic situation which confusedly tends to identify freedom and indetermination. In fact, freedom is indifference, and there are two sorts of indifference.[4] There is the passive indifference of the indeterminate subject which can receive any of several determinations precisely because it is indeterminate. The highest degree of such indifference is realized in prime matter, a pure "out of which" that is not of itself any determinate thing and therefore cannot exist by itself but can receive any essential determination and exist under it. Nothing is further removed from freedom than the indetermination of matter, for freedom is mastery and proceeds not from a lack of determination but from a particularly full and hard kind of determination. A free cause is a superdeterminate cause. The trouble comes from the fact that these two opposite realities—the indifference of indetermination, passivity, inachievement and the indifference of superdetermination which is freedom—have in common the property of being distinct from sheer determinate causality. Further, there is in the human will a combination of active indifference and of passive indifference. The latter is an obstacle to freedom; yet it is not always easy to distinguish, in the twilight, the force which is supposed to be overcoming (i.e., active indifference, that is, freedom) and the force which is supposed to be overcome (i.e., passive indifference, indetermination, perplexity, irresolution) if the former is to assert itself. When psychologists do not altogether deny freedom of choice, they generally trace it to an imperfection or uncertainty of the will, to an element of looseness in its operation. Similarly, many social thinkers, when confronted with a seeming plurality of means, trace it to an inadequate knowledge and fail to see that plurality of genuine means can be caused by excellence of knowledge and power. In both cases a misunderstanding concerning indifference results from an insufficiently elaborate notion of causality.

THE VOLITION OF THE COMMON GOOD

The problem of united action is relative to means. Now it is perfectly evident that all operations concerning means are conditioned and sustained by more basic operations, i.e., the volition and intention of the end.[5] Associates may unify their action by way of authority or have to content themselves with the risky procedures of unanimity; clearly, there would be no action to be unified if these men had not antecedently determined that a certain object should have for all of them the character of an end to be pursued through common action. Thus, beyond the problem of united action, we have to inquire into a more profound issue, i.e., that of the very intention of the common good. We know that authority is necessary, under definite conditions, for the proper working of the means; the next question is whether the proper intention of the common good requires the operation of authority.

If we were concerned with a society including stupid or vicious members, the answer would be so plain as to make the statement of the

---

[4] On the all-important subject of the two indifferences found in the human will, see Thomas Aquinas, *Sum. contra gentes*, i, 82; John of St Thomas, *Cursus philosophicus*, IV, q. 12, a. 2 (Marietti, III, 387); *Cursus theologicus*, i, disp. 24, a. 4 (Solesme, III, 89); I–ii, disp. 3, a. 2 (Vives, V, 373).

[5] Let it be recalled that *volition* is concerned with the end considered absolutely and *intention* with the end considered as term of a means or set of means.

question superfluous. People lacking good will or understanding obviously have to be directed toward the common good; they even have to be compelled not to harm the common good and to serve it positively. The relevant and difficult question concerns a society composed exclusively of good and enlightened people. At first glance, the answer may seem obvious: if all these people are well-intentioned, they *spontaneously* intend the common good and do not need to be directed toward it. By the very operation of their virtue they aim at the common good and want to subordinate to it their private advantages; without such basic volition and orderly subordination, they would be selfish people, bad citizens, or, at best, well-meaning people misled by illusions. Thus all conceivable function of authority, with regard to the volition and intention of the common good, seems to be merely substitutional.

The question with which we are concerned here is one whose difficulty equals its profundity. It has rarely been considered in proper isolation. The preceding discussion removed the risk that it should be confused with the problem of united action, but there remains a risk of confusion with another neighbouring issue. Briefly, most societies are divided into two groups of persons, i.e., those who govern and those who are governed. Now throughout the history of political literature there is a tendency to identify the two following questions: (*a*) whether society needs to be governed and (*b*) whether it needs to be governed by a distinct personnel. In fact, there are many instances of direct government of the multitude by itself; unless it is claimed, arbitrarily enough, that these constitute abnormalities, they should suffice to show that the essence of government abstracts from these two peculiar modalities: embodiment in a distinct personnel, embodiment in the entire multitude. Citizens of a great nation, we obey laws made by a small body of elected legislators; but members of a New England community were no less *governed* by the regulations that the whole community issued in its town meetings. The constitution of a distinct governing personnel has to do with the modalities of authority, not with its functions and the grounds of its necessity. How the confusion takes place is easy to grasp. Wonder is aroused by the power that the few claim to have over the many and that the many acknowledge not too reluctantly. This power, if justifiable at all, should be justified by the requirements of the common welfare. It is realized or strongly suspected that the common welfare needs to be taken care of by a body of public persons. There are instances in which the entire people is such a body; but in most cases and in the most impressive and best-known cases the public persons in charge of the common good are, of necessity, specialized, as it were, in the pursuit of the good which is not special or private but common. Thus, in most cases and in the best known of them, the body of public persons called for by the common good is determinately a distinct governing personnel. The positing of government and the positing of a distinct governing personnel are empirically one conclusion, and experience does not direct attention to the difference of grounds. Further, the operation of a distinct governing personnel implies an element of paradox which will be most felicitously dealt with if, by letting it resolve into the more fundamental issue of government itself, we manage to ignore its specific difficulty.

In order that the problem of authority, with regard to the volition and intention of the common good, may be properly isolated, it is helpful to keep in mind, whenever possible, pictures of government without distinct governing personnel, as in the case of a New England town, a Swiss canton, or a nation deciding an issue by way of plebiscite. The entirely different problem of the necessity of a distinct governing personnel will be discussed in another part of this book.

That virtuous people, as a proper effect of their virtue, love the common good and subordinate their choices to its requirements is an entirely unquestionable proposition. Thus, *in a certain way at least*, the volition and intention of the common good are guaranteed by virtue itself, independently of all authority. Of this *way* we do not know, as yet, anything, except that it is essential and basic; for it is not by accident or in any superficial fashion that the just love the common good and surrender for it their private interests. The problem, accordingly, is to determine whether the virtue of the private person regards the whole of the common good or merely some fundamental aspect of it. If, and only if, the latter is true, authority may have an essential part to play in the volition and intention of the common good. We are wondering, in other words, whether the *way* in which virtue guarantees adherence to the common good is an all-embracing one; should the guaranty supplied by virtue fail to cover some essential aspect of the common good, then direction by authority might be needed, in order that the adherence of society to all essential aspects of its good be steadily assured. The examination of a few typical instances will provide an answer.

Let the first instance be that used by Thomas Aquinas in his inquiry into the general conditions of morality. The question is whether the human will, in order to be good, ought to agree with the divine will *in volito*, in other words, whether it must carry agreement with the divine will so far as to desire the very thing whose coming into existence is desired, or permitted, by the divine will[6] (e.g., if God let me know that he wants my father to die tomorrow at noon, would ethical perfection demand that I should refrain from any action designed to prolong the life of my father beyond tomorrow noon?). Aquinas says that, when a thing is good in one respect and bad in another respect, there is nothing wrong about its being desired by one, to whom it is related in its desirable aspect, and hated by another, who happens to occupy such a position as to regard the thing in its undesirable aspect. Thus the wife of a murderer hates the prospect of her husband's being put to death; she is normally and virtuously concerned with the good of her family, and, from the standpoint which is and ought to be hers, the death of the murderer is an evil. On the other side, the judge, who stands for society, sees in the death of the murderer elements of the common good: justice and determent from crime. The common good, of course, shall prevail, but, significantly, Aquinas considers altogether sound and honest the opposition made to the requirements of the common good by the person in charge of the particular good. The common good itself demands that wives should want their husbands to survive, even though the latter happen to be criminals. *That particular goods be properly defended by*

[6] *Sum. theol.*, i–ii, 19, 10.

particular persons matter greatly for the common good itself. The wife of the murderer, as she fights for the life of the man whom the common good wants to put to death, does precisely what the common good wants her to do. It is in a merely material fashion that she disagrees with the requirements of the common good: by doing what the common good wants her to do, she formally desires the common good. The common good formally understood is the concern of every genuine virtue, but it is the proper concern of the public person to procure the common good materially understood, which the private person may virtuously oppose.

This analysis of human relations receives increased significance from the truth that it is designed to manifest in the relation between man and God. To the question whether the human will, in order to be good, must conform to the will of God *in volito*, Aquinas answers that the only conformity required is formal and that a formal conformity may well be compatible with material disagreement or even demand such disagreement. God, who takes care of the common good of the universe, holds me responsible for some particular goods and wants me to discharge my responsibility. God may want my father to die tomorrow, but he certainly wants me to do all I can to prolong the life of my father; and if I were told by special revelation, under circumstances making for absolute certainty, that the definite will of God is that my father should die tomorrow at noon, it would still be the will of God that I should struggle against the death of my father until it has become a fact.[7]

Let a second instance be drawn from military life, where hierarchical relations are defined with peculiar clarity. A commanding officer is ordered to hold a certain position at all costs. His orders do not mention any circumstances under which he might retreat. We suppose that his will is entirely good. As a good soldier and a good citizen, he wants and intends the common good of the army and of the whole nation at war, viz., victory. It is in relation to the common good of the army and nation that he aims at this particular good, viz., the holding of this position. Without such subordination of purposes he would not be a true soldier and a good citizen. A mercenary or an adventurer might pledge himself to hold a place without caring who wins the war, but not a soldier. Thus the particular good—holding the place—is willed because of the common good, on the ground of the common good, under a determination supplied by the common good. In other words, there is, as a proper effect of military and civic virtue, volition and intention of the common good formally understood.

It is assumed, of course, that the orders are not absurd and that the holding of this position, at all costs, is precisely what the common good requires. But this *material* issue concerns the high command or, according to the felicitous expression recently coined, the *over-all* strategy board, not this particular commanding officer. All are supposed to refer all their actions to victory, but, so far as material objects of intention are concerned, the good to be intended by this officer is the holding of this position and nothing else, until another task becomes him. He is not in charge of determining what operations over-all strategy demands: the high command is.

[7] John of St Thomas, *Cursus theologicus*, i–ii, disp. 11, a. 4 (Vives, VI, 48 B).

This is what becomes tragically clear when those in charge of the common good materially considered fail to fulfil their task. Anxiety fills the soul of particular persons as it becomes increasingly dubious that the objects assigned to their care are what the common good demands. Holding this position one more day will mean the annihilation of the defenders, with no advantage whatsoever; that is clear, but there is no news from the high command. Those whose job it is to care for the common good materially considered have vanished. By now the defender of a particular position has to do two things; (1) to defend this particular position or to counter-attack or to withdraw his unit safely and (2) to decide what is best for the final victory of the army and nation—defending the place to the last man? counter-attacking? retreating? This duality of duties, viz., taking care of both the *particular* good materially considered (defending the position, counter-attacking, organizing a safe withdrawal) and of the *common* good materially considered (deciding whether it is better to hold the position or to counter-attack or to retreat) is known to induce a sentiment of helplessness that the strongest characters alone can overcome. When the private person has to emerge above his capacity and substitute for non-existent public persons, an awe-inspiring solitude makes him realize that the structure of society has broken down.

Lest this example should suggest that the care of the common good necessarily belongs to distinct persons, consider, instead of an army, a group of pioneers in which there is no government except that of the majority. Suppose that, during an initial phase implying a great deal of scattered activity, the group gathers every second day to make decisions concerning common interests. A flood, a snowfall or interference by a party of competitors may make it impossible for the group to convene over a long period. Then each individual will experience the unnatural situation which confronts an army unit when the high command remains silent in spite of the emergency. Private persons have to take care both of their own business and of the public business. Confusion comes to an end when the assembly convenes again and relieves private persons of cares which are not theirs. The same persons, in fact, laboured in isolation yesterday and today act as one public character. But, in isolation, they are normally qualified for the pursuit of particular goods alone; in assembly they are the mind and will to which it pertains to understand and intend the common good; this difference of capacity is all that essentially matters.

An example of another type would be supplied by a school comprising, say, a teacher of English, a teacher of philosophy, a teacher of Latin, a teacher of history and a teacher of mathematics. The good pursued by each of these men is not particular in the way in which the field ploughed by its owner is particular. The teacher of Latin has for his proper purpose the maintenance and promotion of Latin culture in the community; this pertains to the common good, but, inasmuch as it is only one aspect of the common good, the purpose of the Latin teacher remains particular.

Consider now that the frame of mind of a conscientious Latin teacher may conceivably be either of two. There are Latin scholars of whom one says that, if they had their own way, they would convert every youngster into a Latin scholar, regardless of how ignorant their pupils might be in mathematics, modern languages and even Greek. Such ardent characters supply cartoons and comedies with congenial fun, but their social significance is well known to wise people. There is something absolute about their dedication, the urge of which they are possessed is as uncompromising as a categorical imperative, they are determined to crush obstacles; they show, in fact, little consideration for obstacles arising from their own person, and their devotion generally wears them out. They are good teachers of Latin, their better pupils are fairly good. But what is it that inspires them with such fierce determination? Is it just a passion, to be likened to that of the stamp-collector or of the mountain climber? Not necessarily. The toughest and roughest determinations are those derived from a sense for the *function* that one has to fulfil in society. This old scholar who so faithfully, unambitiously, taught Latin so well for so many years: do not believe that he overdoes the importance of classics and ignores that of mathematics. He may be fully aware of the modesty of his job; his occupational conscience may be pervaded with humility. But one day he realized that his unglamorous job, rather thankless, poorly paid and not too highly considered, was needed for the common good and that a society in which a few men appreciate Vergil is, all other things being equal, better than a society in which Vergil is entirely unknown; and, because there is something sublime about the common good, his vocation, from that day on, was animated with a sense of fervour whose expressions were rough and tough, like everything that is concerned with the absolute. Society is well served by such individuals.

There are, on the other hand, men of skill who feel that it is their duty to keep their own concern well within the proper limits of its real importance. If they happen to be Latin teachers, they will refrain from anything that might look like fanatical zeal for Latin; they will not recommend Latin studies except as part of a balanced programme comprising also modern languages, mathematics, history; if they were consistent, they would not recommend any schooling except as a part of a balanced programme of human activities, comprising the proper amount of sleep, sport, social life, etc. Although such fellows, for obvious reasons, never attract much attention, we know them by daily experience. They do not arouse any complaints; they are occasionally congratulated on their wise-looking serenity; they do not accomplish great things; they pass for civilized and enjoy their reputation. Social observers, stirred by the greater accomplishments of barbarians, would wonder what is wrong and would come to understand that some fundamental error causes the dynamism of the particular skill to be extinguished by improper brainwork. What happens here is the fateful accident of *confusion*, which, understandably, blunts every instrument, stultifies every energy, rules out thoroughness and causes forces to compromise before the elements of necessity in them have had a chance to work. No part of the land will be thoroughly tilled unless each labourer has a distinct field to plough. And no function will be exercised with thoroughness unless my function—say, that of teaching Latin—is distinct from any other function and thereby particularized. But if my function is a particular one, if, in other words, the good with which I am concerned is but a particular aspect of the common good, then it is necessary that there be, above me, a person or a group of persons properly concerned, not only formally but also materially, with the whole of the common good.

Again, let it be remarked that the positing of a distinct governing personnel does not necessarily follow. An assembly of specialists, acting as a body, may transcend the division of labour and have for its proper object the whole of the good whose diverse aspects constitute as many proper objects for its members, when the latter are not convened and do not act as a body. For instance, it is not impossible that the general policy of a school be adequately managed by a committee of teachers. When such a committee convenes, the teacher of Latin is no longer a person whose life is dedicated to the maintenance of Latin culture; he is, by now, a faculty member dedicated to the whole purpose of the school, understood and desired in its entirety, with all the relations of priority and subordination that the good of a society implies. Shifting from a particular function to an over-all concern is possible, but generally difficult; the mental habits of the specialists are hard to overcome. Hence the rule that the authority in charge of controlling experts should be made of non-experts. It is understood that the latter are supposed to be expert in a pursuit known to involve special difficulties, viz., that of the good which is not, by any means, special.

The theory emerging from these and such examples and analyses can be summed up in the following propositions:

Under the assumption that the society with which we are concerned is aiming at a common good, it is stated:

1. That virtue implies love for the common good, willingness to sacrifice one's own advantage to its requirements.

2. That the common good may be intended formally without being intended materially.

3. That the virtue of the private person guarantees the intention of the common good formally considered, not the intention of the common good materially considered.

4. That society would be harmed if everyone intended the common good not only formally but also materially; that, in a material sense, particular persons and groups ought to intend particular goods.

5. That the intention of the common good, materially considered, is the business of a public reason and a public will.

6. That the intention of the common good by the public reason and will necessarily develops into a *direction* of society, by the public reason and will, toward the common good considered not only formally but also materially; which is the same as to say that the intention of the common good, materially considered, demands the operation of authority.

Let our exposition proceed, for a while, by way of a comment on these propositions.

The preliminary assumption specifies that the theory holds only for societies aiming at a common good. In fact, many theorists take it for granted that without a common good there is no society. Yet, according to universal and very ancient usage, the term "society" can be predicated of such a partnership as that of a handicraftsman and a moneylender. If a partnership of this sort were relative to a common good, the argumentation which derives the need for authority from the requirements of the common good would be invalidated, for the relation between handicraftsman and moneylender is purely contractual. They exchange promises, but from their promises it does not result that anyone should command and anyone obey. In the incidental case of broken pledges, authority would step in and see that contracts are lived up to; but it would be the authority of civil society, not any authority immanent in the society under consideration. True, it looks as if the moneylender and handicraftsman society was founded for the pursuit of a common good. The gentlemen speak loudly of their common interest. Suppose that in case of prosperity one of them gets 10 per cent. of the invested capital and the other one 20 per cent.; is it not clear that such prosperous returns constitute the purpose for which these men became associates, the common good of their association? The case is of great theoretical interest, because it supplies a perfectly pure example of *pseudo-common good*. One of these gentlemen proposes to get 10 per cent., and this is an entirely private good; the other proposes to get 20 per cent. and this is a no less private good; as to the 30 per cent. which constitutes the sum total of the coveted return, it is a sum of private goods which looks like a common good but is not. It lacks one of the defining features of the common good, viz., the intelligible aspect by which the common good calls for communion in desire and common action. In order that a good be common, it does not suffice that it should concern, in some way or other, several persons; it is necessary that it be of such nature as to cause, among those who pursue it and in so far as they pursue it, a common life of desire and action. Whenever the good interesting several persons or groups causes (or, more precisely, is of such nature as to cause) such common life, it is a genuine common good and renders authority necessary. If, on the other hand, a good interesting several does not call for a common life of desire and action, it does not call for authority either, and it admits of purely contractual relations. Rather than a common good, it is the sum of particular goods that happen to be related to one another. The moneylender is looking for his own income and the handicraftsman is looking for his own income; but their two particular goods are parts of a sum—hence the partnership and the appearance of a common good.

It was often remarked that the expressions "the greatest good of the greatest number" and "the general interest", which prevailed throughout the golden age of individualism, designated a sum of individual goods rather than a common good. Strikingly, the same age and the same schools of thought cherished, in varying degree of radicalness, a contractual interpretation of the state or the ideal of a purely contractual society into which the state would have resolved. This is perfectly logical. Let us say, to sum up, that the ground for the constitution of a society is either the attainment of a common good or that of interdependent private goods; in the first case there is need for authority; in the second, contract suffices. Conversely, if a society needs authority (for essential reasons), it has a common good for its ground, and if a society can afford to be purely contractual, it has no other grounds than the interdependence of private goods.

The difficulties involved in the first statement ("that virtue implies love for the common good . . .") concern general treatises, most properly the treatise on moral virtues. Let us merely remark that the principle of the primacy of the common good, often misunderstood or denied by the theorists of ethics, has, in fact, an extraordinarily powerful hold on the consciences of men. People of debased conduct and sceptical judgement still find it natural to die for their country or for such substitute for a country as a gang. And during the golden age of individualism the conscience of men, in spite of what the theorists had to say, often recognized the common good and served it with devotion under such improper names as "general interest" or "greatest good of the greatest number".

The second statement ("that the common good may be intended formally without being intended materially") expresses a sheer fact and needs merely to be illustrated by examples. This has been done. An army officer, wholly dedicated to victory and determined to hold a certain position according to his orders, may not be intending the common good materially considered; he may not be intending what is actually required by the common good, for new circumstances may require evacuation and withdrawal. And the son of a murderer, himself a good citizen, wants the life of his father to be preserved, even though the common good may demand capital punishment.

The third statement ("that the virtue of the private person guarantees only the intention of the common good formally considered") signifies that failure to intend the common good materially considered is not necessarily traceable to lack of moral excellence. If what victory demands is evacuation and withdrawal, it is up to the high command to issue new orders; and it is up to the courts to see that society is protected by adequate punishment of crime. Any particular difficulty raised by this statement resolves into the difficulties pertaining to statement No. 4 ("that, in a material sense, particular persons and groups ought to intend particular goods"), which is the keystone of the whole theory.

Seemingly, all would be best if each member of a community intended the common good both in formal and in material fashion. Because of the limitations of men, a continual and unfailing adherence of everyone to what is actually demanded by the common good cannot be realized. But why should it not be desirable, if it were realizable? Why should it not be posited in the construct of an ideal community? Why not promoted, in so far as it is realizable, in our imperfect societies? The statement seems to put a restriction on love for the common good, as if too much of it might harm.

It is, indeed, harmful to ignore the laws of the one and the many. These laws are independent of human deficiencies and transcend human affairs; they are metaphysical. Goodness implies unity, but the notion of unity, as divided into "unity of the individual" and "unity of the multitude", involves an order of anteriority and posteriority. The unity of a properly unified multitude is less of a unity than the unity of an individual. The degree of unity that a multitude admits of is the same thing as the kind of unity that it calls for. Although unity is an absolute perfection, there can be too much of it, inasmuch as, beyond a certain measure, the inappropriate kind forcibly displaces the proper one and destruction results. Such is the meaning of Aristotle's celebrated objections to the communism of Plato.

It is easy to see how uniformity can do violence to the nature of multitude and cause waste. The systematic extinction of qualitative diversity impairs the kind of plenitude that it is the metaphysical function of the many to achieve; and if the purpose is to effect the highest degree of unity, a multitude, no matter how thoroughly uniformized, is bound to remain second to individuality, that is, one man would be nearer to the goal than any commonwealth, even though it be made of puppets all carved and dressed after the same pattern. At this point, the statement under discussion acquires a new clarity, for we come to recognize in it a particular case of a familiar, altogether congenial, and almost uncontroverted formula. Imagine a multitude in which all intend the common good, materially as well as formally, and refrain from intending any particular good, even though in merely material fashion; this multitude has achieved thorough uniformity. Its uniformity is the most radical of all and comprises virtually all kinds of uniformity. Behind the uniformity resulting from rationalized industry and mass production, qualitative diversity survives, so long as my heart is filled with love for persons of unique significance; but suppose that, through a skilful arrangement of society, no old man is known to have the distinction of being my father, no man is known to be more of a brother to me than any other man and no boy is known to be more of a son to me than any other boy; permanent grounds for the love of the particular are destroyed. A man may happen to have a special affection for a certain old man, but the common good has a monopoly on permanent grounds for love and devotion. In the order of final causality, the common alone stands; the particular no longer plays the part of a cause. Its causal power has disappeared into the causal power of the whole. But the end is the form of the will and in so far as the whole alone retains the character of an end, only one form is left for all wills.

The construct of a society in which the common good is intended materially by all results from an accident in the treatment of the subordination of causes. When the supremacy of a subordinating cause, its uniqueness, and the unutterable qualitative distance which separates it from the subordinated causes are keenly realized, the metaphysical intellect happens, not infrequently, to lose its balance. An exalted vision of the subordinating cause brings about, after the fashion of a by-product, the impairment and, as a limit, the annihilation of the subordinated causes. In not a few systems of metaphysics or theology, God alone is the genuinely efficient cause, and his sovereign power confronts a universe deprived of causality, of life, of liberty and perhaps of reality. Contrasting with this picture of a waste land, the God of the living, who does not need to lay things waste in order to assert his power, is powerful enough to cause every thing and every act and every modality of every act in a world whose law is one of plenitude and superabundance, in a world full of reality, of autonomy, of activity, of life and of liberty.

A society in which none intends, even materially, a particular good is like a dead world. Would such sacrifices serve any purpose? Far from being genuinely exalted, the common good has become a mere appearance. Common good cannot exist unless it does exist as the good of a multitude; but there is no good "of a multitude" unless particular goods are intended by particular appetites and taken care of by particular agents. The laws of distinction inside the multiple were ignored; confusion ended in destruction.

The *Republic* of Plato supplies a clear pattern of institutions designed to keep down to a minimum all interest in particular goods. On the other hand, Plato perceives with unique keenness the need for distinction in society. The meaning of this contrast can be explained by considering that there are two ways in which a good can be particular: (1) particular, as opposed to common, qualifies the good whose subject is but a part of society; (2) particular, as opposed to "over-all or "whole" or "general"— we do not have very good words to express these important concepts —qualifies the good which is but a part or an aspect of the common good, although its subject is not a part but the whole of society. Referring to the examples described above, let it be said that the welfare of a family, as distinct from the welfare of the state, has the character of a particular good in the first sense; that the objective of an army unit (e.g., holding a strategic position), as distinct from the objective of the whole army and of the nation at war, is likewise particular in the first sense; that the good pursued by an ardent teacher of Latin is particular in the second sense and—in case the latter example is not deemed clear enough—that the objective of the director of public health is also particular in the second sense. Public health is obviously a good whose subject or beneficiary is the whole of society; but this good is not the whole of the common good, it is only an important part or aspect of it. In order to clarify our terminology, we shall, from now on, call "private" the good which is particular in the first sense, "special" the one particular in the second sense, and use the word "particular" itself only to express the likeness, the relative unity, of the "private" and the "special". A homestead owned by a farmer is particular as private; a function exercised by a public servant is particular as special: the terms "homestead" and "function" may be conveniently used as symbols of these two principles of distinction.

In order to remove confusion from their midst, most societies use both principles. Plato opposes the former, or at least opposes several important aspects of the former, and consequently is led to emphasize strongly the latter. That everyone should mind his own business is for him an intrinsic condition of justice; but, with regard to the way of establishing a clear distinction between the business of the one and the business of the other, he tends to rely exclusively upon the division of social labour into functions, as if the division of the land into homesteads should endanger the unity of the commonwealth.

If statement No. 4 is considered established, statements Nos. 5 ("that the intention of the common good, materially considered, is the business of a public reason and of a public will") and 6 ("that the intention of the common good, materially considered, demands the operation of authority") hardly call for elaboration. It is obvious that the common good has to be intended not only formally but also materially; if it is established that it should not be intended materially by particular persons, it follows that a non-particular reason and will ought to be constituted; otherwise the common good, materially considered, would not be intended at all. But what relation will there be between those in charge of the common good and those whose duty it is to intend, in a material sense, particular goods? Clearly, the very principle of the primacy of the common good demands that the intentions of the latter be subordinated to the intentions of the former. The primacy of the common good demands that those in charge of particular goods should obey those in charge of the common good. It is, in the last analysis, as simple as that. And let it be remarked, once more, that these propositions do not imply any definite stand concerning the creation of a distinct governing personnel. Those in charge of the common good and those in charge of particular goods may be distinct groups of persons—this is what happens in most cases; but the private persons who make up the multitude may all convene in a town meeting or *Landgemeinschaft*; they no longer are private persons, they are the public reason and will, endowed with the power to direct private persons toward the common good.

Throughout this inquiry into the intention of the common good, we have been referring both to the particularity of the homestead and to that of the function. Each kind of particularity suffices to make authority necessary. If the particularity of the homestead, i.e., particularity by way of privateness, were done away with—as in a thoroughly communist society—the particularity of the function, i.e., particularity by way of speciality, would still, all by itself, render authority indispensable. Actually, experience does not suggest that the importance of authority declines when functional diversity stands as the only way to remove confusion from society. Authority is overwhelming in the *Republic* of Plato, and it is, to say the least, very strong in all communities which tend to do without the homestead as a factor of distinction. Considering, on the other hand, that diverse functions are, or may be, all relative to the common good, we come to understand that, with regard to the intention of the common good, authority is necessary on two grounds: (1) in order that there be intention of the common good materially considered, and (2) in order that the common good materially considered be intended in its totality and according to all the relations of priority and posteriority, pre-eminence and subordination, that its integrality requires. Think of the various great administrations which constitute the permanent structure of government in modern states: interior, treasury, foreign affairs, army, navy, agriculture, education. The men who make them up are adequately called "functionaries"; their tasks are directly related to the common good, none of them is supposed to labour for any private good, except in so far as he gets a recompense for services that are essentially public. If a cabinet is needed, on top of these administrations, it is not precisely in order that private agents should be directed toward the public welfare; the agents are already public, they are, by occupation, servants of society, and, in so far as they behave ethically, none of their actvities during working hours is related to private purposes. In line with the hypothesis needed in this search for the essential, let us assume, comic though it may sound, that these functionaries are all perfectly competent and thoroughly disinterested. Under such an assumption it is not precisely in order that they be watched, stirred to action, kept from doing harm, encouraged and punished that a cabinet is needed. Yet, although public administrations are, by essence, relative to the common good, as distinct from the private good, and even though we suppose the administrators to be free from private concern, the sheer fact that each administration has a *special* task to fulfil makes it necessary that there be, on top of all departments, a non-departmental agent, a non-specialized agent, or, if this expression is clearer, an agent specialized in having the point of view of the *entire* common good prevail over any special angle.

Thus the proposition that authority is necessary to the intention of the common good has a double meaning. It means, first, that authority is necessary in order for private persons to be directed toward the common good; it means, second, that authority is necessary in order for functional processes, each of which regards some aspect of the common good, to be directed toward the whole of the common good.

Of the three functions of authority that we have surveyed, the first is substitutional, the second is essential and the third deserves to be termed "most essential", since it concerns the most fundamental act of social life. In a society composed exclusively of clever, virtuous and fully mature persons, authority would have no paternal duty to exercise; it would have to effect unity of action whenever the means to the common good is not uniquely determined; it would, above all and first of all, have to procure the intention of the common good. Considered in its essential functions, authority is neither a necessary evil nor a lesser good nor a lesser evil nor the consequence of any evil or deficiency—it is, like nature and society, unqualifiedly good.

The Freedom of Man in the Freedom of the* Church

John Courtney Murray, S.J.

As the standpoint for my remarks I shall assume that we now stand at the "end of modern times". The phrase, in one or other variant, has come into common use. Whether "modern times" began with the fall of Constantinople in the fifteenth century, or with the rise of Gnosticism in the second century, is a matter of dispute. But there is some scholarly agreement today that the spiritual era known as "modern" is running to a close. A new era is beginning. Almost everything about it is unpredictable, save that it will be an era of unprecedented dangers. The danger of violent destruction threatens the physical fabric of civilization. And the spiritual nature of man himself is menaced by more insidious corruptions. I have no wish to be a prophet of *Untergang*; I do not believe that downfall is our inevitable civilization fate. But I do think that confusion is the present civilizational fact. Were it not so, this conference would not have convened.

Is the Problem today rightly identified, in one word, as "freedom"? The point might be argued. In any case, the Problem is not "freedom" in the sense in which modernity has understood the term. So rapidly have the generations slipped beneath our feet that the prophets of modernity and of its "freedom"—the Miltons and the Mills, the Madisons and the Jeffersons—have already begun to seem slightly neolithic figures to our backward glance. Certain of their insights retain validity. But the adequacy of their systems can no longer be upheld. The broad question has arisen, whether the problem of freedom in the post-modern era can be satisfactorily dealt with in terms of philosophies (and theologies) which bear too heavily the stamp of modernity.

The problem does not centre on some minor malfunctions of the mechanisms of freedom. Our "free institutions", in their procedural aspects, are working today as well as they ever have worked or ever will work. Some tinkering with them may be needed. But tinkering is not our full task. It is characteristic of the present moment that all the serious talk is about Basic Issues.

The initial difficulty is that these Basic Issues are not easily located and defined. Perhaps rather abruptly, I shall venture a twofold formulation.

First, the Basic Issues of our time concern the spiritual substance of a free society, as it has historically derived from the central Christian concept, *res sacra homo*, "Man is a sacredness" (only the abstract noun can render the Latin rightly). Second, the Basic Issues concern the fundamental structure of a free society. I do not mean its legal structure, as constitutionally established; few of the real problems today are suscept-

* From *The Modern Age*; see p. x above.

ible of solution, or even of statement, in legal language. I mean rather the ontological structure of society, of which the constitutional order should be only the reflection. This underlying social structure is a matter of theory; that is, it is to be conceived in terms of a theorem with regard to the relation between the sacrednesses inherent in man and the manifold secularities amid which human life is lived.

This twofold formulation is very general. I set it down thus to make clear my conviction that the Basic Issues today can only be conceived in metaphysical and theological terms. They are issues of truth. They concern the nature and structure of reality itself—meaning by reality the order of nature as accessible to human reason, and the economy of salvation as disclosed by the Christian revelation.

But these general formulas may not be useful for purposes of argument. And argument, I take it, is our purpose. Therefore a more pragmatic approach to our problem is indicated. No philosopher today will uphold the crude tenet of an older outworn pragmatism, that whatever works is true. But any philosopher must acknowledge the more subtle truth, that whatever is not true will somehow fail to work. Prof. Hocking has stated the case in his book, *The Coming World Civilization*: "For whatever is real in the universe is no idle object of speculation; it is a working factor in experience or it is nothing. Consciously or subconsciously we are always dealing with it; to entertain false notions about it, or simply to neglect it, will bring about maladjustments which thrust this neglect forward into consciousness. A false metaphysic, engendering empirical malaise, calls for a new work of thought, begetting an altered premise."

The statement suggests a method of inquiry. What are our malaises today? That is, what are the discomforts and uneasinesses that trouble, not the surface of mind and soul, but their very depths? Are these distresses somehow traceable to falsities in the philosophy that has inspired the political experiment of modernity? If so, what new work of thought is needed? And what alterations in the premises of the modern experiment are called for?

A process of questioning, more or less inspired by this method, has been going on of late; and in the course of it many ideas dear to a later modernity have found their way into Trotsky's famous "dustbin of history".

For instance, we no longer cherish the bright and brittle eighteenth-century concept of "reason"; we do not believe in the principle of automatic harmony nor in the inevitability of progress. We have rejected that principle of modernity which asserted that government is the only enemy of freedom. We see that the modern concept of freedom itself was dangerously inadequate because it neglected the corporate dimension of freedom. We see too that modernity was wrong in isolating the problem of freedom from its polar terms—responsibility, justice, order, law. We have realized that the modern experiment, originally conceived only as an experiment in Freedom, had to become also an experiment in Justice. We know that the myopic individualism of modernity led it into other errors, even into a false conception of the problem of the state in terms of the unreal dichotomy, individualism vs. collectivism. We have come to disbelieve the cardinal tenet of modernity which regarded every advance in man's domination over nature—that is, every new accumulation of power—as necessarily liberating. We have begun to understand the polyvalence of power. In fact, we know that we are post-modern men, living in a new age, chiefly because we have begun to see what modernity never saw—that the central problem is not the realization of the Cartesian dream. This dream today is largely reality; man is the master of nature. Our problem now is the dissolution of a nightmare that never visited Descartes—the horrid vision of man, master of nature, but not master of himself.

It may be useful here to carry this process of questioning further, and to an altogether basic level. This can best be done, I think, by viewing the modern political experiment in its continuity with the longer liberal tradition of the West. My generalization will be that the political experiment of modernity has essentially consisted in an effort to find and install in the world a secular substitute for all that the Christian tradition has meant by the pregnant phrase, the "freedom of the Church". This freedom, though not a freedom of the political order, was Christianity's basic contribution to freedom in the political order. Some brief articulation of the concept will initially be necessary. Modernity dropped the phrase out of its political vocabulary, and eliminated the thing from its political edifice, and installed in its place a secular surrogate—this will be my second assertion. Thirdly, I shall attempt to identify some of the more acute stresses and distresses currently being experienced at our present stage in the modern experiment. Finally, I shall attempt to state some of the spiritual issues which lie, I think, at the origin of our empirical malaises. It will be sufficient for my purpose simply to present these issues for argument.

I

In his book, *Libertas: Kirche and Weltordnung im Zeitalter des Investiturstreites* (a broad study of the basic issues involved in that great medieval struggle between opposed conceptions of the nature and order of Christian society which centred around Gregory VII), Gerd Tellenback writes: "In moments of considered solemnity, when their tone was passionate and their religious feeling at its deepest, Gregory VII and his contemporaries called the object towards which they were striving the 'freedom' of the Church." More than six centuries earlier the same idea had inspired Ambrose in his conflicts with Gratian and Theodosius. And eight centuries later, Leo XIII used the same phrase to define the goal of his striving in a more radical conflict between the Church and modernity, now fully developed not only as a spirit but also as a polity. In more than sixty Leonine documents the phrase, the "freedom of the church", appears some eighty-one times.

On any showing, even merely historical, we are here in the presence of a Great Idea, whose entrance into history marked the beginning of a new civilizational era.

It is an historical commonplace to say that the essential political effect of Christianity was to destroy the classical view of society as a single homogeneous structure, within which the political power stood forth as the representative of society both in its religious and in its political aspects. Augustus was both *Summus Imperator* and *Pontifex Maximus*; the *ius divinum* was simply part of the *ius civile*; and outside the empire there was no other society, but only barbarism. The new Christian view was based on a radical distinction between order of the sacred and the order of the secular: "Two there are, august Emperor, by which this world is ruled on title of original and sovereign right—the consecrated authority of the priesthood and the royal power." In this celebrated sentence of Gelasius I, written to the Byzantine Emperor Anastasius I in A.D. 494, the emphasis laid on the word "two" bespoke the revolutionary character of the Christian dispensation.

In his book, *Sacrum Imperium*, Alois Dempf called this Gelasian text the "Magna Charta of the whole 'freedom of the Church' in medieval times". It was the charter of a new freedom, such as the world had never known. Moreover, it was a freedom with which man could not enfranchise himself, since it was the effect of God's own "magnificent dispensation", in Gelasius' phrase. The whole patristic and medieval tradition, which Leo XIII reiterated to the modern world, asserts the freedom of the Church to be a participation in the freedom of the Incarnate Son of God, the God-Man, Christ Jesus.

For our purposes here we can consider this new freedom to be twofold. First, there is the freedom of the Church as a spiritual authority. To the Church is entrusted the *cura animarum*; and this divine commission endows her with the freedom to teach, to rule and to sanctify, with all that these empowerments imply as necessary for their free exercise. This positive freedom has a negative aspect—the immunity of the Church, as the suprapolitical sacredness (*res sacra*), from all manner of politicization, through subordination to the state, or enclosure within the state as *instrumentum regni*. Second, there is the freedom of the Church as the Christian people—their freedom to have access to the teaching of the Church, to obey her laws, to receive at her hands the sacramental ministry of grace and to live within her fold an integral supernatural life. In turn, the inherent suprapolitical dignity of this life itself claims "for the faithful the enjoyment of the right to live in civil society according to the precepts of reason and conscience" (Pius XI). And this comprehensive right, asserted within the political community, requires as its complement that all the intrapolitical sacredness (*res sacra in temporalibus*) be assured of their proper immunity from politicization.

This concept, the *res sacra in temporalibus*, had all the newness of Christianity itself. It embraces all those things which are part of the temporal life of man, at the same time that, by reason of their Christian mode of existence, or by reason of their finality, they transcend the limited purposes of the political order and are thus invested with a certain sacredness. The chief example is the institution of the family—the marriage contract itself, and the relationships of husband and wife, parent and child. Included also are other human relationships in so far as they involve a moral element and require regulation in the interests of the personal dignity of man. Such, for instance, are the employer-employee relationship and the reciprocal relationships established by the political obligation. Sacred too is the intellectual patrimony of the human race, the heritage of basic truths about the nature of man, amassed by secular experience and reflection, that form the essential content of the social consensus and furnish the basic guarantee that within society conditions of freedom and justice, prosperity and order will prevail, at least to some essential human degree.

Instinctively and by natural inclination the common man knows that he cannot be free if his basic human things are not sacredly immune from profanation by the power of the state and by other secular powers. The question has always been that of identifying the limiting norm that will check the encroachments of secular power and preserve these sacred immunities. Western civilization found this norm in the pregnant principle, the freedom of the Church.

I should perhaps emphasize that the phrase must be given its full meaning. As a matter of history, the liberal tradition of Western politics did not begin its lengthy, slow and halting evolution because something like Harnack's wraith-like *Wesen des Christentums* began to pervade the dominions of imperial Rome. This pale phantom would have been altogether unequal to the task of inaugurating a new political history. What appeared within history was not an "idea" or an "essence" but an existence, a Thing, a visible institution that occupied ground in this world at the same time that it asserted an astounding new freedom on a title not of this world. Through the centuries a new tradition of politics was wrought out very largely in the course of the wrestlings between the new freedom of the Church and the pretensions of an older power which kept discovering, to its frequent chagrin, that it was not the one unchallengeable ruler of the world and that its rule was not unlimitedly free.

In regard of the temporal order and its powers and processes this complex Existent Thing, the "freedom of the Church", performed a twofold function. First, the freedom of the Church as the spiritual authority served as the limiting principle of the power of government. It furnished, as it were, a corporate or social armature to the sacred order, within which *res sacra homo* would be secure in all the freedoms that his sacredness demands. Men found their freedom where they found their faith—within the Church. As it was her corporate faith that they professed, so it was her corporate freedom that they claimed, in the face of the public power and of all private powers. Within the armature of her immunities they and their human things were immune from profanation. Second, the freedom of the Church as the "people of God" furnished the ultimate directive principle of government. To put it briefly, the Church stood, as it were, between the body politic and the public power, not only limiting the reach of the power over the people, but also mobilizing the moral consensus of the people and bringing it to bear upon the power, thus to ensure that the king, in the fine phrase of John of Salisbury, would "fight for justice and for the freedom of the people".

This was the new Christian theorem. I leave aside the historical question, whether and to what extent the theorem was successfully institutionalized. What matters is the theorem itself: the freedom of the Church, in its pregnant meaning, was conceived to be the key to the Christian order of society. What further matters is the historical fact that the whole equilibrium of social forces which under the guidance of this theory made (however imperfectly) for freedom and justice within society was destroyed by the rise of the national monarchies and by the course of their political evolution in the era of royal absolutism.

II

The basic effort of modern politics, as I have suggested, looked to a re-establishment of the equilibrium. In a much too rapid description of it, the process was simple. The early Christian dualism of Church and state (or better, the dyarchy of Gelasius' "Two there are") was in a sense retained—that is, it endured in a secular political form, namely, in the distinction between state and society which has been the secular political outgrowth of the Christian distinction between Church and state. However, the freedom of the Church, again in its pregnant sense, was discarded as the mediating principle between society and state, between the people and the public power. Instead, a secular substitute was adopted in the form of free political institutions. Through these secular institutions the people would limit the power of government; they would also direct the power of government to its proper ends, which are perennially those of John of Salisbury—the fight for justice and for the freedom of the people.

The key to the whole new political edifice was the freedom of the individual conscience. Here, precisely, lies the newness of the modern experiment. A great act of trust was made. The trust was that the free individual conscience would effectively mediate the moral imperatives of the transcendental order of justice (whose existence was not doubted in the earlier phases of the modern experiment). Then, through the workings of free political institutions these imperatives would be transmitted to the public power as binding norms upon its action. The only sovereign spiritual authority would be the conscience of the free man. The freedom of the individual conscience, constitutionally guaranteed, would supply the armature of immunity to the sacred order, which now became, by modern definition, precisely the order of the private conscience. And through free political institutions, again constitutionally guaranteed, the moral consensus of the community would be mobilized in favour of justice and freedom in the secular order. This, I take it, has been in essence the political experiment of modernity. It has been an attempt to carry on the liberal tradition of Western politics, whose roots were in the Christian revolution, but now on a new revolutionary basis—a rejection of the Gelasian thesis, "Two there are", which had been the dynamic of the Christian revolution.

I take it, without fear of contradiction, that the rejection of the Gelasian thesis has been common to all the prophets of modernity, from Marsilius of Padua onwards. All of them have been united in viewing the freedom of the Church, in the sense explained, as a trespass upon, and a danger to, their one supreme value—the "integrity of the political order", as the phrase goes. Two citations may be given as illustrative. Rousseau complains: "Jesus came to establish on earth a spiritual kingdom. By separating the theological system from the political system he brought it about that the State ceased to be one, and caused internal divisions which have never ceased to agitate Christian peoples. From this twofold power there has resulted a perpetual conflict of jurisdiction which has rendered all good politics impossible in Christian states. No one has ever been able to know which one to obey, priest or political ruler." Thomas Hobbes put the same issue with characteristic bluntness and clarity: "Temporal and spiritual government are but words brought into the world to make men see double and mistake their lawful sovereign", which is Leviathan, the Mortal God.

In this indictment of Christianity for having made the state "cease to be one", and in this protest against men who "see double", one hears the authentic voice of the secular power as modern history has known it.

It would not be difficult to demonstrate that this monistic tendency is somehow inherent in the state, in two of its aspects—both as an expression of reason and also as a vehicle of power. Nor would it be difficult to show how this monistic tendency has been visible in practically all the states that have paraded across the stage of history, even in states that bore the name of Christian. In any case, the tendency has achieved its most striking success in the modern era. It is the most salient aspect of political modernity. Over the whole of modern politics there has hung the monist concept of the indivisibility of sovereignty: "One there is." This has been true even in those states in which the sovereignty, remaining indivisible, has been institutionalized according to the principle of the separation of powers.

The dynamism behind the assertion, "One there is", has, of course, varied. In the seventeenth and eighteenth centuries it was royal absolutism, whose theorists—Widdrington, Barclay, James I—proclaimed a social and juridical monism in the name of the divine right of kings. In the nineteenth century the dynamism was the Revolution, that whole complex of forces which created Jacobin democracy and proclaimed the *république indivisible* in the name of the sovereignty of the people understood as the social projection of the absolutely autonomous sovereignty of individual reason. In the twentieth century the most successful dynamism has been Soviet Communism, which makes the assertion, "One there is", in the name of the unitary class which is destined for world sovereignty, and in the name of its organ, the Party, whose function is to be the servant and ally of the materialist forces of history.

In the twentieth century too, as the modern era runs out, the ancient monistic drive to a oneness of society, law and authority has also appeared in the totalitarianizing tendency inherent in the contemporary idolatry of the democratic process. This democratic monism is urged in the name of something less clear than the *république indivisible*. What is urged is a monism, not so much of the political order itself, as of a political technique. The proposition is that all the issues of human life—intellectual, religious and moral issues as well as formally political issues—are to be regarded as, or resolved into, political issues and are to be settled by the single omnicompetent political technique of majority vote. On the surface the monism is one of process; Madison's "republican principle" affords the Final Grounds for the Last Say on All Human Questions. But the underlying idea is a monism of power: "One there is whereby this world is ruled—the power in the people, expressing itself in the preference of a majority; and beyond or beside or above this power there is no other."

The inspiration of democratic monism is partly a sentimentalist mystique—the belief that the power in the people, in distinction from all other powers, is somehow ultimately and inevitably beneficent in its exercise. But the more radical inspiration is the new idea, unknown to medieval times, which modern rationalism thrust into political history. Christianity has always regarded the state as a limited order of action for limited purposes, to be chosen and pursued under the direction and correction of the organized moral conscience of society, whose judgements are formed and mobilized by the Church, an independent and autonomous community, qualified to be the interpreter of man's nature and destiny. It has been specific of modernity to regard the state as a moral end in itself, a self-justifying entity with its own self-determined spiritual substance. It is within the secular state, and by appeal to secular sources, that man is to find the interpretation of his own nature and the means to his own destiny. The state itself creates the ethos of society, embodies it, imparts it to its citizens and sanctions its observance with rewards and punishments. Outside the tradition of Jacobin or Communist dogmatism, the modern democratic secular state does not indeed pretend to be the Universe or to speak infallibly. But it does assert itself to be the embodiment of whatever fallible human wisdom may be available to man, because it is the highest school of human experience, beyond which man can find no other School and no other Teacher.

Professor Hocking has put the matter thus: "Outside the Marxist orbit the prevalent disposition of the secular state in recent years has been less to combat the Church than to carry on a slow empirical demonstration of the state's full equivalence in picturing the attainable good life, and its superior pertinence to actual issues. As this demonstration gains force the expectation grows that it will be the Church, not the state, that will wither away. Where the fields of Church and state impinge on each other, as in education and correction, the Church will in time appear superfluous. Where they are different, the Church will be quietly ignored and dropped as irrelevant." This, says Hocking, is the "secular hypothesis". It is, he adds, the premise of the "experiment we call 'modernity'". In the language I have been using, the hypothesis asserts: "One there is by which the world is ruled."

The "one" here (sc., outside the Marxist orbit) is the self-conscious free individual, armed with his subjective rights, whose ultimate origins he may have forgotten but whose status as legal certitudes he cherishes. This individual, the product of modernity, has been taught by modernity to stand against any external and corporate authority, except it be mediated to him by democratic processes, to stand against any law in whose making he had no voice; to stand finally against any society which asserts itself to be an independent community of thought, superior to the consensus created by the common mind of secular democratic society, and empowered to pass judgement, in the name of higher criteria, on this common mind and on the consensus it assembles.

Outside the Jacobin and Communist traditions this "one ruler", the modern man, does not object to religion, provided that religion be regarded as a private matter which concerns only the conscience and feelings of the individual. In his more expansive moments he will not object even to organized religion—the "churches"—provided they accept the status of voluntary associations for limited purposes which do not impinge upon the public order. But he will not tolerate any marring of his image of the world as modernity conceives it—the image of democratic society as the universal community whose ends are co-extensive with the ends of man himself. It is the One Society, with One Law and with One Sovereign, the politically equal people. Modernity has declared the Gelasian doctrine to be heretical and has outlawed it, in the name of modern orthodoxy, which is a naturalist rationalism.

This dominant image of democratic society as ultimately monist in its structure (whatever may be its constituent and subordinate pluralisms), and as ultimately secular in its substance (whatever historical tribute it may have levied on religious spiritualities), represents the refined essence of political modernity. Its significance lies in the fact that it confronts us with an experiment in human freedom which has consciously or unconsciously been based on a denial or a disregard of the essential Christian contribution to human freedom, which is the theorem of the freedom of the Church.

III

We come now to the uneasinesses stirring in the world of post-modern man, and in his soul too. The first may be quickly run over, although it is most profoundly serious. I mean all the uneasiness aroused by our confrontation with international Communism. Communism is, of course, political modernity carried to its logical conclusion. All that is implicit and unintentional in modernity as a phenomenon in what is called the West has become explicit and deliberate in the Communist system. The "secular hypothesis", in Hocking's phrase, has been lifted to the status of a dogma. And Hobbes' prohibition has seen most vicious enforcement; man is not allowed to "see double and mistake his lawful sovereign". The operations of the Communist system would seem to offer an empirical demonstration of the fact that there can be no freedom or justice where God is denied and where everything meant by the freedom of the Church is deliberately excised from the theorem on which the life of the community is based.

The measure of human malaise within the Communist orbit cannot be estimated accurately. In any case, the malaise cannot be geographically contained. Stress and distress are the condition of the whole world. And we ourselves feel them, or at least should feel them, most sharply in the form of the question, whether we are spiritually and intellectually equipped to meet the Communist threat at its deepest level.

Communism in theory and in practice has reversed the revolution which Christianity initiated by the Gelasian doctrine: "Two there are by which this world is ruled." This new system has proposed with all logic an alternative to the basic structure of society, and a surrogate of society's spiritual substance, as these are defined in the Christian theorem. And the question is, whether there are in the spirit of modernity as such the resources whereby the Christian revolution, with all its hopes of freedom and justice, can be reinstated in its course, and the reactionary counter-revolution halted. The issue is clear enough; two contrary views of the structure of reality are in conflict. And the issue is certainly basic—too basic to be solved either by military measures or by political techniques. Free elections, for instance, have their value. But of themselves they leave untouched the basic issue, which is joined between the clashing assertions: "Two there are", and "One there is".

The second post-modern uneasiness derives from the current experience of the "impotence of the state". Here I adopt Hocking's phrase and the thesis it states, as developed in the first part of his book, already cited. (With certain of his subsequent analyses and theses, and with their Gnostic overtones, I have serious difficulties.) The net of it is that the modern state has, as a matter of empirical fact, proved impotent to do all the things it has undertaken to do. Crime and civic virtue, education, the stimulus and control of economic processes, public morality, justice in the order and processes of law—over all these things the modern state assumed an unshared competence. But it has proved itself incompetent in a fundamental sense. The reason is that "the state depends for its vitality upon a motivation which it cannot by itself command". As long as this motivation can be assumed to be existent in the body politic, the order of politics (in the broadest sense) moves with some security to its proper ends. But if the motivation fails, there is no power in the state itself to evoke it.

We confront again the dilemma which modernity resolved in its own sense. Is the life of man to be organized in one society, or in two? Modernity chose the unitary hypothesis, that the state itself is the highest form of human association, self-ruled, and self-contained, and self-motivating. But the unitary hypothesis has not been able to sustain itself under the test of experience. Post-modern man has become most uneasily aware of the limitations of the state even in the discharge of its own functions.

The challenge here is to the validity of the suprapolitical tenet upon which modernity staked the whole success of its political experiment. This tenet, I said, was that the individual conscience is the sole ultimate interpreter of the moral order (and of the religious order too), and therefore the sole authentic mediator of moral imperatives to the political order. But the truth of this tenet, confidently assumed by modernity, is now under challenge from a battery of questions.

Is the failure of motivation within the state somehow due to the falsity of this tenet? Is the pragmatic law in operation—that whatever is not true will somewhere fail to work? Or again, is the individual conscience, in modernity's conception of it, equal to the burden that has been thrust upon it—the burden of being the keystone of the modern experiment in freedom? Is it disintegrating under the burden? If so, what of the free society which it undertook to sustain? Will it perhaps disintegrate in

one or other of the ways in which a political structure can disintegrate—
into a formless chaos or into a false order? Will the modern experiment
then prove to be simply an interlude between despotisms—between the
known and limited despotisms of the past, and the unknown despotisms
of the future, which may well be illimitable? In a word, in consequence
of having been enthroned as the One Ruler of this world, has the
conscientia exlex of modernity succumbed to *hubris*, and is it therefore
headed for downfall—its own downfall, and the downfall of the concept
of the moral order amid the bits and pieces of a purely "situational"
ethics, and the downfall of the political order projected by the spirit of
modernity?

From another point of view the same questions return. It was an
essential part of modernity's hope that the moral consensus upon which
every society depends for its stability and progress could be sustained and
mobilized simply in terms of a fortunate coincidence of individual private
judgements, apart from all reference to a visibly constituted spiritual and
moral authority. Has this hope proved valid? Is it perhaps possible that
the profound intellectual confusions in the mind of post-modern man,
which make necessary today a conference on the essentials of freedom,
are somehow witness to the fact that modernity's hope has proved to be
hollow? If there be no consensus with regard to what freedom is, and
whence it comes and what it means within the very soul of man, how
shall freedom hope to live within society and its institutions?

There is a final malaise upon which I should touch. It is, I think, related to the fundamental ambiguity of modern times. Modernity, I said,
rejected the freedom of the Church, in the twofold sense explained as
the armature of man's spiritual freedom and as a structural principle, of
a free society. Initially the rejection was addressed only to a truth of
divine revelation. The whole system of moral values, both individual
and social, which had been elaborated under the influence of the
Christian revelation were not rejected. I mean here all the values which
form a constellation about the central concept, *res sacra homo.* As a
matter of fact, these values are adopted as the very basis for the modern
political experiment. Modernity, however, has maintained that these
values are now known to be simply immanent in man; that man has become conscious of them in the course of their emergence in historical
experience; and that, whatever may have been the influence of the
Christian revelation on the earlier phases of this experience, these values
are now simply a human possession, a conquest and an achievement of
humanity by man himself. Now that I have arrived, said modernity,
Christianity may disappear. Whatever æsthetic appeal it may still retain
as a myth, it is not needed as a dynamic of freedom and justice in this
world. *Res sacra homo* is now under a new patronage—singly his own.

This is what Romano Guardini has expressively called the "interior
disloyalty of modern times". He means, I think, that there has occurred
not only a falsification of history but a basic betrayal of the existential
structure of reality itself. If this be true, we are confronted by the gravest
issue presented by the whole experiment of modernity. The issue again
is one of truth. Upon this issue hangs the whole fate of freedom and
justice, if only for the pragmatic reason already advanced, that the

structure of reality cannot with impunity be disregarded, even less by society than by the individual.

It will perhaps be sufficient if I simply present the issue as I see it, without undertaking to argue it. Here are its terms. On the one hand, modernity has denied (or ignored, or forgotten, or neglected) the Christian revelation that man is a sacredness, and that his primatial *res sacra*, his freedom, is sought and found ultimately within the freedom of the Church. On the other hand, modernity has pretended to lay claim to the effects of this doctrine on the order of human culture—the essential effect, for our purposes here, being the imperative laid on John of Salisbury's "king" (say, if you will, the state in all its range of action) to fight for justice and for the freedom of the people. In terms of this denial (or ignorance) and of this pretension (or hypothesis) modernity has conceived its image of political man. Justice is his due, and his function too; but not on the title of his sacredness as revealed by Christ. Freedom is his endowment, and likewise his duty; but not on the title of the freedom of the Church. A fully human life is his destiny; but its fulfilment lies within the horizons of time and space.

The question is, whether this modern image of political man be a reflection of reality (historical, philosophical, theological), or a mirage projected by prideful human reason into the *terra aliena* of a greatly ignorant illusion. Undoubtedly, this question will be answered by history, in which the pragmatic law operates. But it would be well, if possible, to anticipate the operation of this law by embarking upon a "new work of thought, begetting an altered premise".

In any case, the sheerly historical alternatives are clear enough. I shall state them in their extremity, using the method of assertion, not of interrogation.

On the one hand, post-modern man can continue to pursue the mirage which bemused modern man. As he does so, a spiritual vacuum will increasingly be created at the heart of human existence. But this vacuity cannot remain uninhabited. It will be like the house in the Gospel, swept and garnished, its vacancy an invitation to what the Gospel expressively calls the "worthless spirit" (*spiritus nequam*). He then will enter in with seven spirits more worthless than himself, and there set about the work that befits his character. He is the Son of Chaos and Old Night; his work is to turn vacuity into chaos.

Less figuratively, if post-modern man, like modern man, rejects the Christian mode of existence, the result will be that an explicitly non-Christian mode of existence will progressively come into being at the heart of human life. It will have its own structure and its own substance. And since it exists, it must manifest its existence and its dynamism. And it will do so—in violence, in all the violence of the chaotic. Violence is the mark of the Architect of Chaos, the Evil One, whose presence in the world is part of the structure of the world. It is not by chance that the mark of violence should have been impressed so deeply on these closing decades of the modern era, and that the threat of violence should hang so heavily over post-modern man as he takes his first uncertain steps into the new era. It was Nietzsche, I think, who said that the non-Christian man of modern times had not yet fully realized what it means to be non-

Christian. But in these last decades the realization has been dawning, as we have watched the frightening emergence and multiplication of that "senseless, faithless, heartless, ruthless" man whom Paul met on the streets of non-Christian Corinth and described in his Letter to the Romans.

This development, into a dreadful chaos of violence in which justice and freedom alike would vanish, is not inevitable. An alternative is possible. The way to it lies through a renunciation by post-modern man of the "interior disloyalty of modern times". Thus the new era would have a new premise on which to pursue the experiment in freedom and justice which political society perennially is. However, I must quickly add that this renunciation is not a political act. If one accepts the doctrine of the Second Council of Orange (A.D. 529) it is the work of the Holy Spirit, who "corrects the will of man from the infidelity unto faith".

Nevertheless, the "new work of thought" to which post-modern man is impelled as he reflects on the increasing fragility of the "secular hypothesis" will not be irrelevant to the fortunes of the future. If only we do not deny our malaises or seek to drown them, the experience of them can be turned to rational account. It is, after all, not beyond the power of reason to recognize illusion when the results of illusion are encountered in experience. Hence reason itself, and its high exercise in argument, could lead us to the recognition of a law, even more basic than the pragmatic law, which our forbears of the modern era most seriously failed to reckon with. It is the law of reality itself: "Only that ought not to be which cannot be." This perhaps would be the altered premise—a rational premise—that a new work of thought might beget.

The Church and Human Rights*

Heinrich Rommen

I

THE perpetual process—Man vs. the State—has entered what would appear to be its last phase: the internationalization of the Rights of Man, their incorporation into the body of positive international law at a time when the international community itself is, however haltingly, feeling its way to a more solidly and homogeneously constituted form than was either the anarchism of the sovereign states or the order of the League of Nations. The Universal Declaration of Human Rights adopted by the General Assembly of the United Nations on 10 December 1948 represents the last phase of the maturing relationship of Man vs. the State. What had been claims of natural law in the eighteenth century and as such had been made the declaratory positive law of the modern state in the Bill of Rights, declarations of fundamental rights and similar instruments is now on the way to becoming binding international law over and above the municipal laws, penetrating even into the hitherto closed domain of municipal law.

But this "internationalization" is not the only new feature. For the Declaration adds to the traditional rights the so-called social, economic and cultural rights such as the right to social security, to a just wage, to equal access to education, etc. Such rights were mentioned in some constitutions made after the First World War and are found specifically elaborated in the new constitutions established after the Second World War, for example, in France and Italy. Nevertheless, the Declaration contains the most extensive list of such rights and, in internationalizing them, exceeds in importance the national constitutional Bills of Rights. These social-economic Rights imply claims of the person to positive action on the side of the State according to the idea of Social Justice; they do not mean, as do the traditional Bills of Rights, to limit the "intervention" of the State or to forbid such "intervention" altogether. But it would be wrong to oppose these two classes of human rights as contradictory to each other. They are actually meant to be complementary to each other in so far as the social-economic rights try to secure for the working classes that human security and dignity which the traditional rights *de facto* secured for the propertied classes. Implicitly the traditional rights had also the character of social-economic rights.

The traditional Bill of Rights directed against absolutism establishes rights "against" the State, that is, against arbitrary, unreasonable, state-intervention into a sacred sphere of personal, "private" individual and group life; they stake out prohibitive rules against State intervention in the substantive rights of Life, Liberty, Property; and they secure those procedural rights which guarantee that criminal justice and the

* From *The Catholic Church in World Affairs*; see p. x above.

administrative actions of the State shall follow strictly formalized procedures which place the burden of proof on the State (which is itself under the law).

In other words, the benefit of the doubt is given to Liberty rather than to the State considered as benevolent guardian. The basis of such a "watchman-state" is, of course, the idea that the citizens, enlightened by their reason and their self-interest, organize themselves in the form of the civil society with full autonomy. The free society of free individuals is the positive value. The State *qua* government, as executor of the laws, is a regrettable necessity. It has to do no more than lend the individuals legal forms for their economic and social intercourse, to adjudicate their legal disputes, and to afford protection to their persons, contracts, property, health; and to enforce moral minima of public conduct, for individuals motivated by their reasonable, enlightened self-interest organize themselves by contracts on the basis of freedom of persons, property and contract into an ever-elastic and ever-changing pattern of socio-economic relations. The principle of perfect competition in the markets of economic goods, of intellectual, political and religious ideas is the automatic regulator compelling the individual interests, without conscious intent, to serve the common interest. Thus would be produced an automatic distribution of rewards and penalties, a social harmony without the benevolent supervision and direction of the State by the enlightened despot, that immediate predecessor of the watchman-state with its centrally planned mercantilist policy, its privileged estates as against the non-privileged third estate and the rightless peasants and dependent artisans.

Furthermore, political rights—those democratic rights par excellence, such as the right to vote and to be elected to public office and the abolition of the privileged estates in favour of the *citoyens* (who now form the self-governing sovereign people)—were also meant in the nineteenth century to ensure the protection of the individual from the "arbitrary", "unreasonable" intervention of the State. The nineteenth century still had the optimism of Adam Smith, the moral philosopher who wanted a system of civil freedom and economic wealth which he thought were inescapably linked together by the laws of nature. The nineteenth-century pleas for general liberty and its accusations against the "State", that is, against the *ancien régime*, were optimistically grounded in the idea that if the natural laws are made the laws of the State, a social harmony continuously preserving itself by reason of the fundamental liberties and the equality of opportunity would arise.

While this theory is logical on the theoretical level, in the concrete historical world the contradictions of the Manchester-system, as it began to be called, became more and more obvious. The old legal estates with their gradations of privilege were superseded, but no society of the free and equal arose. Instead, there came into being a class-society organized around the labour-market with essentially antagonistic interests. Society divided itself into the class of owners of the means of production, and the class of propertyless proletarians, whose basis of existence was limited to short-time labour-contracts made in a highly competitive, hazardous and wildly fluctuating labour-market in which they had no influence. At the same time the progress of industrial technology made capital less mobile and less able to change employment. Thus it became "sunk" capital and developed technological mass-production with monopolistic tendencies as a consequence. This led, then, for instance in the United States, to the paradox that the State had, in the anti-trust laws, to intervene in the supposedly self-regulating society to protect it against its own tendencies. Thus the liberties claimed and realized by business men could not be realized either by the worker or by the small independent artisan; nor, later, by the independent farmer. The workers were forced, after discovering the disadvantageous situation, to utilize their political rights and to set in motion a labour movement which aimed at fuller realization of those personal rights unrealizable under the libertarian principles of the Social Harmony doctrine. But the realization of their rights forced the worker-movement to go beyond the claims for equality of bargaining power by unions, that is, organizations of self-help (often declared in the nineteenth century as inimical to a competitive society in that they implied undue restraints on free trade). The workers received the support of liberals—that new group in our industrialized society who saw that legislation protecting the rights of labour must be as strong as that protecting industry. Bargaining power was equally as important to secure the position of labour as were tariffs and free incorporation of enterprises to secure the position of the business man. The basic structure of competitive society was to be changed to assure the sort of well-rounded socialist order in which there would be an egalitarian distribution of the national income; or it was to be changed, without socialism, to conform to Christian ideas. Christian social principles stood for an economic policy responsible to the principle of distributive justice. By the development of social law in factory and labour-market, Christian social thinkers envisaged the preservation of those liberties which Adam Smith's society could not realize for all. Social law of this sort would evolve a vocational group-order of society in which the rights of individuals were protected by the rights of the self-governing functional groups to which they belonged. They would thus actively participate in the formation of their own destinies. These criticisms of nineteenth-century society by various "under-privileged" groups and by the liberals led, by the end of the First World War, to an increasing acceptance of social and economic rights.

Such rights are considered to be derived from the old rights by interpretation. The first of these new concepts, haltingly and modestly set up, was that of the workers' right to organize into unions and bargain collectively. In addition, it came to be acknowledged that workers might make use of their political rights as citizens to organize labour parties and to work by parliamentary methods for social reform. Rather than to abstain from politics, workers were to participate in promoting the piece-by-piece growth of social legislation. They were also to appoint their representatives to the councils of administrative agencies which the administrative State establishes. This participation in policy-making councils was to be considered labour's collective right to co-determine the socio-economic policy of the admittedly interventionist state—admittedly interventionist because of its controls on money and credit, tariffs and investment, a policy very different from that of the old watchman-state, with its ascetic abstentions from a world that, it was supposed, could run by itself.

These slowly developed social and economic rights are fundamentally different from the rights and liberties of the original Declaration of the Rights of Man. Those were rights against the State, historically against the State of princely absolutism with its privileged classes and its rightless subjects, with its union—nay, even identification—of Church and State, with its general paternalism in education, and in its mercantilist "planned economy". The newly rising social and economic rights of the property-less working-classes and the small family-farmers establish a positive social and economic participation in the administrative State. They seek to allow those who under the *laissez-faire* pattern were helpless, to play a co-operative role in regulating the economic system. The right and duty to work, acknowledged in so many post-World War II constitutions and in Article 23 of the Universal Declaration of Human Rights, means something very different from the "freedom" of the worker to enter the labour-market and accept any wage-offer, even one which gives him only a slight differential above starvation level. The famous "Iron Law of Wages" has given place to a State-initiated policy of full employment, to a guarantee of the right to work and of the right to social security, to unemployment insurance. Such a guarantee would be too costly in a system which permitted chronic or cyclic unemployment. If the right to just and favourable remuneration and to a family-wage is declared as a human right, then the old free labour-market pattern cannot survive; and a just general economic policy by the State becomes necessary so that certain minima of justice in wages are regularly guaranteed. A whole series of social and economic policies may stem from such beginnings: from the radical policy of total planning to the "steered" economy of a Keynesian full-employment economy, or to the Social Market-policy of the Adenauer government in Germany propagated by neo-liberals such as Wilhelm Röpke.

These great changes in the societal order have raised the question, heatedly discussed by Hayek and Röpke on the one hand, and Finer and Woolton on the other, as to whether the fundamental personal liberties of the individual against the State will be able to survive in the face of the radical policy changes required if men are to be guaranteed their social and economic rights. Article 23 of the Universal Declaration, for example, says that everyone has the right to work, to free choice of employment, and to protection against unemployment. It is quite clear that conflicts may easily arise in the realization of these rights; and the question as to which of the rights in a conflict with the others actually cannot be realized without coercion is not easily answered. A man uses, let us say, his free choice to work at a certain skilled job which is rendered superfluous by technological progress. He then acquires the right to protection against unemployment, but on the condition that he accept work in another trade and location. He has, in such a case, suffered a *de facto* loss of free choice of employment. This means, however, scarcely a restriction, and even less a loss, of liberty supposedly possessed in earlier times by the worker. Actually, he was then controlled by the inescapable and for him uncontrollable and unpredictable law of supply and demand for general or qualified labour-power; his free choices were nothing else than a function of the competitive "standards" and migration policies of capital, policies of individual corporations which will now necessarily have to be influenced by the economic policy of the State.

Another characteristic of the twentieth-century Bill of Rights, incorporating these new economic and social developments, is that they consider not only the rights of man as an individual vs. the State, but also his rights as a social being, as a member of a group; as a member of a trade union, as a parent, as a child with the right to education and social protection. Some of these newly declared, not simply newly created, rights were already known as derivations from the venerable old formulas of the Declaration of Rights, of the fundamental rights of modern constitutionalism, inherited from the theory of the natural rights. Such is for instance the right of the parents to determine the education of their children, the duty of the State to provide for universal, even free access to its educational institutions, from compulsory elementary education up to the university. Such were the rights of members of religious, racial and national minorities as written into the minority-treaties, after the First World War, in Poland, Czechoslovakia and other nations; and incorporated in many constitutions promulgated at that time. They have been proclaimed—unofficially—by a commission of the Interparliamentary Union as the substance of the "Declaration of Rights and Duties of Minorities". In particular, such rights of minorities, recognized *de lege lata* in treaties and demanded *de lege ferenda* by the previously mentioned Declaration, included the protection of life and liberty with no discrimination against religious allegiance or forms of public and private worship; the equal protection of the laws, and equality of civil liberties and political rights; the right to the use of one's mother language in private and public life; and the right of groups to found and sustain charitable, religious and educational institutions of their own.

It is significant that these rights were not only to be secured democratically in the municipal law of these countries, but were guaranteed also by international law, though the procedures for their enforcement certainly were not particularly effective. The minorities themselves (though they might acquire the status as "corporations of public law" in municipal law) were not recognized as subjects of international law nor was an individual member of such minorities so recognized. A member of the League might bring a violation of the minority treaties before the Council of the League of Nations as an international dispute or appeal to the Permanent Court of International Justice for a judicial settlement.

A further step towards an international Bill of Rights was the Declaration of International Rights adopted by the Institute of International Law at its meeting in October 1929. It declared that it is the duty of States to give every person the equal protection of the law, the right to Life, Liberty and Property without discrimination as to nationality, sex, race, language, or religion. It declared specifically the right of the individual to religious freedom and to private and public worship, the right to the free use of the language of his choice, especially in schools, and to the citizen's freedom from any deprivation by the State, directly or indirectly, of his civil liberties and political rights. Article 5 states that equality before the law must be so absolute as to exclude any direct or indirect discrimination. The same Institute adopted in 1947 a similar Declaration on the Fundamental Rights of Man as the Basis of Restoration of International Law; for an effective order of the law among the States is considered inseparable from the respect of the human person in the internal order of the State, and progress in international law is understood to be intimately bound to the respect for those inherent rights of the human person which the State must serve.

II

The rise of the totalitarian State has given the idea of fundamental human rights a powerful validation. Yet unfortunately, the novelty of totalitarian ruthlessness and totalitarian expansionist techniques has put the idealism of our human-rights concepts under a most difficult strain. Nevertheless, the future belongs to it; not least because the Church Universal is on its side. The nineteenth-century liberal may scoff at the idea of being backed by the Christian tradition; but the principles of human rights not only stem historically and logically from the venerable idea of the *jura naturalia* developed since the Middle Ages, but Christian religious and ethical concepts have constituted the very inner quickening of the internal history of these human principles. The human rights we now recognize were derived as the logical juridical consequences of Christian ideas. Indeed the history of the great institutions of constitutional law, and of all parts of the law, are themselves parts and effects of the history of ideas, of culture, of developing intellectual and moral "climates". Ideas which have grown up with Christianity—and that means historically, the Catholic Church—are the origin of our human rights. Greek and Roman antiquity was not, to be sure, wholly devoid of notions of personal rights. On the basis of natural law some Greek sophists, the critics of Greek society like Hippias and Alkidamos, conceived the idea of the natural rights of all men. Yet these were sporadic cases. They cannot overbear the general attitude of injustice with which Plato and Aristotle distinguished the Greeks as called to freedom under the laws of the Polis and the rightless barbarians as fit only to be slaves of the Greeks. Furthermore, not even the Greek citizen, free under the laws, supposed himself to be endowed with inalienable, personal, human rights. However "free" the Greek citizens were, as our classical scholars tell us, and the Roman citizens under the Republic, they were free by virtue of the positive laws of their city-states. They were not aware of individual human rights, of rights of man, inalienable in character as against the positive laws. They had not the idea of a sphere of the intimate person, and of the family, staked out by the rights of man; of every man, citizen and alien, Roman and foreigner secure from any arbitrary intervention by the State. Arbitrary is here determined by these rights themselves, not by a mere procedural formality or pure legality. What "rights" there were, were political rights of the citizen established by positive law, not *jura naturalia* which would be the critical norm for the positive law. The *Crito* of Plato is here pertinent. Socrates was condemned to death unjustly, as he and his disciples very well knew and openly affirmed. *Crito* offered Socrates assistance to escape. Socrates refused. The laws of Athens were good and just, he said, even those that were the basis of his condemnation to death. That the jury used these laws wrongly did not free Socrates from obedience to the laws. The idea that the unjustly applied law itself may be wrong, and that it must be critically measured as to intrinsic right or wrong with "the idea of the law" was not mentioned. Nor did Socrates conceive of himself as a citizen possessing the right to criticize the law's justice or to speak in his own defence against an unjust law. Such criticism and such self-defence, constituting the essence of freedom and of legal reform and of progress and of a "personal natural right" against unjust laws, were beyond the comprehension of Socrates. So were the problems of law and person, authority and conscience. The Polis and its laws remained the "omnipotent pedagogue", and the appeal from its laws to the "higher law" in defence of personal rights, in defence of human rights, equal for Greeks and Barbarians, was only sporadically admitted.

Neither did Stoicism, that last and perhaps most significant philosophy of antiquity, co-eval with the idea of the *Civitas Maxima* of the Roman Empire, come to a conception of fundamental and equal human rights, in spite of its universalism and its doubts about the institution of slavery. Though the Stoics formed the *word-vessels*, in which, later, the Church fathers could mould their Christian ideas, what Bergson has to say about them remains true: That not one of the great Stoics thought about tearing down the bars which separated the free citizen from the slaves, the Roman citizen from the barbarian. Christianity had to come in order that the idea of universal fraternity, which implies equal rights and the inviolability of the person, could be realized, however slowly.[1]

For two reasons Christianity must be considered the fertile soil of the idea of the rights of the human person. First Christianity is intrinsically universal; it is ordained for mankind, the community of nations, not to a particular state only; it is above nation-states, national cultures and civilizations. And its purpose is not "secular" or transitory, but perpetual, to be performed within all historical climates whether they be favourable, indifferent, or unfavourable. Its purpose is the salvation of individual souls, however much they be immersed in their specific cultural pattern and "historicity". Within, yet apart from, the Greek Polis and the national and imperial State religions of the Roman Empire, the Christian community grew, its beliefs invalidating (as St Paul made clear) the old, deep distinctions between Greek and barbarian, freeman and slave. And so, since it could not win salvation for its adherents, the State as Polis and as Imperium lost its religious life-centre and became restricted to the control of merely temporal affairs. Still more significant is the assumption of the Christian that he must serve his divinely revealed truth, a truth which gives to the Church a priority over the State and over man-made, pagan forms of State-religion. The *Libertas Christiana* was established to affirm the right in conscience of the Christian to turn the citizen's allegiance away from compulsory State worship and toward a God who

[1] *Les deux sources de la morale et de la religion*, p. 72.

had revealed not only himself but the form which worship of him must take.

The Church of the Martyrs is in a particular sense the Church of the Witnesses. There was, of course, no subjectivism and sectarian individualism in the Church, which is itself the Holy People, the Mystical Body of Christ, the *Communio Sanctorum*, with sacramental law and hierarchical order. The *Libertas Christiana* could not be conceived as against this divine Law and the hierarchical constitution of the Church. The juridical objectivism of this institution divinely "founded", is irreconcilable with subjectivist sectarianism. Against any claims of the divinity of Emperor, Polis or Empire, that is of the temporal State, the Christian demanded his Liberty, the Church her *Libertas*.

It is an outstanding characteristic of the Roman Church that, in contradistinction to the Eastern Church's lack of resistance against Caesaropapism, it led an interminable fight for the *Libertas Ecclesiae*. The names of such Popes as Gelasius, Gregory the Great, Gregory VII, Innocent III, stand for this steady struggle for the *Libertas Ecclesiae* from the deadly embrace of the political power which at that time did not hate the liturgical life and the spiritual character of the Church, but tried to use it for its own purposes, at times sincerely believing in the Church's divine mission and under other circumstances, such as the presumptions of Frederick II, using it merely to secure itself.

Libertas Ecclesiae has had two significant meanings in history. First, it has always implied a community, the Church, not to be identified with any transitory political "life-form"—neither with feudalism nor with the Carolingian ideal, the *Civitas Dei*. *Libertas Ecclesiae* meant that, whatever its positive legal guarantees might be, the Church understood itself to have its own divine mission to fulfil—a mission that set it apart as different from and ultimately independent of, the world and the world's historical structures, civil and cultural. Man was thus made a citizen of two worlds: one spiritual and the other natural and secular, distinct, though not wholly separate from each other. There stood the Church, to which a man gave devotion, spreading the gospel, inspiring men and women, providing a regimen of sacramental life and moral rectitude, influencing peasant and knight, noble and serf, burgher and tradesman, to transcent their "natural" lives and so save their souls. *Libertas Ecclesiae* meant that the Church could thus work upon a succession of civilizations and cultures, teaching, forming, educating, inspiring, but always maintaining as its *Libertas* an ultimate aloofness, a *diastasis*, so that her own substance and life, her constitution and law, could not be drawn wholly into any civilization (such as feudalism) to perish with it when it should come to an end.

And so the second meaning of *Libertas Ecclesiae* came to be freedom of the spirit for the religious man against secular Powers and Dominations. The act of Faith and the life which it initiates must be free from secular oppression. Man is not wholly immersed in his biological-national or even cultural forms of life; man transcends with his person, with his conscience, all such historical, accidental conditions of existence. Such ideas were inconceivable to the ancients, to whom politico-cultural existence and "religion" were one, though there may be prefigurations of these ideas in sophist and Stoic philosophy.

It might be pointed out here that the pagan Roman Empire came to realize with a premonitory clarity that with the Church, the *Ecclesia*, and its demand for *Libertas*, whether of herself as *Corpus* or of her members as individual citizens, an "incompatible" element had entered the pagan world. Rome, as is evidenced by her Pantheon, was tolerant and indifferent to the national religions of the people it subjected to its political rule. But it reacted almost instinctively against that small *secta Christianorum* and persecuted this "Church of the Martyrs" with the full might of its police apparatus. Even the philosopher emperor, Marcus Aurelius, participated in this persecution. It was a unique fact that none of the many "sects", oriental or occidental, were made to suffer as was the *secta Christianorum*, though it never ceased to pray for the secular ruler and preach civil loyalty to the temporal laws. This had been taught by St Paul and St Peter, by Clement I, and by Justin, the martyr, in his famous Apologia for the Christians. The reason for the persecution was that Christianity put intrinsic limits to the powers of the Realm: not only the limits of the natural law as it was already known but also those of the divine law of the Founder of its Church. The latter took precedence in any conflict with the "temporal" law. The great struggle between the spiritual law of the Church and the temporal law of the secular State began. And it should be made clear that the *Libertas Ecclesiae* included the religious liberty of the Christian against the secular authority—not, of course, as the Reformation redefined the phrase: as religious liberty in the sense of freedom from the authority of the Church. The Christian conscience must be free to live according to the revealed law, just as the Church must be free and untrammelled to follow its divine mission.

Constantine in his famous Edict of Toleration of Milan (A.D. 311) wanted to make the Church and her moral authority a political prop for his imperial rule, and her bishops and dioceses administrative props for the political structures of the decaying Realm. Thus arose the great danger of Caesaropapism: that the Church might become part and parcel of the Realm as a political structure. In that event, the bishops and the pope would assume the functions of political administrators and morale builders of the Empire, and mass-conversions would make the Empire nominally Christian, but in reality still temporal and secular.

We see, thus, how the painful and often disappointing struggle for the *Libertas Ecclesiae* within the Western and Eastern parts of the Empire began. The final issue of the struggle in the West might be called successful; but in the East, where it ended with the submission of the Orthodox Church to the Byzantine emperors, the result was failure.

From the beginning, in the West, the Latin Church was essentially successful in its struggle for the *Libertas Ecclesiae*. However, the waves of the migrating Germanic tribes early flowed over the ruins of the Western Realm, and upon this tide arose the civilization of the Middle Ages. And then the struggle for the *Libertas Ecclesiae* began again in earnest.

The natural piety of the Germanic tribes together with their conversion to Christianity produced the idea of the Holy Roman Empire. Charlemagne meditated upon the *Civitas Dei* of St Augustine and, misinterpreting it, made the great design for his and his successors' political plans. To the time of Ludwig the Bavarian in the fourteenth century, this idea of the Holy Empire, the *Sacrum Imperium*, was the formative dream of the German Emperors. It harboured immense dangers for the *Libertas Ecclesiae*. Among the threats with which it was pregnant were the character of the Germanic law and the natural piety with which the Germanic tribes were willing to accept the Emperor as the Vicar of God on earth, and the feudalistic concept of the majesty of the Emperor.

During these dangerous centuries there were, none the less, some significant victories for true Christian liberty. Great Christian champions appeared in the persons of Gregory VII, Alexander III, and Innocent III. There was Gratian's treatise on canon law. Scholasticism arose. New religious orders arose. The Franciscans especially aided in the struggle. And as the cities grew, the striving for the *Libertas Populi* also grew apace. So, likewise, did the *Libertas Ecclesiae* find its supporters.

We must not be confused by the fact that this struggle for the *Libertas Ecclesiae* was conducted in the terms of the medieval civilization and in its frame of reference. When the disputants of those times spoke of *Potestas*, they did not mean a Machiavellian power for power's sake, amoral and meaningless. *Potestas* meant liberty to the disputants. *Libertates* and *Potestates* as legal terms are often interchangeable. In the letters of a Gregory VII, the *Potestas Ecclesiae* as opposed to the *Potestas Imperii* is treated substantially as the *Libertas Ecclesiae*, as the concept that the Church as a spiritual society with its canon law, its sacerdotal offices, and its jurisdictional autonomy, must be freed from the interference of the "sacred" majesty of the Emperor. Thus *Potestas* was conceived of as serving the *Libertas Ecclesiae*, not as a power to be used for its own sake.

That in this struggle the legal forms of the feudal order which was so dangerous to the *Libertas Ecclesiae* were used as weapons by the popes to protect this *Libertas*, is again quite understandable, though it led to tragic consequences: a widespread secularization of the Church which necessitated the not always successful reform movements of which the last, in the sixteenth century, led to the final dissolution both of the unity of the Church and of the unity of the *Sacrum Imperium*. Gregory VII, Innocent III and Alexander VI (in his famous Motu Proprio *"Inter cetera"* 1493) used the feudal legal forms to dispute the claims of the Emperor, based on a sacralized feudal law, because the propagandists of the Emperor were not less theoretical than those of the popes, and all were influenced more or less by a misinterpretation of the Augustinian *De Civitate Dei*.

Scholasticism, from Peter Abelard on to St Thomas Aquinas and John of Paris, distinguishing sharply, as it did, between nature and grace, philosophy and theology, faith and reason, criticized at least implicitly the Augustinian devaluation of nature, reason and philosophy and arrived at a different elaboration of the *Libertas Ecclesiae* from that of the theocratical partisans of the Pope. In the thinking of the Scholastics, the political order, the *civitas*, belongs to Nature. So does political authority, which derives its competency from the people whose temporal common good it serves. Political authority is autonomous in its ordering of the temporal common good; it is legitimized and limited by the natural law and by the revealed divine law, but not, *prima facie*, by the canon law. Scholasticism insisted upon the distinct natural and temporal character of political life as opposed to the supernatural and spiritual character of the Church. It was on philosophical grounds, rather than upon the basis of the positive public law of the Empire, that the Scholastics considered that the duties and rights of subjects and of political authority are independent of the supernatural order of Grace. The later Wycliffian doctrine that the prince who lives in mortal sin cannot demand the allegiance of his subjects was explicitly opposed by the Scholastics' view.[2] St Thomas states that neither simple misbelief nor even the apostasy of the ruler *eo ipso* destroys the duty of political loyalty due to such a ruler by his Christian subjects. But it is, he says, possible that the apostate ruler may by declaratory judgement of ecclesiastical authority be pronounced deposed as a punishment for his apostasy. Thus only according to the positive public law of his times is such a declaratory judgement recognized; for it was the Church which blessed the covenant of Prince and People in the sacral act of crowning and taking the respective oaths; thus it was considered the competency of the Church to declare the breach of covenant if and when the prince apostatized.

The temporal common good was considered a genuinely independent, though natural, value. It is natural, John of Paris says, that nations, since they are different in character and in way of life, should have their own states and different constitutions, because what suits one people may not suit another. Consequently, there is little room for a universal monarchy with the Emperor as Lord of the World, as Head of Christendom. Still less would there be room for a sacral monarchical ruler, quasi-divinely instituted by such rites of consecrating and crowning an Emperor as those upon which Eichmann reports so interestingly.[3]

The Scholastics were equally indifferent, philosophically, both to the Papocaesarism of the Curialists who would have made the Pope the overlord of Church and World and to the Caesaropapism of the Legists who would have wished the sacred Emperor to be the overlord of the World and Church. Though they made obeisance to the general political ideas of their time and to the positive public law of their feudal world, and might have appeared, at times, to be partisans of the claims of the Pope or of the Emperor, philosophically they distinguished sharply between the Church universal as a spiritual society and the pluralism of temporal secular states.

The introduction and assimilation of Aristotle's *Politics* into the medieval world of political ideas was certainly, though by no means intended to be, a revolutionary act, because it deprived the temporal ruler, whether Emperor or King, who did not recognize a political superior, of the particular sacral character which was claimed by and for him since Charlemagne. The Scholastics thus brought back the principle that the *Libertas Ecclesiae* is best guaranteed by the restriction of political authority to its proper field, the temporal common good. Such con-

[2] *Summa Theologica*, II, II, quaest. 12, a. 2.
[3] *Die Kaiser-Kronung im Abendland*, I, pp. 23 ff.

sideration of the common good might or might not include the idea of
religious homogeneity.

Thus we see that the Church was not considered the source of the
State, nor its superior. The Church was considered to be ordained to the
realization of a value much higher than that of the State, but it does not
follow that the State is subordinate in causality to the Church. It is
simply that the Church enjoys a higher dignity.[4]

III

It would not be too far fetched if we were to say that the struggle for
the *Libertas Ecclesiae*, which practically often meant the many *libertates*,
immunitates and *privilegia* of ecclesiastical office holders, courts and the
canon law they administered, worked also in favour of the many tendencies of cities and vocational groups which, before A.D. 1000, granted
liberties, immunities and privileges for cities and their inhabitants, for
the guilds and their members, and for the rural yeomen-farmers, from
the typical burdens of feudal law and feudal lords. The Magna Carta of
1215, which King John was compelled to grant, is the most famous, but
by no means a singular, example of such charters of liberties, immunities
and privileges. It was significant mostly for the simple fact that, by reason
of particular circumstances, it endured the many political upheavals
which occurred between 1215 and 1789, while other similar charters were
buried by political changes such as monarchical absolutism and wars of
religion.

The many charters of "liberties, rights and franchises", of "immunities
and privileges", which we encounter in the history of the Middle Ages,
more and more frequently, from the tenth century on, originate almost
always as the result of the demands of burghers or members of merchant
and trade guilds to be freed from the bonds of feudalism. If one studies
the slow development and enlargement of such liberties and immunities,
one can see how each additional liberty frees man further from the many
bonds of feudalism, until the self-government and the *Libertas populi*
of the medieval city (and not seldom, also, of the yeoman in rural dis-
tricts) is accomplished.

The legal device by which such liberties were acquired sometimes took
the form of perpetual privileges granted by the feudal lord or the overlord to immigrants, as with the newly-founded towns and villages in East
Germany; sometimes the granting of such freedoms was the price paid by
a feudal prince for financial or military help by burghers of an already
existing town; and sometimes these expansions of freedom came as a
result of a peace-treaty after a successful rising of the citizenry against
the lord, as was the case in the famous *Conjuratio Magna pro Libertate*
in Cologne against the Lord-Archbishop (A.D. 1112). By reason of their
origin such liberties might appear as only corporate liberties of the city
and not as subjective liberties and rights of the individual citizens. But
the sources, on the contrary, tell us that though these liberties were
acquired through the mediation of the city, they nevertheless were *jura*
singulorum and as such recognized, when the cities became sovereign, as

[4] John of Paris, *Treatise on the Royal and the Papal Power*, Goldast, II, p. 134.

valid also against the city-government. We find also that many charters speak of "all free citizens, wealthy and poor", or "without consideration of rank and avocation".

Among the types of liberty thus gained in the Middle Ages, we find freedom from feudal services and taxes; freedom of movement (important for merchantmen and trades-journeymen); freedom to acquire, hold and dispose of movable and immovable property; freedom from unreasonable and oppressive taxation; and the right (*jus*) to be tried by the city-court and by one's own peers, even though the accuser may be the feudal lord or his successor. Furthermore, no one might be deprived of life, or property or suffer damage to his body except by formal trial before a lawfully constituted court; that is, there was to be no punishment *sine legali judicio*, a standing formula since Otto III's privilege to the citizens of Cremma (A.D. 996). Freedom from arrest without proven cause and right to bail had already been recognized in the eleventh and twelfth centuries, though that freedom harks back to the eighth Council of Toledo (A.D. 683). The famous Golden Bull of Hungary (A.D. 1222), by no means a copy of or derived from the Magna Carta, also contains a clause against arbitrary arrest and is in many respects as elaborate as is the Magna Carta. The freedom from search is also recognized in many parts of the Continent before A.D. 1215. The equality of all men—Jews and heretics as well as Christians—before the Law was fully recognized in the famous German Law-text, the *Sachsenspiegel*, and by the equally famous Superior Court of Magdeburg, the decisions of which had the rank of ruling cases. (It would, of course, be wrong to forget the political disabilities of Jews or Saracens in the Middle Ages.)

Not only serfdom, so typical of the socio-economic feudal system, but even slavery, was still customary in the Middle Ages. The latter came into being mostly as punishment, or as a consequence of men's being taken prisoners of war. These survivals of injustice are evident from the discussion of the theologians, who rather uncritically, yet with an uncomfortable conscience, seem to accept the Aristotelian doctrine of "natural" slavery, though they make it less provocative by explaining it as being not *in prima intentione naturae* but being caused by original sin and thus belonging to the *jus gentium*, that rather opaque body of law somewhere between natural and positive or civil law. Yet the *Sachsenspiegel* declared simply "that slavery and also serfdom have their origins in unrighteousness. They have been introduced by force. What earlier times regarded as unlawful custom wants now to be held for law" (II, 42, 6). Such ideas about the institution of serfdom and slavery were more widespread than conservative theologians allow us to assume. Witnessing to this are the many peasant-risings and their legal claims, which after the Flemish rising (1323) become more and more vocal. Against the increasing demands made of the feudal lords the "old liberties and rights" are stressed. But not only these. The natural and the divine law is more and more quoted.

The "Reformation of Emperor Sigismund", a widely read pamphlet written by a cleric in A.D. 1480, affirms that servitude is against the Divine and the Natural law, and that it is an unbearable crime for a Christian to say to another Christian, "Thou art mine". To fight against servitude is a divine work. The propaganda of the *"Bundschuh"*, the secret society of the rebellious peasants, also declares serfdom to be intrinsically wrong since all men are created free by God. And the third Article of the famous Twelve Articles of the Peasants (1525), at the start of the Great Peasant War, condemns serfdom as un-Christian, since "we are all, rich and poor, redeemed by Christ's precious blood; and, therefore, according to Holy Writ, 'We are free and will be free.' "

We come to the conclusion that all through the Middle Ages, not only in towns and cities, but also in whole territories, a struggle for securing the rights of life, liberty and property was going on. This struggle was not one of whole nations, for the nation-state had not yet developed. It was a struggle of smaller communities, of the members of certain strata in a hierarchical society. The Magna Carta was only one among many charters claiming rights against governmental authority, and its particular dignity rests more on the fact that it was never wholly submerged by princely absolutism than on the fact of its uniqueness. Furthermore, the struggle for securing such "positive" rights, liberties and immunities was not initiated by a powerful radical ideology as was the case in the eighteenth century. It was more a pragmatic and concrete struggle for the specific rights of groups, of guilds, of settlers, of members of the nobility, of cities and towns and of the yeomanry against the feudal order.

However, we should not assume that motives of a spiritual and philosophical character were absent in this struggle. On the contrary, Christianity certainly contained such motives. However much the individual might be immersed in his group and conditioned by his station in that stable and "hierarchical" society of the Middle Ages, he transcended all these circumscriptions by his particular dignity as a Christian called to a higher citizenship in the true city of God, in the Church considered as the "Holy people" and in the Heaven beyond. The Middle Ages were the era of never-ceasing social criticism of all institutions which stood in the way of the realization of this dignity. Feudal institutions slowly yielded to the critical attacks Christianity made upon them. Still more important, the Church itself survived a life-and-death struggle against its own feudalization. Finally, the medieval social order and its institutions as the effect of the Church's influence, proved to be incapable of enduring. They had to be—and were slowly—transformed or abolished as a consequence of Christian ideas. Before God there is no discrimination of worldly rank and family status. The asceticisms of the friars constituted a constant criticism, not only of the old religious orders, but of all of feudal society. The friar's preaching, while no summons to revolutionary action, chipped steadily away at the ideological foundations of feudal society, at the superior-blood *mystique*, at the hereditary pride of belonging to the leading families, at the identity of status and wealth, at the *splendor familiae*, at the contempt for the lowly born serfs. The friars praised "poverty", and they glorified the poor as the particular "children of God". It is very difficult for us today to understand the tremendous effect of the sermons of the friars, those wandering preachers, with their blistering attacks upon the society in which they lived. In a society of lavish "conspicuous consumption", of the wealth of the few and the poverty and servile status of the many, suddenly the "poor of and in

Christ" appeared, recruiting especially from the ranks of the upper strata of medieval society. It is no wonder that these great spiritual movements —some of them regrettably turning into heretical sectarianism like that of Waldo's followers—became the parents of more democratic and individualistic trends in philosophy and politics. Poverty meant freedom not only from wealth but from the society that made feudal status and wealth the basis of inequality and serfdom. John of Salisbury and Bernard of Clairvaux had already praised the "poor"! John also had fought for the *Libertas conscientiae* under God against its violation by the political power of the Emperor who demanded obedience as the *Vicarius Dei* on earth. Bernard had praised the spiritual man who is truly free, because he is, like a Stoic, indifferent to the "World", and he found in the "poor" Pope the true vicar of Christ, the crucified.

Thus it was not strange that the first effort to give the charters of liberties a philosophical understructure was made by the friars, especially by William of Ockham. The latter developed a well-constructed theory of "natural rights". They are to be considered powers or faculties based on the Natural Law as an objective rule. They empower or authorize a person to act, to own a thing or to dispose of it. Such a right is a liberty as distinguished from a *licentia*. The latter is merely a permission to do something granted by a revocable *gratia* of a superior and is distinguished from a right by the fact that only the latter can be enforced by action before courts. Such a natural right is a subjective, individual or collective liberty based on those objective rules of Natural Law which lay upon all the obligation to respect this right.

Ockham distinguished between natural and positive man-made rights. To the former belong especially liberty and property. Liberty is the right to independence, initiative and self-determination, flowing from the rational nature of man. It follows that slavery and all forms of servitude must be products of man-made laws and cannot be based upon Natural Law. Natural liberty can only be lost by voluntary action, i.e., by contractually giving it up to another person; or a person can be deprived of it judicially *ex justa causa et culpa* and for no other reason. Likewise Ockham contended that the right to private property is a natural right. Under a slight but significant change of the previous scholastic doctrine, which ascribed property as an institution either to the *jus gentium* (following the Roman Law) or to mere human law, Ockham said that under the conditions of fallen human nature private property becomes not only a useful, convenient institution, but a strictly necessary one. It is thus of divine ordination as a dictate of right reason. The concrete positive law regulating the use, the forms, the acquisition and the disposal of property are of course of mere human law. Yet anterior to these human laws of property is the natural right to property given by God and nature. Nobody consequently may be deprived of this right without his consent (*volenti non fit injuria*) or without just and reasonable cause in formal procedures. Ockham thus gave the positive *jura et libertates*, mostly "granted" or acquired by agreement and thus somewhat weak, a sound foundation in Natural Law. They are not to be delivered to the whims of discretionary authority, but they are to be understood as true rights, of which the holders cannot be deprived without just cause established

400 The Political Order

before courts or by the vote of assemblies. A mere contention of a discretionary authority was not sufficient to deprive a person of these rights since he was protected by the right to vindicate them in courts of law.

We must not make the mistake of imputing modern ideas to medieval writers even though, like John of Salisbury, they use a term like "freedom of conscience" or, like Gregory VII (in his letter to the people of Venice) a term like "*Libertas populi*". We can make no simple identification of liberty, in the modern sense, with medieval man's longing for his liberties. What medieval man wanted was the securing of his economic and civic activities within the hierarchical society for any egalitarian liberty or liberal democracy such as we conceive of in modern times. He wanted to secure his concrete liberties. He had no idea of himself as a solitary self-centred individual, nor as an agent in the building and reforming of society and the State. He had scarcely any conception of himself as an individual capable of self-determination and self-fulfilment in all the fields of human endeavour—cultural, political, social and economic. The liberties which he conceived of were to exist only within the basic framework of a "sacral" society—concrete freedoms from restrictions upon economic and civic activities.

IV

In the light of this discussion we may better understand that most troublesome institution of the Middle Ages—the Inquisition, which seems in so stark a contradiction to modern liberty of religion and of conscience. Let me say at once that I will not defend the Inquisition. The greatest majority of Catholic theologians agree about the dark side of this historical, non-essential, institution of the ecclesiastic society. It would be easy to collect condemnations of this institution by famous theologians; and I am sure that, so far as theology is concerned, it will be adjudged a regrettable affair of the past. But, while the Inquisition certainly is indefensible, it is not inexplicable.

The Inquisition was, as the same suggests, a judicial inquiry about religious dissent, about the propagation of heretical sectarian doctrines. Religious dissenters, heretics, were from time to time persecuted after the Church became the Church of the Realm, because religious heterodoxy was all too easily construed to be political disloyalty or as an attack on the religious political substance, on the way of life of a society in which religion and politics, canon and civil law, the Emperor's and the Pope's office, were so intertwined *de facto* that the violations of the laws of the one were all too easily considered also violations of the laws of the other. Canonical excommunication often drew after it such civil law consequences as dissolution of the bonds of political allegiance, and political crimes such as tyranny, or civil crimes such as murder and rape, were often followed in turn by canonical punishment.

The unity of that politico-religious society, under the impossible ideal of realizing the *Civitas Dei*, was almost totalitarian in character. In spite of the clear distinction between the competencies and powers of the distinct societies, Church and Empire, and between the *Libertas Ecclesiae* and of the sacerdotal office and the Canon Law, the unity—if not the identity—of both societies in Christendom with the pre-eminence of either Emperor or Pope was much more effective than the fine distinctions of the schoolmen or the longing of Saints for the spiritual Church. To belong by baptism to the Church was all too easily considered the basis of political homogeneity and loyalty. To be a Christian was the condition of political rights.

This strong feeling of unity, religious and political, which was by no means foreign even to that strange "un-Christian" Emperor Frederick II, led easily to the civil intolerance and persecution of non-conformists which is associated with the Inquisition. If even the sincere ruler is perchance convinced that religious heterodoxy is necessarily also political disloyalty, or that religious unanimity or conformity is the *prima facie* basis of political unity and of civic loyalty, then religious heterodoxy becomes all too easily proof of political disloyalty and revolutionary conspiracy. This was the case in the Middle Ages, as it was the case in Elizabethan England, and in Calvin's Geneva. Only when the Church and State are understood to be independent societies, their laws different in competencies and object, with the duties of citizen and the right of secular authorities based on natural law not on supernatural authority, only then is it possible to distinguish and to keep apart the two societies, their laws, authorities and allegiances.

Practically this was not done in the Middle Ages. Consequently, Jews and Mohammedans could not acquire civil rights, though they might be —and mostly were—protected in their rights to life, to certain granted liberties and to property. They could not be compelled to have their children baptized. Their religious services were to be tolerated. On the other hand, heretics, i.e., validly baptized persons who in spite of several formal summonses to give up their heterodox opinions stubbornly persevered in them, presented a presumably homogeneous society with a dangerous problem.

The approach of the theologians and churchmen was to a degree rather legalistic. The Christian promised at baptism to remain faithful to the Faith. Ergo, he was held to keep it and if he became heretical, he had broken his promise; he consequently ought by spiritual and secular law to be compelled to honour his promise and desist from heresy. Furthermore, because of the unity of civil and religious society, he who violated the faith by public or external heresy was also held to have committed a crime in temporal law, because heresy was by all medieval theologians considered as a disturbance of the public order of Christianity. Consequently, heresy was first an affair for the spiritual courts; and after being established there, became an affair of the temporal courts by reason of the public law of Christendom. But infidels and Jews were to be tolerated.

Such was the way of thinking from the first Christian Emperors all through the Middle Ages, up to the victory of civil tolerance. And this thought was common to Lutherans, Calvinists and the New England divines as well as to Catholics. Rightly or wrongly, in those universally Christian societies, the question as to whether a man shocked by ecclesiastical abuses, could in sincere conscience fall into "heresy" (and thus be subjectively not guilty of heresy) was never seriously discussed. Such involved psychological questions were scarcely aired in such a non-indi-

vidualist society. It should be remarked also that in medieval society a
critique of religious abuses could usually be made within the Church,
issuing even in reform movements, without being considered heretical.
The similarity and the difference between St Francis and Waldo are
striking in this respect.

If punishment of heretics in the canonical sense by secular punishments (which rarely included capital punishment) had been carried on
for centuries, what made the Inquisition so abominable to modern man
and so to be regretted by modern theologians?

I think it must be said that the peculiar horror of the Inquisition was
a matter of two things.

First, there was the introduction and ecclesiastical sanction of torture
as a means of getting evidence not only from suspects but even from
mere material witnesses. Torture (*quaestio*) had become a means of
getting criminal evidence in the old Roman Empire predominantly for
capital crimes and high treason (as with the Christian martyrs). Ulpian
was full of misgivings about this *res fragibilis* and St Augustine com-
plained bitterly about the misery caused by it to innocent people.[5] The
non-Romanized Germanic tribes did not use torture. But this was more
because they did not yet know public criminal prosecution, leaving the
prosecution of crimes to the violated person or his family. Oaths and
ordeals were the customary means of evidence.

When the public peace in the eleventh and twelfth centuries was
disturbed so wantonly by the robber-barons and the feuding lords, the
public authorities had to take over public prosecution of crimes. Thus a
new mode of procuring evidence became necessary—the official search for
it, or "inquisition" (inquirere), regardless of the request of the violated
person or his kin. Hence arose the questioning of witnesses to get evidence
against the arrested suspect, to get a confession, the queen of all evidence.
To get a confession, torture began to be used and looked upon as necessary for criminal justice.

By the beginning of the thirteenth century, torture had thus re-
appeared. The *Sachsenspiegel* (1220) ignores torture, but some thirty
years later the *Schwabenspiegel*, influenced by Roman law and by Curial-
ism in its political theory, recommends it, as do some other Germanic
laws, not similarly influenced. The Roman Inquisition was an institution
that slowly developed, in the form of special regional courts with a
supreme tribunal in Rome, for the detection of the many, rather secret,
heretical movements sprouting everywhere at the end of the twelfth
century. Its tribunals superseded the ordinary episcopal courts which had,
up to then, rather inefficiently and often very arbitrarily tried to stamp
out heresy. The real black mark against the Inquisition was the order by
Pope Innocent IV in the Bull, *Ad Extirpenda* (1252), to apply torture
as a means of getting evidence from suspects, not only for self-incrimina-
tion, but also for denunciation of fellow-heretics. This order was directed
to all courts, secular and spiritual, not only to the tribunals of the Inquisition; it thus gave torture a kind of supreme sanction. The Bull
cautioned against excessive use of torture. A confession could be accepted
only after, not during the torture, and outside the torture-chambers. It

[5] *De Civitate Dei*, XIX, C. 6.

was to be "free and spontaneous" and without the infliction of "force or fear". That sounds like bloody irony and can only be condemned as hypocritical. Even if we give the inquisitors every benefit of the doubt and assume that they followed to the letter the rules that torture should only be applied as a means of last resort, we may be sadly certain that, between the fervour of the heretic and the fanatical passion of the defenders of the faith, the laws were not seldom flaunted.

Secondly, the Inquisition employed the shocking device of having the death penalty pronounced and executed by the temporal authority. But what if the temporal power was not itself convinced of the victim's guilt, or wanted to be more merciful, or tried to save a heretic for political reasons? In that case, the temporal authorities themselves could be declared *"Fautores haeresis"* and would become subject to prosecution by the Inquisition. This was indeed a vicious circle.

That it seemed such to the people of the Middle Ages is doubtful. The heretic was considered an actively subversive agent. At least he was so considered by the ruling classes, who at that time often composed the higher clergy and the higher political authorities. They were thus connected by common family and political interests. Not a few heresies, all those, for instance, which contained Manichean tendencies or those which argued that by mortal sin dominion was lost or those which denied the sacredness and the goodness of oaths—in a society that was based on a pyramid of oaths and allegiances—were *de facto*, within the moral and ideological framework of that practically universal and single society, Christendom, subversive of that historical stage of human development. In that sacral society, in which the Faith was the very foundation of religious and social homogeneity, heresy could be considered with some reason not only as a danger to the Faith, but as a political and social danger as well. Repressive action will in similar cases always be taken even by political authority.

What the forms of repression in any society will be is not a theoretical question, but depends on the general moral temper, the intellectual climate, the humanist tendencies of a given civilization. Two hundred years ago we had cruel penal justice even for a mere youth of fourteen years of age. One hundred years ago we still had legal slavery in this Christian country, in spite of the idealism of the founding fathers and great liberal Bills of Rights in state and federal constitutions. Thirty years ago those of us with awakened consciences smarted under the Sacco-Vanzetti case. Today our consciences are disturbed by the fanaticism of anti-communists who appear ready to play havoc with our liberties. On the other hand, one has only to study the penal part of the Canon Law, up to the presently valid code, and the Concordats with even predominantly Catholic countries, in order to know that the modern Bill of Rights and the inviolability of the sincere conscience must be jealously respected by a Catholic civilization, if ever the dream of a wholly Catholic world is to be realized.

v

Everywhere under absolute monarchy, even those rights and liberties which were generally respected in the Middle Ages were often submerged by the *Raison d'État*. Religious toleration was first accepted by so-called Catholic States in Poland and in Switzerland after a victory of the Catholic party. The Edict of Nantes was made long before Protestant states showed any signs of tolerance; its breach was condemned by Catholics with the same feeling of shame as Protestant liberals might feel about the persecution of Catholics in Elizabethan or Puritan England. The cause of such persecution, of course, was the assumption that only religious conformity to the Church of the Prince who had become definitely the spiritual authority in Protestant states and who claimed at least the control of the jurisdictional, the external, organizational life of the Catholic Church within his nation or territory, could guarantee unquestioning political loyalty and filial submission to the Father-Prince. Religious dissent, recognizing especially the Pope's jurisdictional primacy *in spiritualibus* was considered as incompatible with this kind of political loyalty. Hence the era of State-Churchdom.

But such an identification, based essentially on a mockery of the Divine Right, was in contradiction not only to the Scholastic political theory, but came into increasing conflict with the "Spirit" of the times. The Enlightenment, with its Deism, its criticism of revealed religion (of whatever Christian denomination), and with its nurturing of non-conformity, did much to destroy the idea of a state Church. When Canisius in 1550 recommended that the Inquisition, spiritual in character, be introduced in Germany to fight against the spread of Protestantism (a spiritual counter-attack similar to what Luther had recommended against the *Schwarmgeister*), Ignatius of Loyola advised firmly against it. But "Divine Right" Kings had no qualms. They were willing to see religion made political, and the Church debased to an instrument of thought control at least so far as its organizational relationship to the Crown was concerned.

Thus the dubious unity of Church and State was attacked from two flanks: from the idea of the *Libertas Ecclesiae* and from the individualist rationalism of the philosophers who wanted to destroy both Absolutism and its ideological prop, the Church. The *écrasez l'infame* of Voltaire meant the destruction of both. Furthermore, the ruling classes of the Ancient Régime apostatized in great numbers and went over to unbelief. Everyone wanted Freedom—the rising entrepreneurial class from the planned economy of princely mercantilism; the philosopher, from a rather inefficient censorship of literature and sciences; the freethinker, from what he considered an enforced religio-political ideology; and the rationalist, from the servitude of Reason to a State-religion. "Man is born free, but everywhere he is in chains."

The "Christian Monarchy" itself was already "secularized"; it had lost its concrete legitimacy in the intellectual world of the ruling classes in the eighteenth century, however much the simple faithful, the farmers and artisans, still lived secure in their traditional faith.

Thus became explainable the enthusiasm of the Great Revolution, the Declaration of the Rights of Man and of the Citizen, and the falsification of freedom of religion into persecution of the Church and of religious belief. And thus also it becomes understandable that Catholic writers and churchmen should not have greeted the Revolution with complete trust, however much not a few of them were ready to accept the *Novus ordo saeclorum* in its initial liberating epoch.

In the Anglo-Saxon countries the Revolution was not a violent break with the past and a radical (if shaky) new construction, but a slow evolution, and the traditional forms were slowly (as by a kind of osmosis) transformed. The free non-conformist groups had done their part to save the intellectuals as well as the masses from a hasty Erastian identification of State and Church. Thus, in those countries, it was not only anti-religious Rationalism that pleaded for freedom but the Christian consciences of non-conformists; there an amicable separation of Church and State could be accepted by practically all as a rule of political prudence.

It was different in Continental Europe. There the Restoration and political romanticism followed as a violent reaction against the terror and against the revolutionary promulgation of the civil religion in 1792 which secularized Gallicanism. And the romantic political writers of that period (and many churchmen who misread the signs of their time) thought that by such a re-establishment, a bygone historical form of political and social life could be simply continued, and that the positive gains of the Revolution (what was genuinely humane and Christian in the new order) could be simply suppressed. They did so in an unforgivable misinterpretation of the conservative character of the Church, of its *Libertas*, of its ability and duty to adapt its external forms of pastoral service, its teaching and its missionary work to social changes, in that they, at least implicitly, contended that the new secular, not necessarily "secularized", state with its Bill of Rights, its civil tolerance, its democratic constitution was intrinsically anti-Catholic.

In addition they were guilty of a methodological error. They pleaded that the new Democracy with its equal protection of the law, with its political and legal equality of all citizens, with its personal and political rights of the individual, was born tainted with the quasi-original sin of godless Revolution. They asserted, consequently, that its characteristic institutions could only be interpreted and applied in the spirit of a rationalist and often violently anti-Christian ideology. The Church in France insisted on interpreting the new democratic institutions as intrinsically unacceptable, as if contaminated with injustice from their very origin.

But this was a great error. Delivery from State-Churchdom, from Absolutism, from a Régime which was already "secularized" and morally corrupt, and a turning to greater freedom was a historical and moral necessity. Furthermore, political institutions such as the Bill of Rights, representative government and political equality in their positive constitutional form are not absolutes. They are not metaphysical or theological truths. They must be judged according to their concrete service to that common good to be realized in and by an historical society. They are practical maxims restricting government, organizing it, legitimizing it.

Thus tolerance is a practical maxim, not a metaphysical absolute truth. It might at one period in history be based on a great respect for the individual conscience, even though that conscience might lead the individual to errors not found in the ages of faith. It might be based, at another time, on a judgement of prudence that tolerance is more favourable for the common good than is enforced conformity. It might be based, falsely, on theological indifferentism, that is the thesis that there is no true religion, that objective truth is a fiction; the State, then, would assume a neutrality that must eventually lead to a new quasi-religion, a Rousseauist *religion civile.* This neutrality can easily show the same disregard for the religious convictions of Christians as was shown in times of intolerance. But only this one kind of tolerance—that based on indifferentism—leads to evil consequences. The other bases of tolerance (since they represent non-trespass on the individual conscience) are unassailably right. In other words tolerance is a practical prudential maxim which takes into account the inviolability of consciences, the common good and the interests of religion and public morality. Even the most tolerant or free state cannot afford absolute tolerance even toward "private" religion. For such absolute total tolerance would issue in anarchy just as surely as absolute intolerance issues in tyrannical totalitarianism.

Furthermore, the criticism by theologians and Popes of the wrong philosophy out of which decent political institutions historically sprang should not have led to the rejection of the positive institutions themselves.

The Belgian Charter of 1830 contained all the usual liberties, of religion, of conscience, of speech, of press, of assembly. The Cardinal Archbishop of Malines wrote to the National Congress which was deliberating upon the new constitution: "We do not want any privileges. Perfect liberty with all the consequences—that is what we want." Another Catholic publicist wrote: "The Liberty of all has become the condition of the Liberty of us Catholics." Another succinctly states: "To demand freedom of opinion does not mean to assert that all opinions are equally good. . . . Wherever a society has ceased to be unanimous in its religion, a positive religion ceases to be a social law and the State, the necessary expression of all the needs of that society, must restrict itself to protect the civil security of all citizens without discrimination." Gregory XVI, certainly a conservative, author of *"Mirari vos arbitramur"*, when informed by Cardinal Sterkx about the proposed Charter, declared that he had no feeling of uneasiness *(inquietude)* whatever about it. And the great Catholic leader, Deschamps, stated in 1856 that no pontifical utterance existed regarding any incompatibility of the Charter with Catholic doctrine and that there was not the slightest papal reservation about taking an unqualified oath to the Charter.[6] Similar views may be found among theologians and representative authors in Germany, France, Switzerland, the Netherlands and, of course, in England and the United States.

A certain diffidence against such utterances stems from a feeling that they might be only the products of clerical opportunism. Those who are thus suspicious will recall Montalembert's famous plea for the "Free Church in the Free State", which was later adopted by Cavour in his fight against the papal temporal sovereignty. Doubters will also remember our modern American principle of the absolute separation of Church and State. But it would be only common sense to say that the situation in a predominantly Catholic country is a special case. If a people is universally Catholic, then it is quite clear that that fact will find reflec-

[6] Georges Goyau, *Catholicisme et Politique* (Paris, 1923), pp. 112 ff.

tion in its political life and in its laws, since the common good of such a people will contain religious elements. To demand under such conditions absolute separation of State and Church and a-religious public schools would be simply ridiculous.

In our days Spain is often cited as an example of Catholic opportunism in regard to the Bill of Rights. Yet religious freedom is guaranteed to all Spaniards with the qualification that religious dissidents from the State-religion shall have only the right to private worship, in simple prayer-houses. In the *Civiltà Catolica* Father Cavalli (in agreement with the great majority of the Spanish bishops) criticized this "legal" tolerance granted to the small Protestant groups (perhaps one thousandth of the population, half of them alien residents), saying that they deserved only a practical tolerance (*tolleranza di fatto*). But that is by no means an official opinion of ecclesiastical authority, as has been pointed out repeatedly by recognized theologians.[7] Also in contradiction to Cavalli's ideas is the weighty opinion of the late Archbishop McNicholas of Cincinnati that "if tomorrow the Catholics constituted a majority in our country, they would not seek a union of Church and State. They would then as now uphold the Constitution and all its amendments, recognizing the moral obligation imposed on all Catholics to observe and defend the Constitution and its amendments."[8] In this respect there are numerous testimonies of similar bearing from members of the hierarchy in many countries. The only State where a different attitude partly prevails is Spain. But Spanish practice is not to be identified either with Catholic doctrine or with universal Catholic practice.

St Thomas defended the natural right of the parents to determine the education of their children, and asserted that to baptize the children of Jews or Saracens against the will of their parents represented a grave violation of this natural right. This right was positively recognized in the order to the civil governor of Rome by the latter's temporal ruler, Pope Benedict XIV, in 1747, concerning baptism of Jewish children. Children of Protestant parents cannot, therefore, be compelled by the State against the will of the parents to attend Catholic public schools.

A great confusion comes into this question of precedence of religion by a common misuse of the term "heretic". A heretic, as was said above, is a baptized and therefore lawful and *bona fide* member of the Church. The heretic makes, as the Greek word implies, a choice; he chooses on his own authority, in contradiction to ecclesiastical authority and tradition, certain parts of the whole body of doctrine, denying others or distorting and misinterpreting established parts of the doctrine. (The apostate repudiates the whole of the faith.) It is essential to the definition of a heretic that he formerly held the doctrine of the Church and that, then, he should have made a personal choice, substituting his private opinion on a doctrine of faith for that of the Church. It is essential, further, that he should stubbornly persist in his "private" choice despite being formally and thoroughly informed of the error of his opinions.

---

[7] *Vie Intellectuelle*, October, 1948, 294 ff.; Father Pribilla's essay on "Tolerance" in *Stimmen der Zeit*, April, 1949; Franz Thyssen in *De Situatie van de Protestanten in Spanje*, Utrecht, 1951.
[8] Wilfrid Parsons, *The First Freedom*, p. 83.

Consequently, there is at least an implied supposition that he continues to hold to his wrong opinion in spite of better knowledge. It is essential also that the heretical opinion be externally manifested; otherwise it is a violation of the moral law of Faith known only to God. The external heresy is, therefore, punishable *in foro externo* because in this sense heresy is a violation of the social order and the established faith and doctrine of the Church in subordinating this doctrine and faith to one's own "private" faith and doctrine. What punishment is inflicted for the offence of heresy in canon law, for instance automatic excommunication or the latter after a formal trial or administrative procedure, or what civic consequences, if any, the sentence of ecclesiastical tribunal or administrative authority will have, are to a great degree a matter of changing positive law, both canon and secular. Pius XII in addressing the Roman Rota, the Supreme Court of Canon Law, stated that the offence of heresy cannot leave the Church indifferent. "Without doubt," said the Pope, "the tribunal charged with the defence of the Faith has in the course of centuries taken forms and methods not required by the nature of the things but nevertheless explainable in the light of particular circumstances. . . . If it may seem to the modern mind that the repression of delicts damaging to the Faith has, in past centuries, gone beyond just limitations, modern society shows generally in this respect insensibility and excessive indifference." The Pope then cited Lactantius (fourth century): "There is no need for violence and injustice, because religion cannot be imposed by force . . . therefore, nobody is kept with us against his will." He concludes: "If the Church after having gained certitude about the fact of heresy and apostasy punishes those guilty, for instance, by excommunicating them from the Church, then the Church remains strictly within the domain of its competencies, within its domestic jurisdiction, as it were" (*Allocution* of 6 October, 1946). Let that stand by itself.

Now all citizens who are born Protestants, Old Catholics, etc., are by definition not heretics. The German language calls them more appropriately *Andersgläubige*. The official liturgical and diplomatic language of the Church uses the term "dissident brethren" for individuals and Protestant "Congregations", "dissident oriental Churches", "dissident Churches".[9] They never subjectively and externally belonged to the Church, though their baptism might be valid; they have never had full knowledge of the full Faith and did not make a "choice". They are objectively "in error" though subjectively they are of sincere conscience. Any attempt to violate their conscience even by indirect political pressure would be objectively wrong. "A society in which the only means to make a career would be to be a Catholic would be a society in which the right of sincerity is menaced."[10] Furthermore, a Protestant as long as he sincerely believes in the divine truth of his religion is, according to Catholic doctrine, not even permitted deliberately to doubt it. This right of sincere conscience in matters which do not directly concern the secular public order, or, to use a more appropriate term, the temporal common good has to be respected by State and Society. The "persecution" of heretic

---

[9] M. J. Congar, O.P., *Divided Christendom*, 1939, Appendix IV.
[10] J. Leclercq, *Vie Intellectuelle* (February 1949), 109.

in the Middle Ages by the secular branch was a consequence of a practical identification of Church-"State"-Society, just as the persecution of Catholics in some American colonies was based on the identification of Society with a particular Christian sect. With the victory of the doctrine of two perfect societies, Church and State (each sovereign and independent in its own field and thus separate, though co-operating for the same people who are members of both), it is quite clear that personal rights of all, especially the freedom of conscience, have to be protected against unjust and unconstitutional intervention. For the essentially secular State had, in matters of religion, no original competency after the Church was instituted by God. Even in a "Catholic" state the government has no right to violate the consciences of the religious minorities as long as their external acts do not disturb the public order.

It would be well, if all exaggerated claims of absolute rights of religion, speech and press were dropped. Not even the most liberal democracy recognizes an absolute right of subversive conspiratorial groups to freedom of speech, press and assembly. To change the constitution only the use of constitutional means is permissible. An absolute freedom of religion, of speech, of the press is recognized in no liberal democracy; but these rights, meaningful only in politically organized society, are always restricted by the values which are the substance of the constitution and the essential parts of the common good. Jefferson, in his rationalist optimism about the victory of truth and reason in free discussion with error and unreason, is only right as long as Robert's rules of parliamentary procedure are observed and as long as spurious fanaticism and passions do not drown the sincerity of open reason.

Much misunderstanding, and the fear that the Church and Catholics do not sincerely and without surreptitious mental reservation recognize the freedom of religion, of conscience, of speech and of the press stem, I think, from a lack of judicious information, for which indubitably not a few Catholic writers may be involuntarily responsible. Especially in the great struggle of the nineteenth century over the ideas of 1789, the conservative anti-revolutionary writers have contributed much to this misinformation, for they appeared to be, as they certainly wished, the standard-bearers of the official Catholic doctrine. Yet partisan as they were, propagandists more than scholars, they often were not only far off the mark, but they lacked especially the judicious circumspection, the sensitivity for the fine nuances, the prudent comparison and evaluation of apparently superficially discordant doctrinal utterances which only a mind trained in scholastic distinctions can harmoniously unite into a balanced body of doctrine. On the other hand non-Catholics are full of old tales, remembrances of bygone times, of prejudices confirmed by the careless conservatives mentioned above.

In fine, let me state expressly that the French Declaration of the Rights of Man in 1789 voted by the bishops and by the clergy of France and the modern Bills of Rights from that of 1688 to those of the new constitution enacted in many countries after the Second World War contain no phrase, no word that expressly and necessarily implies a formal negation of Catholic doctrines. These documents hold that the freedom of religion from state intervention, that is, civic freedom of religion, not based on theological indifferentism, is best protected by political freedom; that freedom of the press is good in itself; that freedom of speech and of discussion is essential to the growth of individual persons as well as to the furtherance of the common good which, today, is not entrusted to the hands of a divine right monarch (always a suspect figure to serious Catholic theologians) but to the peoples who have grown mature. As to freedom of speech, let me recall the instruction of Pope Paul III on the rules of debate for the Council of Trent: that each member should have the right to full freedom of speech in all matters before the Council and that nobody should be silenced even if he uttered a manifest heresy, as long as he promised to submit to the final decisions of the Council.[11] Consequently the Church also accepts fully the human rights as declared in the Universal Declaration of December, 1948. No religious community has suffered more than the Church in the totalitarian states, because the latter better recognizes the Church's defence of human rights than do its detractors in the democracies.

VI

About the Church's attitude to the so-called socio-economic rights only a few words have to be said. These rights are, for the most part, the direct and indirect consequences of the basic organizational pattern of that particular historical socio-economic order which is called Capitalism, free enterprise system, free market economy, etc. Its rise from the pre-capitalist order was, as has been said above, simultaneous with democracy and a strongly individualistic conception of natural rights. In apparent contradiction to the democratic ideology and to the economically relevant personal rights was the situation of modern workers, that is, the earlier artisans and guildsmen, the earlier (before the liberation of the peasantry) serf or agricultural servant and the small craft-shop-owner, dispossessed by the rise of the factory system. They all appeared now with the legal mark of the free seller of labour-power as a quasi-commodity in the economic system. As was said above, they only theoretically were profiting from the new rights; actually their condition was that they only rarely could use these rights. Quite significantly they called themselves "wage-slaves".

Thus the specific social problems of Capitalism arose. And society was much more conscious of them, because the tremendously increasing productivity of the socio-economic system offered a good chance to rid society of the phenomenon of mass-poverty in spite of the Ricardian-Malthusian pessimism which considered it as institutionally conditioned. Furthermore, the very ideological basis of democracy, of *weltzugewandte* piety, and the highly increased appreciation of personality opposed the blatant misery of the industrious masses caused by their ruthless exploitation. The Church was from the beginning somewhat suspicious and uncertain of this new order. It was inspired, *de facto*, though not by any intrinsic necessity, by a whole mixture of ideas and motives of which at least some, such as the threatening materialism of an acquisitive mind, the extreme individualism, and the attempt to substitute for the moral law the

[11] Theiner: Introductio, **XIX**.

economic law, were unacceptable to the ethics of the Church. Furthermore, if we consider the high social mobility, the horrible industrial slums, the dissolution of the family and the hardening of human relations in factory and slum, the destruction of the old order to which the pastoral methods of the Church had adapted themselves caused almost insuperable difficulties for pastoral work. Additional causes were the dissolution of traditional forms of social life, of manners and customs which, with their religious foundation, had earlier been strength and comfort in trials, the *Vermassung* and the wildness of leisure time pleasures, the impossibility of meeting mass-misery by the usual means of charity and of reaching pastorally the tempted souls in tremendously enlarged parishes. Faced with these almost insurmountable difficulties, some Catholics (a minority), politically alienated from democracy and romantically glorifying the medieval social and political order, out of protest against capitalism remained in an ineffective negative position. Others, troubled in their consciences and eager to help immediately, and not particularly concerned about ideologies, embarked on programmes of social action. Their main argument was the mutual interdependence of morality and a decent living-standard: the old maxim of St Thomas that without a minimum of earthly goods, determined by the particular socio-economic civilization, the practice of the virtues would require ethical heroism which cannot be demanded generally nor for any length of time. After some discussion, which the history of Catholic social thought extensively reports, a general agreement was reached for furthering the self-help organizations of the workers (unions, co-operatives) and for imperiously demanding, on the basis of distributive justice, social legislation to suppress obvious social injustices, to prepare a more just social order and above all to foster the self-help organization of the workers. All efforts and plans for overcoming the violent class-conflicts issuing *de facto* in the class-struggles so typical of the capitalist class-society should be encouraged. For example, practical co-operation of employers and employees for the particular common good of their industry and vocation within the framework of the national and even of the international common good should be developed.

The famous Social Encyclicals, "Rerum Novarum" of Leo XIII (1891) and "Quadragesimo Anno" of Pius XI, are not so much documents that originate and give initiative to these efforts; rather, they sanction or approve the efforts already successfully made, they encourage and they warn of extreme demands and wrong ways and means. Thus, they can only be appreciated against the background of the history of Catholic social action originating in the free initiative of laymen, workers, intellectuals and industrial entrepreneurs, and of priests and bishops motivated mainly by moral and pastoral reasons.

Catholic social thought and action, based firmly on theology and on natural law approved by the supreme authority, and reliably directed by it, has thus recognized for many decades that all social actions aims at the restoration and preservation of the human personality and dignity of the worker as man, as a Christian, and as citizen, in the factory, in the political community, in "society". While equally rejecting Marxism and the concept of the absolute rights of private property, Catholic social thought stresses the private and the social character of property, and demands the "redemption of the proletariat by a wide distribution of industrial property and the introduction of institutions which fulfil for the individual, but especially for the family, the main property-function, namely: secure liberty and social security. It is the duty of the State, by legislative intervention and by an active economic policy, so to arrange the social order that the demands of social and distributive justice in our society may be realized under full realization of the rights of the workers and of other classes such as the family-farmer, the small businessman and the independent craftsman. The right to associate freely in trade unions, the right to a just wage which will include the right to a family-wage and a decent living-standard, and finally, the right to strike, if that is the only means to realize these rights, were all recognized long before actual legislation acknowledged them. Similarly the state, in the interest of the common good, is strictly obliged to realize social justice. All have a right to participate in the common good on the basis, first, of their dignity as men and citizens, and then according to their own contribution to it in their various vocations and professions. If a whole class or group by reason of the malfunctioning of the (free) social order of the market society does not participate according to its functional contribution in the common good, then the state has by corrective legislation the duty to make the social order work justly. The state should not violate the principle of subsidiarity, but should put at the disposal of the injured groups such social institutions as credit unions, which they may administer themselves.

Catholic social thought early recognized the right to social security in its various aspects. Much of the modern social security legislation in many countries has been developed, if not always under the initiative of Catholic social reformers, always at least with their fervent support. There is not a single human right enumerated in Articles 22 to 28 of the Universal Declaration which Catholic social reformers, when it was in their power, had not already put in legal form many decades ago, in national laws and constitutions. Proof of that is that the modern constitutions which contain more elaborated catalogues of social and economic rights, the Weimar constitution of 1919, the French and the Italian constitutions of 1946 and 1948, the Bonn Constitution of 1949 of Western Germany, have all been established under the decisive influence of the Christian democratic parties, "the democratic parties of Christian inspiration", whose political programmes are profoundly influenced by the traditional ideals of Catholic social thought. What is especially meritorious in these programmes is a zealous defence of free social action of social groups, wherever they satisfactorily can realize justice, as against a so-called social progress ideology which wants to charge the administrative State with all these tasks, making it a bureaucratic care-for-everything State (*Versorgungstaat*). Characteristic, furthermore, is its recognition of the rights of groups (the family, the religious community, the universities and the free schools, of the municipalities), in other words, of a kind of social federalism somewhat akin to Jeffersonian ideas and hostile equally to *laissez-faire* individualism and to those Marxist ideas of socialist uniformity and mass-collectivism which prepare for the ascendancy of the totalitarian state.

In the struggle for an effective bill of human rights honest men everywhere will find—and will be glad to do so—a mighty ally in the Church. Catholics will find in this struggle their inspiration in the Faith; honest men, in the social doctrine of the Church which being based also on the Natural Law common to all men, can give by its long and tried experience and practically proven prudence, powerful support to the "recognition of the inherent dignity of all members of the human family (as) the foundation of freedom, justice and peace in the World" (Preamble of the Universal Declaration).

ЈARPER ✦ ᴄORCҺBOOKS

The New American Nation Series, edited by Henry Steele Commager and Richard B. Morris.

American Perspectives series, edited by Bernard Wishy and William E. Leuchtenburg.

The Rise of Modern Europe series, edited by William L. Langer.

Researches in the Social, Cultural, and Behavioral Sciences, edited by Benjamin Nelson.

The Library of Religion and Culture, edited by Benjamin Nelson.

‡ Harper Modern Science Series, edited by James R. Newman.

Not for sale in Canada.

3

4

6

RICH NEUMANN: The Archetypal World of Henry Moore. *107 illus.* TB/2020

ERICH NEUMANN: The Origins and History of Consciousness Vol. I *Illus.* TB/2007; Vol. II TB/2008

C. P. OBERNDORF: A History of Psychoanalysis in America TB/1147

RALPH BARTON PERRY: The Thought and Character of William James: *Briefer Version* TB/1156

JEAN PIAGET, BÄRBEL INHELDER, & ALINA SZEMINSKA: The Child's Conception of Geometry ° TB/1146

JOHN H. SCHAAR: Escape from Authority: *The Perspectives of Erich Fromm* TB/1155

Sociology

JACQUES BARZUN: Race: *A Study in Superstition. Revised Edition* TB/1172

BERNARD BERELSON, Ed.: The Behavioral Sciences Today TB/1127

ABRAHAM CAHAN: The Rise of David Levinsky: *A documentary novel of social mobility in early twentieth century America. Intro. by John Higham* TB/1028

THOMAS C. COCHRAN: The Inner Revolution: *Essays on the Social Sciences in History* TB/1140

ALLISON DAVIS & JOHN DOLLARD: Children of Bondage: *The Personality Development of Negro Youth in the Urban South* ‖! TB/3049

ST. CLAIR DRAKE & HORACE R. CAYTON: Black Metropolis: *A Study of Negro Life in a Northern City. Revised and Enlarged. Intro. by Everett C. Hughes* Vol. I TB/1086; Vol. II TB/1087

EMILE DURKHEIM et al.: Essays on Sociology and Philosophy: *With Analyses of Durkheim's Life and Work.* ‖ *Edited by Kurt H. Wolff* TB/1151

LEON FESTINGER, HENRY W. RIECKEN & STANLEY SCHACHTER: When Prophecy Fails: *A Social and Psychological Account of a Modern Group that Predicted the Destruction of the World* ‖ TB/1132

ALVIN W. GOULDNER: Wildcat Strike: *A Study in Worker-Management Relationships* ‖ TB/1176

FRANCIS J. GRUND: Aristocracy in America: *Social Class in the Formative Years of the New Nation* TB/1001

KURT LEWIN: Field Theory in Social Science: *Selected Theoretical Papers.* ‖ *Edited with a Foreword by Dorwin Cartwright* TB/1135

R. M. MACIVER: Social Causation TB/1153

ROBERT K. MERTON, LEONARD BROOM, LEONARD S. COTTRELL, JR., Editors: Sociology Today: *Problems and Prospects* ‖ Vol. I TB/1173; Vol. II TB/1174

TALCOTT PARSONS & EDWARD A. SHILS, Editors: Toward a General Theory of Action: *Theoretical Foundations for the Social Sciences* TB/1083

JOHN H. ROHRER & MUNRO S. EDMONSON, Eds.: The Eighth Generation Grows Up: *Cultures and Personalities of New Orleans Negroes* ‖ TB/3050

ARNOLD ROSE: The Negro in America: *The Condensed Version of Gunnar Myrdal's An American Dilemma* TB/3048

KURT SAMUELSSON: Religion and Economic Action: *A Critique of Max Weber's The Protestant Ethic and the Spirit of Capitalism.* ‖ ° *Trans. by E. G. French; Ed. with Intro. by D. C. Coleman* TB/1131

PITIRIM A. SOROKIN: Contemporary Sociological Theories. *Through the First Quarter of the 20th Century* TB/3046

MAURICE R. STEIN: The Eclipse of Community: *An Interpretation of American Studies* TB/1128

FERDINAND TÖNNIES: Community and Society: *Gemeinschaft und Gesellschaft. Translated and edited by Charles P. Loomis* TB/1116

W. LLOYD WARNER & Associates: Democracy in Jonesville: *A Study in Quality and Inequality* TB/1129

W. LLOYD WARNER: Social Class in America: *The Evaluation of Status* TB/1013

RELIGION

Ancient & Classical

J. H. BREASTED: Development of Religion and Thought in Ancient Egypt. *Introduction by John A. Wilson* TB/57

HENRI FRANKFORT: Ancient Egyptian Religion: *An Interpretation* TB/77

G. RACHEL LEVY: Religious Conceptions of the Stone Age and their Influence upon European Thought. *Illus. Introduction by Henri Frankfort* TB/106

MARTIN P. NILSSON: Greek Folk Religion. *Foreword by Arthur Darby Nock* TB/78

ALEXANDRE PIANKOFF: The Shrines of Tut-Ankh-Amon. *Edited by N. Rambova. 117 illus.* TB/2011

H. J. ROSE: Religion in Greece and Rome TB/55

Biblical Thought & Literature

W. F. ALBRIGHT: The Biblical Period from Abraham to Ezra TB/102

C. K. BARRETT, Ed.: The New Testament Background: *Selected Documents* TB/86

C. H. DODD: The Authority of the Bible TB/43

M. S. ENSLIN: Christian Beginnings TB/5

M. S. ENSLIN: The Literature of the Christian Movement TB/6

JOHN GRAY: Archaeology and the Old Testament World. *Illus.* TB/127

H. H. ROWLEY: The Growth of the Old Testament TB/107

D. WINTON THOMAS, Ed.: Documents from Old Testament Times TB/85

The Judaic Tradition

MARTIN BUBER: Eclipse of God: *Studies in the Relation Between Religion and Philosophy* TB/12

MARTIN BUBER: Moses: *The Revelation and the Covenant* TB/27

MARTIN BUBER: Pointing the Way. *Introduction by Maurice S. Friedman* TB/103

MARTIN BUBER: The Prophetic Faith TB/73

MARTIN BUBER: Two Types of Faith: *the interpenetration of Judaism and Christianity* ° TB/75

ERNST LUDWIG EHRLICH: A Concise History of Israel: *From the Earliest Times to the Destruction of the Temple in A.D. 70* ° TB/128

MAURICE S. FRIEDMAN: Martin Buber: *The Life of Dialogue* TB/64

FLAVIUS JOSEPHUS: The Great Roman-Jewish War, *with The Life of Josephus. Introduction by William R. Farmer* TB/74

T. J. MEEK: Hebrew Origins TB/69

Christianity: Origins & Early Development

AUGUSTINE: An Augustine Synthesis. *Edited by Erich Przywara* TB/335

ADOLF DEISSMANN: Paul: *A Study in Social and Religious History* TB/15

8

9

Code to Torchbook Libraries:

TB/1+	: The Cloister Library
TB/301+	: The Cathedral Library
TB/501+	: The Science Library
TB/1001+	: The Academy Library
TB/2001+	: The Bollingen Library
TB/3001+	: The University Library

A LETTER TO THE READER

Overseas, there is considerable belief
that we are a country of extreme conservatism and
that we cannot accommodate to social change.

Books about America in the hands of
readers abroad can help change those ideas.

The U. S. Information Agency cannot,
by itself, meet the vast need for books about
the United States.

You can help.

Harper Torchbooks provides three packets
of books on American history, economics,
sociology, literature and politics to
help meet the need.

To send a packet of Torchbooks [*] overseas,
all you need do is send your check for $7 (which
includes cost of shipping) to Harper & Row.
The U. S. Information Agency will distribute the books to libraries, schools, and other
centers all over the world.

I ask every American to support this
program, part of a worldwide BOOKS USA campaign.

I ask you to share in the opportunity to
help tell others about America.

                    EDWARD R. MURROW
                    Director,
                    U. S. Information Agency

[*retailing at $10.85 to $12.00]

PACKET I: *Twentieth Century America*

   Dulles/America's Rise to World Power, 1898-1954
   Cochran/The American Business System, 1900-1955
   Zabel, Editor/Literary Opinion in America (two volumes)
   Drucker/The New Society: *The Anatomy of Industrial Order*
   Fortune Editors/America in the Sixties: *The Economy and the Society*

PACKET II: *American History*

   Billington/The Far Western Frontier, 1830-1860
   Mowry/The Era of Theodore Roosevelt and the
     Birth of Modern America, 1900-1912
   Faulkner/Politics, Reform, and Expansion, 1890-1900
   Cochran & Miller/The Age of Enterprise: *A Social History of
     Industrial America*
   Tyler/Freedom's Ferment: *American Social History from the
     Revolution to the Civil War*

PACKET III: *American History*

   Hansen/The Atlantic Migration, 1607-1860
   Degler/Out of Our Past: *The Forces that Shaped Modern America*
   Probst, Editor/The Happy Republic: *A Reader in Tocqueville's Americ*
   Alden/The American Revolution, 1775-1783
   Wright/The Cultural Life of the American Colonies, 1607-1763

*Your gift will be acknowledged directly to you by the overseas recipient.
Simply fill out the coupon, detach and mail with your check or money order.*

HARPER & ROW, PUBLISHERS · BOOKS USA DEPT.
49 East 33rd Street, New York 16, N. Y.

Packet I ☐   Packet II ☐   Packet III ☐

Please send the BOOKS USA library packet(s) indicated above, in my
name, to the area checked below. Enclosed is my remittance in the
amount of _____ for _____ packet(s) at $7.00 each.

_____ Africa   _____ Latin America

_____ Far East   _____ Near East

Name_____

Address_____

_____

NOTE: This offer expires December 31, 1966.